REDEEMERS
BOURBONS
&
POPULISTS

LOUISIANA STATE
UNIVERSITY PRESS
BATON ROUGE

REDEEMERS
BOURBONS
&
POPULISTS

Tennessee

1870–1896

ROGER L. HART

ISBN 0-8071-0079-X
Library of Congress Catalog Card Number 73-91776
Copyright © 1975 by Louisiana State University Press
All rights reserved
Manufactured in the United States of America
Printed and bound by Kingsport Press, Kingsport, Tennessee
Designed by Albert Crochet

To My Parents

Contents

Maps and Charts

Tables in Text

Preface

The purpose of this book is to discover the patterns of politics in Tennessee during the generation after Reconstruction and to determine how political forces reflected deeper social tensions. At first I expected to find politics a battleground for economic class interests. Instead, my conclusions fit better into a status-anxiety framework of explanation, although I hope that I have escaped dogmatism and preserved the complexity and uniqueness of my subject.

Tennessee Populism can best be understood as one of a series of political dislocations following the Civil War. The Republican ascendency of the late 1860s was, of course, a shock to antebellum ruling elites. In 1870 former Confederate Redeemers threw the scalawags out but failed to build a coalition strong enough to contain the growing controversy over payment of the state debt. The collapse of the Redeemers necessitated a Democratic reorganization. The consequent Bourbon restoration of 1882 created a party based squarely on antebellum Democratic doctrines and predominantly hostile to the dynamic, industrialist nationalism of the Republicans and their New South sympathizers. The Farmers' Alliance was in harmony with Bourbon Democratic policy until the farmers appeared to place their movement above party unity. Their rough treatment at the hands of Democratic leaders in 1892 produced the People's party, whose grievances were tied more to state than to national issues. The Republican party, meanwhile, continued to provide a more vigorous and more clear-cut alternative to the Democrats. The Republicans were swamped and the Populists were sunk in the William Jennings Bryan silver tide of 1896.

These political developments are related less to the opposition of

economic interests than to traditional group loyalties. The memory
of close antebellum campaigns outlived the old Whig party, and the
trauma of secession and war gave rise to the deepest and most
enduring partisan identifications. Race was not often a divisive issue
in politics, because all significant white groups were racist and because the blacks were almost inarticulate and powerless. But though
blacks seldom appeared in public political roles, they loomed large
in the minds of the whites, upon whom they had a profound and
incalculable effect.

I am indebted to the Tennessee State Library and Archives for
its fine collections and gracious staff, particularly Miss Kendall
Cram and Mrs. Harriet C. Owsley, both of whom were most patient
and generous. I am also grateful to librarians elsewhere, especially
at the Firestone Library of Princeton University and the Memphis
Public Library. My use of a computer in statistical analysis would
have been impossible without Mrs. Shirley Gilbert of the Office of
Survey Research at Princeton University. Arthur S. Link, James M.
McPherson, and J. William Berry offered many helpful suggestions.
This study was guided by Sheldon Hackney, who was at the same
time critical and encouraging and who shared with other good teachers the role of exemplar. My mistakes are my own.

REDEEMERS
BOURBONS
&
POPULISTS

1

The Redeemers

In retrospect, the year 1870 appears to be the beginning of a long era in the history of Tennessee. Contemporaries, however, could have felt few certainties about their future. Tennessee was a proud old state, mother of more presidents than any other except Virginia, but it had recently endured division and defeat. A major battleground of the Civil War, the state suffered its own miniature civil war, with a large minority of mountain dwellers stubbornly hostile to the southern Confederacy. The bitterness was exacerbated after Military Governor Andrew Johnson yielded power in 1865 to Governor William G. Brownlow, an ardent Republican whose hatred for rebels was fully reciprocated. Brownlow and his Unionist white supporters had a low regard for the black freedmen, who, though enfranchised early, won no recognition or power in state government. When Brownlow became United States senator in 1869, he was succeeded as governor by D. W. C. Senter, who restricted martial law and began to restore voting rights to former Confederates. Even in East Tennessee, a politician remarked, the "suffrage revolution [was] . . . crushing everything before it." Senter's policy split his party but created conservative voters, and he was elected over a Radical to a full term in 1869.[1]

The conservative legislature elected with Senter summoned a constitutional convention to meet in January, 1870. The convention fully reflected the downfall of the Radicals; there were no black delegates and only four white Republicans. William B. Stokes, Senter's de-

1. A. A. Kyle to Andrew Johnson, July 12, 1869, in Andrew Johnson Papers, Library of Congress. For the period 1865–1870, see Thomas B. Alexander, *Political Reconstruction in Tennessee* (Nashville, 1950).

feated opponent, and other leading Radicals were excluded. The victorious conservatives, in and out of the convention, included various distinct groups. First, there were old Whig Unionists like Senter, John Baxter of Knoxville, and John Netherland, some of whom would later find their way back to a less Radical Republican party. Other old Whigs had gone with the Confederacy, though usually after opposing secession. Strong before the war, and the strongest group in 1870 because of their middle position, they included men like former governor Neill S. Brown, his brother John C., James D. Porter, and General W. H. Jackson. A third group of conservatives, the friends of former president Andrew Johnson, was less distinct because it included not only Unionist Democrats like Johnson, but also Democrats like George W. Jones, who had gone with the South, and even a prominent former Confederate Whig, A. S. Colyar. Finally, the most extreme conservatives, in terms of their distance from the Radicals, were the secessionist Democrats, represented in the convention by a relative moderate, former senator A. O. P. Nicholson. Former governor Isham G. Harris, General W. B. Bate, Peter Turney, and other fire-eating rebels were still in temporary eclipse. From the conservative viewpoint, Senter deserved the most credit for "redeeming" Tennessee from Radical rule. The name of Redeemer, however, has clung not to Senter but to the men he ushered into power, especially an unstable coalition of the second and last groups of conservatives: former Confederate Whigs and secessionist Democrats.

When the convention met in early 1870 the Redeemer coalition was yet unformed, but most conservatives agreed on basic goals. Most of the South was under either direct military rule or civilian Radical government. Tennessee had not been included in military reconstruction, having ratified the Fourteenth Amendment at Brownlow's urging, but Congress had demonstrated its readiness to intervene to prevent the resurgence of former Confederates elsewhere in the South. Now most of Tennessee's congressional delegation was urging federal action to nullify the conservative election victory of 1869. The convention, however, was reportedly "bent on cleaning out if possible every vestige of Radicalism" from the state constitution. How far could the convention go without provoking the Radicals in Washington? "Shall we disfranchise the negro?" one conservative asked. "Shall we repudiate the state debt? Shall the judiciary continue elective? Shall the present incumbents be turned out of office? These are questions that will have to be acted on." [2]

The crucial issue was the relation of race to voting rights. The conservatives agreed on full political rights for former Confederates, but differed on the question of black suffrage. Perceiving a "threatening attitude of the [national] Radical leaders toward Tennessee," a Memphis moderate warned that the federal government was "determined to enforce its pet dogmas" and urged the convention not to disfranchise blacks.[3] A. O. P. Nicholson disavowed full social or even civil equality for blacks but declared bluntly that if disfranchising some whites was wrong, then barring blacks from voting was wrong too. More typically, the dominant moderate group argued from expediency, not principle, and pled for acceptance of the inevitable. The suffrage committee recommended a nondiscriminatory voting clause, but a group of diehards on the committee who asserted "that the negro race is the lowest order of human beings" brought in a minority report. They called for a separate referendum in which the people would cast ballots for "Negro [*i.e.* universal] suffrage" or "white suffrage." When George W. Jones of Lincoln county moved for the adoption of this minority report, convention president John C. Brown remarked that they had "arrived at the most important business of the session," and suspended the rules limiting time for debate. On the assumption that a separate referendum would disfranchise blacks, the moderates defeated the committee minority and their supporters. The new constitution would not contain an explicit racial bar to voting.[4]

If the hottest issue before the convention was outright racial dis-

2. Memphis *Avalanche,* January 13, 1870; New York *Herald,* quoted in Nashville *Union and American,* January 18, 1870. All citations of newspapers publishing both daily and weekly editions are to the daily editions unless otherwise specified. J. W. Head to Johnson, August 17, 1869, in Johnson Papers.

3. Memphis *Avalanche,* January 9, 1870.

4. Nashville *Union and American,* January 25–28, 1870; *Journal of the Proceedings of the Convention of Delegates Elected by the People of Tennessee, to Amend, Revise, or Form and Make a New Constitution for the State* (Nashville, 1870), 97, hereinafter cited as *Convention Journal,* 1870; Memphis *Avalanche,* January 22, 1870. Some delegates who later became Republicans were considered conservatives rather than Radicals in 1870.

crimination in the franchise, one of the major secondary questions
was the poll-tax requirement for voting. For many, the poll tax was
not primarily a racial matter in 1870. A Memphis newspaper opposed to the clause declared, "The probability is that the proportion
of whites and blacks to be affected by this poll tax will be about equal.
. . . [T]he tendency is to establish, for practical purposes, that poverty is a crime[.]" A few of the staunchest backers of the white
franchise clause were adamantly opposed to the poll tax; in fact, after
its approval G. W. Jones stormed out of the hall and went home,
refusing to sign the constitution or even to accept his per diem
allowance. Jones's old friend Andrew Johnson, no champion of
rights for blacks, declared that he opposed the new constitution
because it would strengthen "aristocrats" by making the franchise
"an article of merchandise to be bought and sold for a price fixed
by law." [5] A historian of the poll tax in the South concluded that
it was "difficult to connect the poll tax with Negro suffrage" in the
convention. This view is supported by the absence of a statistically
significant correlation between the roll-call votes on the white franchise clause and on the poll tax.[6]

Table 1
VOTING ON WHITE FRANCHISE CLAUSE,
1870 CONSTITUTIONAL CONVENTION, SHOWING 1860 SLAVE
POPULATION OF DELEGATES' HOME COUNTIES [7]

	Average Percentage Slaves in Home Counties, 1860
For white franchise; for poll tax	35
Against white franchise; for poll tax	25
For white franchise; against poll tax	27
Against white franchise; against poll tax	11

5. Memphis *Avalanche,* February 3, 1870; Nashville *Union and American,* February 17,
1870; Johnson to G. W. Nixon, March 4, 1870, in Johnson Papers.

6. Frank B. Williams, Jr., "The Poll Tax as a Suffrage Requirement in the South,
1870–1901" (Ph.D. dissertation, Vanderbilt University, 1950), 76; *Convention Journal,* 1870,
pp. 159–60, 169–70.

7. *Ninth Census. Volume I: The Statistics of the Population of the United States, Embracing the Tables of Race, Nationality, Sex, Selected Ages, and Occupations* (Washington, D.C.,
1872), 61–63, hereinafter cited as 1870 Census, *Population; Convention Journal,* 1870, pp.
159–60, 169–70.

On the other hand, there is evidence that while these two roll calls were not directly interconnected, they may each have been related to race. Table 1 shows that delegates from blacker counties tended to favor a more restrictive franchise, one way or the other. But the lack of clear evidence of a racist purpose for the poll tax in 1870 does not prove that it would not be used against blacks later.

Although the roll-call divisions on the white franchise and on the poll tax do not show a significant intercorrelation, each of them is similar to divisions on other questions. Delegates supporting a white franchise tended also to favor a plan to turn all responsibility for public schools over to the counties as shown in Table 2. Here, too,

Table 2

VOTING, 1870 CONSTITUTIONAL CONVENTION, ON WHITE FRANCHISE AND COUNTY CONTROL OF PUBLIC SCHOOLS [8]

		White Franchise	
		Yes	No
Schools Wholly	yes	15	16
under County	no	4	35
Control			$\phi = -.43$ *

* For explanation of ϕ (phi), see Appendix A.

there seems to be a connection with race: the average percentage of slaves in the 1860 population of the home counties of delegates voting for both measures was thirty-seven, compared to a statewide percentage of twenty-five. Less surprising is the high correlation ($\phi = -.48$) between the white franchise roll call and the vote on whether to exclude blacks from juries and public office.[9] Thus there was a loose group of delegates ready to fight various kinds of outside interference in their local communities. Using the three roll calls on the white franchise, exclusion of blacks from public office, and local control of schools, the delegates can be divided into two groups, the nationals (against racial discrimination and for a state school system) and the locals.

The ghost of the once-powerful Whig party still walked in Tennessee. One Redeemer worried about "a feeling among some, that

8. *Convention Journal,* 1870, pp. 159–60, 314.
9. *Ibid.,* 159–60, 314, 341; 1870 Census, *Population,* 61–63.

Democrats, and particularly those who were such 'antebellum' would perpetually be excluded from voice and counsel in 'things.' " [10] Thomas B. Alexander has pointed out the disproportionate influence of old Whigs in Tennessee after 1865 and has provided a convenient list of prewar party affiliations of many 1870 convention delegates.[11] Was the convention divided on the lines of the antebellum parties? One way to find out is to correlate the national-local groups with antebellum party affiliations, where known. The result is to reveal no relationship (see Table 3). By 1870, old party lines were being blurred in some cases by more immediate issues.

Table 3
NATIONAL-LOCAL GROUPS AND ANTEBELLUM PARTY
ATTACHMENTS, 1870 CONSTITUTIONAL CONVENTION [12]

	Whigs	Democrats	Unknown/Young
Nationals	9	7	12
Locals	9	6	26
Unclassifiable	2	1	3

The poll-tax division correlates with a different set of roll-call votes. One of the more heated questions concerned taxation: agricultural interests wanted mercantile property to be taxed at a higher rate than farmland, but the merchants insisted that would be unfair. Another unsuccessful taxation provision was to allow the legislature to exempt manufacturing property from taxation for five years. The poll-tax advocates tended to take the capitalist positions on both of these tax matters. Also, poll-tax advocates tended to favor long terms for judges. Using the poll-tax division and the roll-call votes for five other issues related by the delegates' voting to the poll tax, one can arrange the delegates along a scale with the defenders of commerce and a restricted franchise at one end and the champions of agricul-

10. "Whit" [W. C. Whitthorne] to John C. Burch, June 30, 1869, in Johnson Papers.
11. Thomas B. Alexander, "Persistent Whiggery in the Confederate South, 1860–1877," *Journal of Southern History,* XXVII (1961), 305–29; Thomas B. Alexander, "Whiggery and Reconstruction in Tennessee," *Journal of Southern History,* XVI (1950), 291–305; list in Alexander, *Political Reconstruction in Tennessee,* 251–52.
12. *Convention Journal,* 1870, pp. 159–60, 314, 341; Alexander, *Political Reconstruction in Tennessee,* 251–52. For sixteen members whose ages were available, there was a two-year difference in average age between locals and nationals.

ture and democracy at the other.[13] Let us call those at the first end
the mercantile group and their foes agrarians.

This mercantile group seems vaguely Whiggish in outlook, and
the agrarians more Jacksonian. Table 4 shows that this set of roll

Table 4

MERCANTILE-AGRARIAN DIFFERENCES, 1870 CONSTITUTIONAL
CONVENTION, AND ANTEBELLUM PARTY ATTACHMENTS [14]

	Whigs	Democrats	Unknown/Young
Mercantile	11	5	13
Agrarian	5	6	19
Unclassifiable	4	3	9

calls does reflect antebellum party loyalties: old Whigs more than
old Democrats tended to vote with the mercantile group. It is significant that the convention was not fully in the control of Whiggish
mercantile types on these six roll calls, three of which they lost.

These two different divisions among the delegates—the local-
national and mercantile-agrarian polarities—prefigured Tennessee
politics for the next generation. Since the two divisions cut across
each other, they make four groups that form a regional pattern.
Cotton-planting West Tennesseeans were mostly local mercantile
men, and delegates from the mountainous, Unionist eastern end of
the state were mostly of the opposite national agrarian type; Middle
Tennessee had a mixture including the bulk of the other two groups.
The diversity of the state's white conservatives was reflected in the
convention, where men like Neill S. Brown, A. O. P. Nicholson, and
John Baxter (all national mercantile) often had their way, and such
delegates as John Netherland (national agrarian), James D. Porter
(local mercantile), and G. W. Jones (local agrarian) often did not.
Mercantile men were not always dominant, and "industrialists" are
invisible, if the term implies an active, major material interest in
manufacturing. The new constitution included specific authorization
for a tax on incomes from stocks and bonds and forbade the further

13. The five other issues are the three mentioned in this paragraph, plus a vote on the
legal rate of interest, and a division over whether the secretary of state would be elected by
the people or the legislature. *Convention Journal,* 1870, pp. 119, 169–70, 219–20, 274, 282,
326.

14. *Ibid.*; Alexander, *Political Reconstruction in Tennessee,* 251–52.

use of the state's credit on behalf of private persons or corporations. The conservatives of 1870 do not fit a simple mold.[15]

In late March, 1870, about a month after the convention adjourned, the new constitution was approved in a referendum. It won by a three-to-one landslide, but despite the enfranchisement of former slaves, the total vote was less than the turnout for the 1859 gubernatorial election. A new supreme court and lower state judges would be elected in August and take office by September, but Governor Senter and the conservative legislature were allowed to finish their terms, so their successors did not take office until October, 1871. "The 'nigger' question," remarked the Memphis *Avalanche,* was "practically out of the way," an observation as devoid of accuracy as of taste, but there was a sense in 1870 of a new beginning, a new regime in which the thorny franchise problem had been solved by letting all adult males vote who paid the poll tax.[16]

After the conservative victory it was not clear what would happen next. The state's most famous Democrat was advised privately that "the Whigs [should be] indoctrinated with the idea that they must adopt the Democratic name, or, become Radicals[.]" Memphis editor A. J. Kellar, a former Confederate, speaking for many old Whigs, refused to be indoctrinated. He denied another editor's charge that he was a Radical by retorting that secession Democrats were as bad on one extreme as Radicals were on the other. Kellar's *Avalanche* denounced "Bourbonic," proscriptive, "simon-pure" Democrats and argued for continuation of the Conservative party which had backed Whigs Emerson Etheridge and D. W. C. Senter for governor in 1867 and 1869 when Democrats were keeping their heads down. Kellar accused one prewar Democrat of being afraid of the old Whig party and secretly plotting the revival of the Democratic party. In reply, a Nashville Democrat saw "persistent efforts" in West Tennessee "to induce the old Whigs to believe that the Democrats were going to

15. Tennessee Constitution of 1870, Article II, Sections 28, 31. This analysis of the constitutional convention is based on a small number of roll-call divisions because few important issues were taken up by the delegates, who made only minor changes in the 1834 constitution.

16. Alexander, *Political Reconstruction in Tennessee,* 233; Robert H. White (ed.), *Messages of the Governors of Tennessee,* VI (Nashville, 1963), 30; Memphis *Avalanche,* April 21, 1870. The poll-tax requirement for voting was practically a dead letter until 1890.

form a 'third party' which was to be irreconcilable to the constitution, laws, and government of the United States in general, and to old Whigs in particular." He indignantly reported that in one historically Democratic county, "every county officer is an old-line Whig." [17] If these journalists did not take old party jealousies entirely seriously (Kellar was not really an old Whig), at least they expected their readers to do so.

The Whig and Democratic wings of the Conservative movement appeared to be on collision course over the August election for the six new supreme court seats. Kellar opposed a plan for nominating a party slate, believing that old Democrats would control a convention. After the convention, however, the *Avalanche* heartily endorsed the body's nominees: Kellar explained that he had not realized that the nominees would be such fine upstanding independents.[18] Since one of the six had been a fire-eating secessionist in 1861, very likely there was a compromise which left the old Whig moderates satisfied. The Conservative nominees easily defeated their Republican opponents.

Meanwhile, three Confederate generals were running for governor. William B. Bate was an ardent old-line Democrat who had stumped for Breckinridge in 1860 and who had offered a battalion within a week of Fort Sumter. William A. Quarles had been a Democratic state committeeman while Andrew Johnson was governor in the 1850s. Now he wrote Johnson to ask for help, invoking their old party, and hinting that Quarles was a potential victim of the same men who had greatly embittered Johnson by blocking him from the Senate in 1869. The third general was John C. Brown, younger brother of a former Whig governor and president of the recent constitutional convention. Bate dropped out a month before the nominating convention, suddenly discovering, he said, that the Fourteenth Amendment barred him from office.[19] There remained the possibility of a Whig-Democratic split behind Brown and Quarles.

17. John Williams to Johnson, July 2, 1870, in Johnson Papers; Memphis *Avalanche,* July 6, 9, 24, 1870; Nashville *Union and American,* August 6, 20, 1870.
18. Memphis *Avalanche,* June 26, July 3, 12, 14, 1870.
19. *Dictionary of American Biography,* II, 42; Philip M. Hamer (ed.), *Tennessee: A History, 1673–1932* (New York, 1933), I, 518, and II, 539; William A. Quarles to Johnson, July 21, 1870, in Johnson Papers; Nashville *Union and American,* August 16, 1870.

Democrats were upset by things Brown's friends said. The Memphis *Avalanche,* for example, mentioned a recent Madison County sheriff's race, in which a Conservative beat ten others in the general election, as proof that conventions and nominations were unnecessary. Another Brown man, answering criticism that the candidate's relation to the Democratic party was unclear, said, "It is sufficient to know that General Brown is a Conservative," that he opposed Brownlow, and that he was also against an effort to convert the conservative supreme court nominating convention into a partisan Democratic body. Indeed, a group of Brown newspapers, headed by the *Avalanche,* appeared to favor him because he was not connected with secessionist Isham G. Harris, nor with Harris' enemy but fellow Democrat Andrew Johnson. Brown moved to conciliate the Democrats, telling a Knoxville audience that though he had been raised a Whig, now he did not mind being called a Conservative or a Democrat or anything else, as long as the Radicals were beaten. Later he went much farther in a public statement in which he admitted general doubt about whether he would go before a Democratic convention, but he eased this doubt by stating flatly that he was a Democrat because the only alternative was Radicalism. The next day General Quarles quit the race. "The withdrawal of Quarles was by some arrangement with Brown I have no doubt," wrote A. S. Colyar, "and the effort on his part will be to throw his vote to Brown." [20] Quarles indeed turned up as president of the September convention which nominated Brown by acclamation.

The convention, called Democratic and Conservative to please both sides, had Whigs and Democrats sharing key spots. General Bate was made a special delegate-at-large so he could sit on the platform committee, of which the Whig chairman reported a platform denouncing Reconstruction and Radicalism and blasting at the old-time Democratic targets: national banks, tariff protection, and centralization of government. "The past is buried forever," said Brown with a straight face.[21]

20. Nashville *Union and American,* August 9, 1870; Memphis *Avalanche,* July 28, August 4, 12, 27, 1870; A. S. Colyar to Johnson, August 30, 1870, in Johnson Papers.
21. Nashville *Union and American,* September 14, 1870; Memphis *Avalanche,* September 14, 15, 1870.

All this harmony was unwelcome to Colonel Colyar, who had hoped to see Bate control the convention, driving angry Brown men to support an independent Colyar candidacy. In a speech preceding the convention, Colyar advocated stopping the manufacture of furniture and other consumer products at the state prison, and using the convicts in coal mines and iron mills instead. He asserted that the free workers and the state would both profit by the change, but he did not mention his own great investments in iron and coal.[22] After Brown's nomination, Colyar went ahead with his independent race, objecting to the platform's implicit hostility to greenback currency and especially to its demand that the southern states "be immediately restored to their rights . . . as sovereign States of the American Union." He claimed that the word *sovereign* connoted the right of secession. Such quibbling probably fooled nobody. A. J. Kellar thought he saw "a harmony of action as well as a unity of purpose between Mr. Colyar and the ex-President." The *Avalanche* presses had scarcely printed these words when Johnson spoke in Gallatin, objecting to the same "sovereign states" clause and hinting that his senatorial defeat might somehow be reversed.[23] An alliance between these two men—Confederate Whig and Unionist Democrat—seems implausible, but they cooperated against Brown and the Redeemers.

General Brown's first campaign speech stressed the need for unity against the wicked Radicals, and denied that any Tennesseean still believed in secession, pointing out that Clay, Jackson, Stephen Douglas, and Johnson himself had called the states "sovereign." Brown also advocated working convicts in the mines, to save the state money. Colyar took note and immediately withdrew from the race, explaining that he and Brown agreed on these points. Privately, Colyar told Johnson that he had quit because of "the almost univer-

22. Colyar to Johnson, May 19, 1870, in Johnson Papers; Nashville *Union and American,* August 14, 1870. For details of Arthur S. Colyar's entrepreneurial career, see Clyde L. Ball, "The Public Career of Colonel A. S. Colyar, 1870–1877," *Tennessee Historical Quarterly,* XII (1953), 23–47, 106–28, 213–238; Constantine G. Belissary, "The Rise of Industry and the Industrial Spirit in Tennessee, 1865–1885," *Journal of Southern History,* XIX (1953), 193–215; Thomas Woodrow Davis, "Arthur S. Colyar and the New South, 1860–1905" (Ph.D. dissertation, University of Missouri, 1962). Davis is good on Colyar but not always reliable on the larger political context.

23. Nashville *Union and American,* September 16, 18, 1870; Memphis *Avalanche,* September 16, 1870.

sal request from our friends in East Tennessee," but the colonel was more interested in his mines than in politics.[24]

The Republican party remained as Brown's only obstacle. Their mostly white convention endorsed public schools and the proposed Southern Pacific Railroad, and then nominated William H. Wisener, antebellum Whig speaker of the Tennessee House of Representatives and uncle of the chairman of the 1870 Conservative supreme court nominating convention. A patrician scalawag, Wisener attacked the poll tax and the Ku Klux Klan. Brown won by almost as large a landslide as had the new constitution, and his party did very well in the congressional races, taking six of the eight seats. Two of the six winners were old Whigs, three were Democrats (one had been for Douglas in 1860), and the other was a Union veteran of unknown party. One of the Whigs had a hard fight for the nomination from the Memphis district against a man backed by former Governor Harris, and then won the election mainly because the Republicans were split between a strong black candidate and the incumbent, a former Union general.[25] The elections of 1870 reveal a shift of power toward former Confederate leaders, and to some degree toward antebellum Democrats, but there was no total, thoroughgoing change, and no one seemed anxious about the long wait until General Brown's inauguration.

The nature of the new Democratic-Conservative coalition may be illuminated by a look at his administration. The choice of the state treasurer was in the hands of the legislature, which elected William H. Morrow, an associate of A. S. Colyar in the business of digging coal with rented convicts. As chairman of the six-man Agricultural Commission, Brown appointed General William H. Jackson, an old Whig who lived as a gentleman farmer on a beautiful stock-raising plantation near Nashville, inherited from his father-in-law. When the legislature reestablished the post of state school superintendent in 1873, Brown filled it with an old Whig journalist from Knoxville whose paper had been one of Brown's earliest supporters in the 1870

24. Memphis *Avalanche,* October 4, 1870; Nashville *Union and American,* October 4, 1870; Colyar to Johnson, October 5, 1870, in Johnson Papers.

25. Memphis *Avalanche,* September 21, 25, October 6, 25, 1870; White (ed.), *Messages,* VI, 134.

campaign. For a vacant judgeship Brown picked a Yale graduate of prominent family, an antebellum Democrat and businessman. Despite his platform, it would appear that Governor Brown, who spent most of his first major legislative message on state finances and taxation, placed his confidence in the sort of business and professional men who looked forward to a New South.[26]

Those accustomed to thinking of the Patrons of Husbandry as militant agrarians would not expect Tennessee Grangers to be friendly with Brown and his New South friends. In fact, however, the governor's patricians and the Grange leaders were in some cases the same men, which may indicate that neither group fits the old stereotype. Agriculture Commissioner Jackson was addressed as "brother" by Grange officers, and spoke to the members of the need for low taxes to attract capital. One of the officers of the state Grange was running the state immigration bureau, a characteristic New South project; another was a Harvard Law graduate. A state Grange president had been trained at a Louisville medical college. An 1874 "gathering of Grangers and citizens generally" at Manchester heard about a possible Grange cotton mill, and bought enough subscriptions to show "that the Grangers are terribly in earnest as to the establishment of manufactures." [27] Grange leaders and Redeemers were not sharply divided by backgrounds or by attitudes.

A few days before Governor-elect Brown arrived in Nashville to take office, his brother introduced Carl Shurz for a speech at the capitol, where the Missouri senator called for sectional reconciliation and attacked the Grant administration. Shurz's admirers soon organized a Re-Union and Reform Association, which was opposed

26. A. M. Shook to J. D. Porter, January 25, 1877, in Correspondence of the Governor's Office of Tennessee (hereinafter cited CGO), Tennessee State Library and Archives, Nashville (hereinafter cited TSLA); W. S. Speer, *Sketches of Prominent Tennesseans: Containing Biographies and Records of Many of the Families Who Have Attained Prominence in Tennessee* (Nashville, 1888), 12–15, 445–51; Memphis *Avalanche,* February 8, July 9, 1870; White (ed.), *Messages,* VI, 140–57.

27. W. Maxwell to W. H. Jackson, August 22, 1873, in Harding-Jackson Papers, Southern Historical Collection, University of North Carolina Library, Chapel Hill; undated speech by W. H. Jackson to Patrons of Husbandry at Bell Buckle, in Harding-Jackson Papers; C. W. Charlton to J. C. Brown, January 11, 1873, CGO, TSLA; William Waller (ed.), *Nashville in the 1890's* (Nashville, 1970), 247; TSLA, *Biographical Directory, Tennessee General Assembly: (Preliminary, No. 22) Giles County* (Nashville, 1970), 28; Nashville *Union and American,* July 5, 1874.

by old Democrats like Andrew Johnson and Nashville editor John
C. Burch, but spearheaded by A. S. Colyar and Henry S.
Foote, a former United States senator from Mississippi. They were soon
joined by Emerson Etheridge, the conservative candidate for governor in 1867, by Knoxville businessman John Baxter, and by Thomas
A. R. Nelson, briefly a member of the new conservative state supreme court. Of these five most important Tennessee Liberals, Foote
had been a Douglas Democrat in 1860, and the others were old
Whigs. Baxter put out a circular letter saying that a "disorganization
of the Democratic party" was "essential to the defeat of the Radicals." "The Democratic party cannot elect a Democratic Presidential ticket," agreed the Memphis *Avalanche*. "The Democratic voters
can elect a Liberal or Reform ticket with the support of Liberal
Republicans." This argument carried weight: the Liberal Republican
convention at Cincinnati nominated Horace Greeley in early May,
1872; a few days later the Tennessee State Democratic Convention
endorsed Greeley while affirming the "integrity of the Democratic
party"; by the end of May Governor Brown claimed that the state
was practically unanimous in support of Greeley.[28] The attempt to
form a new conservative Liberal party failed because it succeeded
too well, attracting so many Democrats that they took control.

Although Tennessee Conservatives thus became united on presidential politics, it seemed that Brown might have competition for
renomination. Several possible challengers were rumored, including
Andrew Johnson, General Bate, and especially General Benjamin
Franklin Cheatham. An antebellum Democrat, Cheatham announced his candidacy a month before the scheduled state convention and asked that it be postponed; but the request was denied and
he gave up. Once again, John C. Brown was nominated for governor
by acclamation. A group of Greeley Liberals met later in Nashville
and chose a candidate who did not run. In a replay of 1870, A. S.
Colyar announced as an independent, campaigned against Brown,
and withdrew five weeks later. The Republican candidate, running

---

28. Memphis *Avalanche,* September 21, October 15, December 9, 1871, February 6, March
29, May 10, 29, 1872; Baxter quoted in Thomas B. Alexander, *Thomas A. R. Nelson of East
Tennessee* (Nashville, 1956), 161.

on Grant's ticket, more than doubled Wisener's vote of 1870, and Brown's margin of victory was cut by almost two-thirds.[29]

Soon after Brown's renomination, however, Cheatham had another opportunity. Congress gave Tennessee a tenth representative, to be elected at large. Some said former governor Harris might run, but since Cheatham was a determined candidate, Harris never made a public move. The general's friends ran his campaign on "the idea," as one of them put it, "that an *old fashioned Democrat & a true Confederate cannot be wrong.*" They hoped to tap the strong sentiment for the Lost Cause, the feeling that "a true, faithful soldier, with rank or without it," was "a man worthy to be trusted in any capacity." Cheatham had to rely heavily on his reputation, because he was an inexperienced public speaker, as even his backers admitted.[30]

Liberal Republican Henry Foote entered the congressional race in the hope of being a Tennessee Greeley but, ironically, had his Liberal support wooed away by a man who had opposed nomination of a man like Greeley for president. Andrew Johnson, prodded by editor John C. Burch of the Nashville *Union and American*, began an energetic effort to return to the House of Representatives as John Quincy Adams had done. State Democratic Chairman Burch supported Johnson as he stumped Middle Tennessee, but was also loyal to the party's upcoming special nominating convention, despite Johnson's dim prospects there.[31]

Johnson had other friends, more Whiggish or Unionist in background than Burch, who might have backed someone like Foote. Some of them thought Burch was ready to betray Johnson and take the congressional nomination himself. A. S. Colyar was unconcerned about Johnson's slender prospects in the convention and suggested that the candidate should avoid "a convention gotten up by tricksters." This was the policy followed at the August meeting, where

29. Memphis *Avalanche*, April 10, 11, 17, 30, May 10, 1872; Nashville *Union and American*, August 13, September 1, 8, October 6, 1872; White (ed.), *Messages*, VI, 282.

30. Rolfe S. Saunders to Johnson, June 16, 1872, F. C. Dunnington to L. D. Deavenport, May 29, 1872, in Johnson Papers, emphasis original; Memphis *Avalanche*, July 7, 1870, September 15, 1872; Nashville *Union and American*, October 11, 1872.

31. T. W. Dick Bullock to Johnson, May 24, 1872, Burch to Johnson, May 22 and 25, 1872, in Johnson Papers; Memphis *Avalanche*, December 9, 1871, May 25, August 19, 1872.

only about half the state's counties voted. Johnson delegates refused committee appointments after Burch picked Isham Harris and General Bate to head the key committees. The Redeemer convention nominated Cheatham almost unanimously, with a scattering of votes for old Whig John M. Fleming of Knoxville. Johnson launched an independent race, using as his theme the need to bring government closer to the people. He called for direct election of the Senate, and compared his fight against conventions to Andrew Jackson's against caucuses. In a similar vein, he castigated "a military ring being gotten up in this State for the purpose of getting the officers in power." [32] The Johnson strategy was both to discredit the Cheatham convention and to neutralize the appeal of former Confederates.

Republican Horace Maynard made it a three-way race, but the real struggle was between Cheatham and Johnson for the Democratic and Conservative voters. Harris, Bate, and the other old secessionist leaders were firmly in Cheatham's camp, and so was Governor Brown, who was influenced, among other things, by a personal misunderstanding with Johnson. Most of the Democratic press, including Burch's *Union and American,* favored Cheatham; Johnson had only a handful of weeklies and two city dailies, including A. J. Kellar's Memphis *Avalanche.* Kellar himself ran as an independent for Congress against the regular party nominees from the Memphis district, but withdrew at the last minute with a plea for support for Johnson to beat the "rings and caucuses." Colyar stumped for Johnson after quitting the gubernatorial race.[33] The sensation of the campaign was an anti-Johnson speech by state party committeeman F. C. Dunnington which attempted to indict him as a Federalist centralizer, contrary to Johnson's own Democratic professions, and as a violator of his own much-vaunted constitutional principles. The Cheatham forces flooded the state with reprints of Dunnington's speech, and got local orators to follow Johnson and repeat its themes.

32. John Netherland to Johnson, June 20, 1872, H. H. Ingersoll to Johnson, June 24, 1872, Colyar to Johnson, June 20, 1872, all in Johnson Papers; Memphis *Avalanche,* August 22, September 17, 1872; Nashville *Union and American,* August 22, 1872; Johnson campaign speech in White (ed.), *Messages,* VI, 234–39.

33. Burch to Johnson, May 25, 1872, in Johnson Papers; Williams to J. C. Brown, undated, CGO, TSLA; Memphis *Appeal,* September 11, 1872, quoted in White (ed.), *Messages,* VI, 277–78; Memphis *Avalanche,* October 25, November 2, 1872.

A Giles county voter declared bitterly that any southern man supporting Johnson was "writing traitor upon the tombstones of his
comrades who fell in what he and they thought a righteous cause." [34]
Johnson might have rebutted the charge of being a party disorgan-
izer, but the past was too big a burden for him to carry.

Those who warned that Democratic-Conservative unity was
necessary to defeat the Republicans were correct (see Map 1). Maynard won the at-large seat with a plurality because Johnson pulled
in about one vote in five. [35] Analysis of the returns (see Appendix B,
Table 2) reveals that in East Tennessee Maynard got his fellow
Whigs, generally from the white Unionist counties; Cheatham won
the secessionists from former slaveholding areas; and Johnson took
the Unionist Democrats. All this is predictable. In Middle and West
Tennessee, Maynard's appeal to old Whigs was weak, but he drew
support from blacks and former Unionists. Cheatham did best there
in the white counties and in Middle Tennessee among former secessionists living on poor land. Johnson, outside East Tennessee, ran
relatively well in counties with good farmland, which might be partly
accounted for by Johnson voters in cities and towns (which were
always surrounded by high-priced farmland). He also did well in
West Tennessee among former rebels—an indication that despite
Cheatham's campaign, Johnson's attacks on political privilege and
manipulation could sometimes override hostility to the North.

Although Johnson lost his race, he gave the Redeemers a severe
jolt. "Everything looks well," a supporter told him. "The fruits of
your canvass have already made all the leaders from [Isham] Harris
down quite sick." The new state senate had only twelve regular
Democrats, with seven Republicans and six Johnson independents.
The lower house contained thirty regular Democrats, nineteen Johnson men, and twenty-six Republicans including the first black man
ever elected to a Tennessee legislature. [36] The Johnson bloc, with the
balance of power, won both speakerships and influenced legislation:

34. Dunnington speech in White (ed.), *Messages,* VI, 256–66; J. C. Shackleford to Johnson,
September 15, 1872, in Johnson Papers; Nashville *Union and American,* October 16, 1872.
35. White (ed.), *Messages,* VI, 282.
36. Colyar to Johnson, January 21, 1873, L. C. Houk to Johnson, November 21, 1872,
in Johnson Papers; Nashville *Union and American,* November 2, 1872.

18

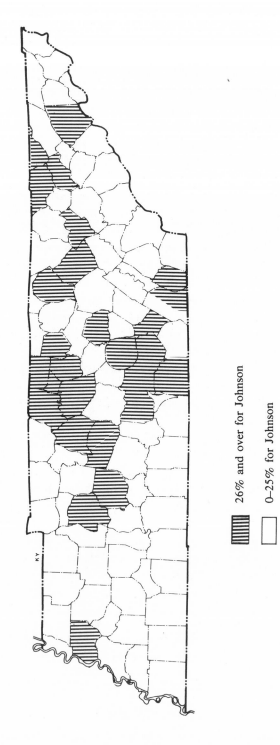

Map 1

SUPPORT FOR ANDREW JOHNSON IN 1872 CONGRESSMAN-AT-LARGE ELECTION

▐ 26% and over for Johnson

☐ 0–25% for Johnson

Source: Manuscript election returns, Archives Division, TSLA.

a landmark act of 1873 reestablished the office of state school super-intendent, which the Redeemers had abolished. With respect to state politics, the most important law of 1873 provided for new bonds to fund the state debt. Although later excoriated as was the famous "Crime of '73," by which Congress demonetized silver, the Funding Act of 1873 attracted no more attention at the time than did the act of Congress. It was passed in the Senate by a vote of fourteen to ten, and in the House by forty-four to twenty-four, with Republicans voting most heavily in favor.[37] Like the demonetization of silver, the Funding Act attained new significance largely because of the economic depression beginning with the crash of late 1873.

Tennessee's debt, which the 1873 act converted into new 6 percent bonds, had been incurred mostly for railroad construction, both before the war and during the Republican Brownlow administration. It amounted to over $39 million in 1869, or about thirty times the total 1870 budget of the state government. Hard times made farmers resent having to pay taxes over to bondholders, and suspicion of corruption under Brownlow and animosity toward railroad influence helped make the state debt a volatile issue for the rest of the 1870s.[38]

One politician ready to profit from disenchantment with the Funding Act was Andrew Johnson, who cited Jefferson's doctrine that it was wrong to hand a public debt down to a second generation, and denounced the Act as "a measure to rot the people and make them slaves of the bondholders." He was bored with living in Greeneville, where, he told his daughter, "I am as solitary as though I were in the wilds of Africa," and so he was receptive to urgings that he run for Senator Brownlow's seat. He was supported by A. S. Colyar, who wanted to "sweep the state against the extremes," and who got in touch with two leading Liberal Republicans and

37. *Journal of the Senate of the Thirty-Eighth General Assembly of the State of Tennessee* (Nashville, 1873), 242, 300; *Journal of the House of Representatives of the Thirty-Eighth General Assembly of the State of Tennessee* (Nashville, 1873), 359, 412 (hereinafter cited as *Senate* and *House Journals*).

38. William A. Stanton, "The State Debt in Tennessee Politics" (M.A. thesis, Vanderbilt University, 1939), 31–32; James E. Thorogood, *Financial History of Tennessee since 1870* (Sewanee, Tenn., 1949), 236. For details on background of state-debt controversy, see Alice Lynn, "Tennessee's Public Debt as an Issue in Politics, 1870–1883" (M.A. thesis, University of Tennessee, 1934); S. J. Folmsbee, "The Radicals and the Railroads," in Hamer (ed.), *Tennessee*, II, 659–73; Stanton, "The State Debt."

called a statewide meeting of Johnson men in the spring of 1874. Other friends of Johnson, however, feared that the "Colyar Radical faction" would only help the "Bourbons," or, in another case, pledged him support "in our hills and hollows among the 'one gallis [*sic*] fellows'—as we have been termed." [39] An issue which could pull these disparate elements together against the Redeemers was the state debt.

Johnson's major opponent in the senatorial race was John C. Brown, whose dedication to sound finance and state credit remained unshaken. He had won no gratitude from Johnson's friends by backing Cheatham in 1872, and now helped them by basing his campaign on a defense of the unpopular Funding Act. Johnson and Brown stuck to relatively substantive issues like the state debt, unlike their rival John H. Savage, whose face always seemed to be turned resolutely backwards. These three ran openly for the Senate, but Johnson early expected old Whigs W. H. Stephens of Memphis and E. H. Ewing of Murfreesboro to oppose him, and General Bate was quietly lining up support. [40] The multiplicity of candidates indicates that the Redeemers had not made the Democratic-Conservative party a disciplined or monolithic organization.

The themes of Johnson's campaign were an attack on illicit privilege or power, and a certain kind of nostalgia. He charged that while United States bondholders were paid in gold, crippled soldiers got depreciated greenbacks, and he denounced national banks, monopolies, and Crédit Mobilier. The former president told a crowd of farmers he preferred his tailor's garb to the regalia of military glory. He advocated the election of the president and the Senate directly by the people, and accused Brown of being "at the head of this clique that is trying to control the state," mentioning a "conspiracy" in his recent defeat for the Senate. [41] Deploring the current indistinct party

39. Lynn, "Tennessee's Public Debt," 8, 22; Johnson to daughter (copy), June 13, 1871, C. J. Moody to Johnson, November 19, 1872, Joseph H. Thompson to Johnson, January 17, 1873, Colyar to Johnson, June 13, 1873, February 23, 1874, R. C. Russ to Johnson, June 8, 1874, J. M. Carmack to Johnson, March 29, 1874, Orville A. Nixon to Johnson, March 31, 1874, all in Johnson Papers; Memphis *Avalanche*, May 8, 1874.
40. Nashville *Union and American*, July 12, 1874; Memphis *Avalanche*, October 13, 31, 1874; Johnson to Andrew Johnson, Jr., January 10, 1874, in Johnson Papers.
41. Memphis *Avalanche*, May 10, 11, 17, September 22, 1874; Nashville *Union and American*, October 7, 1874. See the perceptive characterization of Johnson in Eric L. McKitrick, *Andrew Johnson and Reconstruction* (Chicago, 1960), 85–92.

lines, Johnson reminisced about the years when everyone knew what
a Democrat stood for—or rather against:

> In those old days when you called a man a Whig, the term had an
> association of ideas in it. You thought of Clay, of protective tariff, of
> a line of improvements by the Federal government which were advocated
> by that great party. When you called a man a Democrat, you meant
> anti-protection, anti-banking, and direct opposition to all the principles
> of the great Whig party. Now the Whig party is gone, but we have still
> left what is called the Democratic party, but is there any distinct and
> definite set of ideas associated with it? . . . What has become of the great
> Democratic party? [42]

The upheavals of war and Reconstruction had transformed the
political landscape, and the old Jacksonian trumpeted like a last
mastodon looking for his vanished herd.

Ironically, in view of his rhetoric and his past, Johnson drew
support from Republicans in 1874 who hoped to hang onto his
coattails. In Bedford County the Republican legislative ticket was
so much more pro-Johnson than the Democratic nominees that
Johnson's Democratic friends planned to vote Republican. In Memphis, Liberal Republican Emerson Etheridge headed a GOP-backed
legislative ticket pledged to Johnson and fully in accord with his
low-tax views on the state debt. Pro-Johnson Democrats in Bedford
and Shelby counties arranged for extralegal senatorial primaries on
election day to keep Johnson men in the party.[43] Johnson apparently
lost the primaries in Bedford and in Sumner, where he defeated Bate
eight to one in the county seat but lost many rural boxes. In Shelby
County the victorious Johnson drew over 90 percent of his strength
from the city of Memphis, while Brown the Redeemer found the
majority of his votes in country districts. The former president's
agents lobbied with newly elected legislators, especially in East
Tennessee, until they converged on Nashville in January.[44]

The capitol galleries were packed as Johnson's foes, arguing that

---

42. Nashville *Union and American,* October 7, 1874.

43. *Ibid.,* October 25, 28, 1874; Joseph H. Thompson to Johnson, October 31, 1874,
J. M. Carmack to Johnson, November 13, 1874, in Johnson Papers; Memphis *Avalanche,*
October 22, 24, 1874.

44. Nashville *Union and American,* November 4, 1874; Memphis *Avalanche,* November
4, 1874; E. C. Reeves to Johnson, December 8, 11, and 15, 1874, J. H. Thompson to Johnson,
December 10, 1874, in Johnson Papers.

he was no true Democrat, tried in vain to organize a caucus against him. He led a field of ten on the first ballot, so his opponents concentrated on Brown, who approached Johnson on the thirty-fourth ballot and then withdrew. The anti-Johnson men then voted mainly for Bate and Stephens, then for Bate, who could not quite win the swing votes for a majority. Finally Bate quit and Johnson was elected senator on the fifty-fifth ballot. The voting shows a strong regional tendency: the candidates' first-ballot votes came from their home areas, with the partial exceptions of Johnson's Memphis men, pledged by the primary, and of Brown's votes, about half of which were scattered. On the final ballot not one House member from Johnson's heavily Republican eastern division opposed him. Since there is no relation whatever between the antebellum parties of senatorial candidates and the prewar alignments of their legislative supporters' constituencies, it seems that old party memories had been superseded in 1875 among the political elite by what V. O. Key, Jr., called "friends and neighbors" localism. Another factor in the election was the resistance by former Unionist Democrats, and some Whigs, to a solidification of party lines on the blue-grey division. After Johnson's victory, a minor East Tennessee politician explained that he had lost elections because he "had fool Radicals on one side and fool Rebels on the other to contend with," and rejoiced that "Democracy now in Tennessee does not mean Rebel only." [45] Just as northern Republicans wavered between hoisting the bloody shirt and trying to bury it, so Tennessee Democrats would disagree for years to come over whether to emphasize the war or forget it. The Redeemers used war sentiment more than Johnson did.

There were perhaps even more candidates for governor than for the Senate. As late as six weeks before the 1874 nominating convention, a leading newspaper mentioned thirteen Democratic-Conservative possibilities, most of whom were seriously running. [46] At the convention James D. Porter of Henry County led on the first ballot, but with fewer than a quarter of the votes. Of the other ten the

45. Memphis *Avalanche,* January 7, 19, 20, 1875; *House Journal,* 1875, pp. 106–107, 167–68, 176–201; *Senate Journal,* 1875, pp. 125, 179, 188–210; V. O. Key, Jr., *Southern Politics in State and Nation* (New York, 1949), 37–41; Benjamin G. Owen to Johnson, January 28, 1875, in Johnson Papers.

46. Nashville *Union and American,* July 8, 1874.

strongest were two old-line Democratic state judges, David M. Key and A. S. Marks, and two old Whigs, John Netherland of upper East Tennessee and Dorsey B. Thomas, Democratic-Conservative state chairman in 1872 and reportedly the "favorite of the Grangers." By the thirteenth ballot all had dropped out except Thomas and Porter, but an old Whig railroad attorney from Clarksville, James E. Bailey, had been put in the running. Then someone withdrew Thomas' name and cried "I now go for Porter—run him in!" Porter fell short of the required two-thirds, but Bailey withdrew. On this last ballot, Bailey, a strong defender of paying the state debt, drew nearly all his strength from East Tennessee and the tobacco counties bordering Kentucky. At least two delegations controlled by Johnson men voted for Bailey, despite Johnson's stand on the debt. Perhaps the explanation lies in the claim by a Chattanooga newspaper that East Tennessee voted for Bailey to oppose Isham G. Harris, who voted first for a Memphis neighbor and then for Porter, a secessionist ally of Governor Harris in 1861. Porter astutely made a point of complimenting Johnson on the stump, and won the election easily. The hottest public issue was the pending federal civil rights bill, which Republican nominee Horace Maynard endorsed and which the Democrats used as a campaign target.[47]

The significance of the 1874 convention is that it marks the beginning of a retreat by the party from John C. Brown's strong state-credit position, as well as a step toward rehabilitation of secessionists. The delegates rejected Bailey, who agreed with Brown, and nominated Porter with the help of Harris and of Thomas, an outspoken foe of the Funding Act. When Maynard attacked the Brown administration and the Funding Act in a campaign debate, Porter made no effort to defend Brown; later he practically disavowed the incumbent. "I am not the champion of Governor Brown," he said. "I am the Democratic candidate for . . . Governor." In his first message to the legislature, Governor Porter insisted that taxes be kept down, but also condemned debt repudiation; he was less inflexible about the debt than Brown but did not encourage the growing sentiment for repudiation.[48]

47. *Ibid.*, August 20, September 30, 1874; Memphis *Avalanche,* July 19, September 1, 18, 20, 1874; Nashville *Republican Banner,* quoted in Memphis *Avalanche,* August 27, 1874.
48. Memphis *Avalanche,* October 3, November 1, 1874; White (ed.), *Messages,* VI, 415.

Porter appointed General B. F. Cheatham superintendent of prisons, but most of old Whig Porter's other appointments were Whiggish, and many went to staunch state-credit men. This was very
likely a factor in the decision of Dorsey B. Thomas to oppose Porter
for reelection in 1876 as an independent candidate. Thomas' platform was simple: a low twenty-cent tax rate was enough to pay
current expenses, and the bond interest coupons did not need to be
paid in full. Thomas was supported by A. J. Kellar, A. S. Colyar,
and other friends of the late Andrew Johnson, who had died in the
summer of 1875. A former Union general and a black man also
opposed Porter, but the Republican organizations in most counties
turned out their voters for Thomas, who picked up only about
enough low-tax Democrats to offset the limited appeal of the two
maverick Republicans. Porter won by about the same big margin he
had enjoyed in 1874, but Thomas' bolt was a sign of discontent with
the continued strength of the Brown-Bailey doctrine of the state
debt's inviolability.[49]

The Redeemer coalition was still strong enough a few weeks after
the 1876 election to control the Senate seats through the legislature.
Former governor Harris managed to get Democratic members to
elect him easily on the first ballot with what was, for the 1870s, an
extraordinary display of near unanimity. The election for the remain-
der of Andrew Johnson's term was more typical, stretching out for
dozens of ballots. General Bate led on the first vote, but was over-
taken by James E. Bailey, the ally of John C. Brown who had lost
out to Porter in the 1874 convention. A. J. Kellar and others tried
on behalf of David M. Key the same tactic which had won the seat
for Johnson two years earlier, but this time not enough Democrats
joined the Republicans, and Bailey was elected.[50] The 1877 election
was a triumphant comeback for Harris, proving that secession was

49. Memphis *Avalanche,* November 1, 5, 1876; Hamer (ed.), *Tennessee,* II, 682; *Cumber-land Almanac* (Nashville, 1877), 20–22.

50. *House Journal,* 1877, pp. 67–68, 107; *Senate Journal,* 1877, pp. 81, 112, 133; C. Vann
Woodward, *Reunion and Reaction: The Compromise of 1877 and the End of Reconstruction*
(Boston, 1966), 49–50. Contrary to Woodward's interpretation, that Key was tied closely to
the Redeemers in the Compromise of 1877, he appears here as the foe of Redeemer Bailey.
Perhaps Key had been working with the Harris-Porter wing of the Redeemers (Porter had
appointed Key to Johnson's seat). But in 1877 Key's closest allies were enemies of the whole
Redeemer coalition.

losing its remaining stigma. Bailey's victory over Bate and Key showed that an old Whig, state-credit-flavored Redeemer could still hold his own.

For a generation, historians of the post-Reconstruction South have been working in the light of C. Vann Woodward's monumental synthesis. In contrast with the older view that the Redeemers who deposed the Radicals were reactionary but honest aristocrats, Woodward maintained that they were Whiggish capitalist types "who laid the lasting foundations in matters of race, politics, and law for the modern South." This interpretation holds much truth for Tennessee, and the name *Redeemers* has been used here for the conservative coalition which controlled most major public offices from 1870 through 1877 under the Conservative and Democratic label. But Woodward's path-breaking generalizations have permitted a few misconceptions about Tennessee, partly because the work of Dan M. Robison on the period 1886–1896 has been anachronistically applied to the 1870s. Following Robison's terminology, Woodward referred to the Redeemers, particularly Governors Brown and Porter, as the "Whig-industrialist wing of Tennessee Democrats." [51] This term is partially accurate, but it must be qualified.

First, not all the Redeemers were Whig-industrialists. Brown and Porter became deeply involved in railroad and mining enterprises, it is true, and Porter asked the legislature to aid the Southern Pacific Railroad; [52] but the corporation offices they held after leaving politics do not establish that they were agents of capitalism while governor. General Cheatham, backed by Brown for Congress in 1872 and appointed to office by Porter, was an old Democrat and not a prominent businessman. Other antebellum Democrats linked to the Redeemers but not to industry include John C. Burch, state Democratic-Conservative chairman in 1872 and Brown's appointee to the comptrollership; powerful Memphis journalist M. C. Gallaway; and A. O. P. Nicholson, chief justice of the new state supreme court. Most of these men of the business and professional class had no industrial interests. Former governor Harris and General Bate

51. C. Vann Woodward, *Origins of the New South, 1877–1913* (Baton Rouge, 1951), 3, 22.
52. White (ed.), *Messages,* VI, 420–21.

were powerful, though not dominant, members of the Redeemer coalition, but no one was more clearly associated with the Old South than they. The first convention that nominated John C. Brown hardly showed itself as industrialist when it condemned tariff protection and national banks;[53] nor did the constitutional convention of which he was president.

A second and more important qualification is that not all Whig-industrialists were Redeemers. A. S. Colyar has been implicitly called the "leader" of the Redeemers, but in fact he ran abortively against Brown twice, backed Thomas against Porter in 1876, and aided Johnson both in 1872 and in his successful Senate race against John C. Brown. A. J. Kellar, though not an old Whig like Colyar, thought he could hear "a few good old Whig principles once more making music in the air"; his great interest in the Texas and Pacific Railroad involved him deeply in the Compromise of 1877 which put Rutherford B. Hayes in the White House and D. M. Key in the cabinet. But Kellar was a consistent Johnson man after 1870 and backed Thomas in 1876. His cooperation with Hayes's attempt to build a neo-Whig conservative party in the South was intended not to strengthen the Tennessee Redeemers, but rather to undermine them by securing, as he put it, a "reorganization of party lines." Kellar's newspaper took an inflationist, or "western," view of the money question, and the colonel himself ran for Congress on the Greenback ticket in 1878.[54] Other big businessmen were Republicans, including wealthy Memphis wholesaler William R. Moore, Tennessee Coal and Iron Company general manager A. M. Shook, and Knoxville bank president John Baxter.

The Tennessee Redeemers, then, as a group, although more Whig-gish and more favorable to capitalist enterprise than the Bourbon Democrats of the 1880s, cannot be called simply Whig-industrialists. Though the Redeemers looked to the future in some ways, they can be seen partly as beneficiaries of negative attitudes about the past:

53. Memphis *Avalanche,* September 14, 1870.

54. Woodward, *Origins of the New South,* 3; see Woodward, *Reunion and Reaction,* passim; Memphis *Avalanche,* December 20, 1876, April 3, 27, May 2, June 10, 1877, November 5, 1878. Kellar's simultaneous support for the Compromise of 1877 and opposition to the Tennessee Redeemers were not contradictory, because the latter were mostly more inclined to support Tilden than Kellar's man Hayes for president.

their power was based primarily on a reaction against the national Republican victories of 1860–1865 and the state Republican rule of 1865–1869; and secondarily on wariness of those who had led Tennessee on the disastrous course of secession in 1861. The first attitude barred them from effective cooperation with Republicans, and lasted for decades; the second was much weaker and practically disappeared among Democrats after 1876. As it did, men like Isham G. Harris became more powerful, eventually taking over the state Democratic party after it was shattered by the state-debt issue.

2

The Low-Tax Revolt

Andrew Johnson had several reasons for savoring his election to the Senate in 1875, one of which was his defeat of John C. Brown, who had called Johnson "the father of repudiation in Tennessee." [1] Johnson's victory not only was a severe setback to the Redeemer coalition, but also indicated the rising opposition to their policy of paying the state debt in full. Advocates of scaling down the debt, calling themselves low-taxers, dislodged the Redeemers from the governorship in 1878. Ignoring the refusal of the voters to accept even a compromise debt plan in an 1879 referendum, the Redeemers pressed ahead with a counterattack to regain control of the Democratic party in 1880. They prevailed, but at the high cost of driving many low-tax Democrats into open rebellion. The consequent rivalry of two separate Democratic parties in 1880 allowed the Republicans to elect a governor, and encouraged them to seek an understanding with state-credit Democrats for a new majority coalition. For a short time a major political realignment seemed possible. But Democratic leaders quickly rebuilt their party in a new shape and ended the low-tax revolt by annexing it.

A key figure in the revolt and in the subsequent Democratic reorganization was crusty old Colonel John H. Savage of McMinnville. Born in the year of the Battle of New Orleans, he commanded troops in the Mexican War and then represented his hilly district in Congress as a Democrat. He was fond of remembering his antebellum expertise in the fine points of dueling and could carry a grudge: after some difference with Andrew Johnson in the mid-1850s, Savage

1. Quoted in Woodward, *Origins of the New South,* 91.

never spoke to him again. During the Civil War Savage blamed Governor Isham Harris for his loss of a coveted Confederate army promotion, tried repeatedly to goad the governor into a duel, and later spurned Harris' offer of reconciliation. Characteristically, Savage charged that Harris was part of a "deliberate design to insult and humiliate" him.[2] In the wider world, the colonel's keen eye for malice detected a "conspiracy of modern Shylocks, who seek . . . [to] impose unjust burdens, and take from a people the fruits of hard, but honest toil, so that they cannot support and educate their families." It is not surprising that a man of such temperament believed that the Funding Act of 1873 was evidence of "a ring of politicians and speculators" who "were made rich by selling out," in disregard of "the widow, the orphan, and the aged man and woman tottering to the grave."[3] Savage admitted in a candid moment, "In regard to democracy it is one of my gravest sins that I have been a partisan, often clouding my better judgment and instincts."[4] The old campaigner was in the vanguard of the low-tax Democrats who fought against paying the whole state debt.

Legislators backing Savage for the Senate in 1875 were, along with Johnson's men, those who voted most heavily for a measure debilitating the 1873 Funding Act. Despite the depression, the state had already funded $6.66 million of old bonds but began defaulting on interest payments in 1875.[5] The bondholders, who were organized and quite alert to their interests, suggested that the legislature send a committee to confer with them, which it did. Since they were not

2. *Biographical Directory of the American Congress, 1774–1927* (Washington, D.C., 1928), 1495; [John H. Savage], *The Life of John H. Savage: Citizen, Soldier, Lawyer, Congressman: Before the War Begun and Prosecuted by the Abolitionists of Northern States to Reduce the Descendents of the Rebels of 1776, Who Defeated the Armies of the King of England and Gained Independence for the United States, Down to the Level of the Negro Race* (Nashville, 1903), 70, 145 (quote), 162–63; [Savage], *Col. Savage's Defense: He Is Not an Enemy of Senator Harris: Harris' Friends Make War on Him* (N.p., [1888]); Nashville *Union and American,* October 9, 1874.

3. [Savage], *Speech of Hon. John H. Savage, as Delivered in the Senate and Before the People, on the So-Called State Debt Question* (McMinnville, Tenn., 1879), 9; Savage, *The Power to Tax Is the Power to Destroy* (McMinnville, Tenn., 1876), 5.

4. John H. Savage to Howell E. Jackson, November 24, 1881, in Harding-Jackson Papers.

5. *Acts of the State of Tennessee, Passed by the Thirty-Ninth General Assembly: 1875* (Nashville, 1875), 3 (hereinafter cited as *Tennessee Acts*); *House Journal,* 1875, pp. 115–16, 635; William R. Garrett and A. V. Goodpasture, *History of Tennessee, Its People and Its Institutions, from the Earliest Times to the Year 1903* (Nashville, 1905), 264.

receiving any interest, the bondholders proposed the issue of new bonds to carry a rate of interest beginning at 3 percent and increasing at five-year intervals to 6 percent. The result of the conference, however, was a report to the 1877 legislature outlining a plan to fund the debt at sixty cents on the dollar and 6 percent interest (or, in short, sixty and six, or 60–6). This plan the lawmakers rejected. Instead, they forbade all further interest payments except to Tennessee educational institutions and cut the tax rate from forty cents on the hundred dollars to ten cents. Governor Porter's veto was ineffectual because simple majorities could override it. He re-called the legislature into extra session twice in 1877, but it refused proposals for funding at 60–6 and at 50–6. The ground of battle had shifted: whereas earlier the question had been the importance of paying the debt in full, now the debate was over whether to scale it to sixty cents on the dollar or less.[6]

The Redeemers were sitting atop a party rumbling with discontent. True, four of the state's five big newspapers favored holding the line at sixty cents, as did most prominent Democratic officeholders. But about a third of the Democrats in the lower house, including supporters of Bailey, Bate, and Key for the Senate, petitioned two low-tax leaders to publish their speeches. A. S. Colyar and Colonel Savage both mounted insurgent campaigns for the gubernatorial nomination, challenging Redeemer control of convention delegates at the county level.[7] The party delegates assembled in Nashville in August, 1878, prepared for a battle.

Most of the Memphis delegates were destined to a much longer absence than they expected. Following the first death from yellow fever on August 13, the city was electrified by panic: a single railroad sold $35,000 worth of tickets in two days. Those who were able fled the city, leaving behind thousands of poorer citizens, mostly black and Irish. A total of about 17,600 were stricken in the epidemic, and by September the two-page *Avalanche* was nothing but a death regis-

6. Hamer (ed.), *Tennessee,* 682–83; Garrett and Goodpasture, *History of Tennessee,* 263; J. Q. A. Remine to J. D. Porter, April 4, 1877, J. A. Turley to Porter, January 12, 1877, in CGO, TSLA.

7. Memphis *Avalanche,* June 5, November 25, December 1, 1877, January 15, August 16, 1878; *House Journal,* 1877, pp. 67–68; Nashville *American,* August 13, 1878.

ter, listing scores of new casualties each day. The yellow fever epidemic of 1878 and its milder recurrence the next year not only dealt Memphis a terrible economic blow, but permanently altered the nature of its population.[8]

Against this grim backdrop, the convention in Nashville fully reflected the confusion in the Democratic party. The Savage-Colyar forces made a strong but futile effort to elect the temporary chairman and control the credentials committee. While another committee hammered out the platform, Senator Harris begged the convention to put party unity above the debt question, and the body complied by adopting a platform designed to satisfy both sides and inspire neither. This superficial unity collapsed over a routine resolution endorsing the incumbent Democratic administration. Ironically, Governor Porter, who had dissociated himself from John C. Brown in 1874 because of Brown's strong state-credit views, now found himself the target of a low-tax movement which had become much bolder and stronger since then. Nearly a third of the delegates opposed the normal courtesy of endorsing Porter.[9] Most of them were concentrated geographically in Colonel Savage's secessionist, antebellum Democratic district, but other anti-Porter delegates came from counties quite different (see Appendix B, Table 4). So far, it appeared that these low-taxers had at least a veto over the nomination, which required a two-thirds majority.

Competing with Savage and Colyar were two Knoxville men, one of whom, John M. Fleming, was the candidate most closely identified with past Redeemer administrations. On the first ballot Fleming's vote was matched by that of John A. Gardner of Weakley County, who also had Redeemer connections but who had taken a strong low-tax stand on the state debt. Savage and Colyar were nearly tied for third place. Of these top four candidates, each drew over three-fourths of his votes from his own grand division of the state, except

8. Memphis *Avalanche,* August 18, 1878; Gerald M. Capers, *The Biography of a River Town: Memphis: Its Heroic Age* (Chapel Hill, 1939), 195, 198. Capers, who has written the best account of Memphis' yellow fever epidemics, believes that they, not the Civil War, divided the history of the river city into two distinct periods. So many Irish died, and so many Germans moved away, that the city lost what degree of cosmopolitan diversity it possessed and became a "southern Middletown . . . hopelessly provincial." See pages 186–209.
9. Nashville *American,* August 16, 17, 1878.

Fleming, who got over half his votes outside his own East Tennessee.[10] The bulk of the anti-Porter delegates went to Savage and Colyar, but most of Gardner's men had voted to endorse Porter, and
generally the comparison of voting on the resolution for Porter and
on the nomination indicates that the delegates were not firmly
managed by factional leaders. Furthermore, regional and personal
loyalties still overshadowed the state-debt issue so that neither side
was able to unite on a candidate.

On the second day of balloting Savage withdrew and most of his
votes went to Gardner, who seized the lead. In the midst of much
uproar, someone nominated Judge Albert S. Marks of Franklin
County, but Gardner, Fleming, and Colyar briefly held their forces
in line. Then began contrived bandwagons designed to roll to victory:
first for a Nashville man, then for state-credit man John V. Wright,
and finally for Judge Marks. The last one worked. With several
former Savage delegations leading the stampede on the twenty-
second ballot, Marks was nominated and the Redeemers lost control
of the Democratic party.[11]

The low-tax Memphis *Avalanche,* which was trying to channel
discontent into the Greenback party, bitterly commented that low-
taxers Savage and Colyar were "slaughtered" in the convention.
Redeemer candidate Fleming lost also, however, and Marks won as
a true dark horse, partly because he was understood to be the author
of the platform—one ambiguous enough to be palatable to nearly
all shades of opinion. Perhaps the last-minute show of strength by
state-credit man Wright spurred the low-taxers to try Marks as a
compromise. Four years later the Nashville *Banner,* which had reason to divide Marks and Colyar, asserted that Colyar would have
been nominated in 1878 except that Marks was beyond the reach
of the telegraph and could not withdraw. That was an exaggeration,
but Colyar did criticize Marks harshly in 1878 for "violating family
ties." [12] Marks's friends at the convention may have reminded Colyar
delegates that Marks's mother was the colonel's first cousin and that

10. *Ibid.,* August 17, 1878; Lynn, "Tennessee's Public Debt," 35.
11. Nashville *American,* August 18, 1878.
12. Memphis *Avalanche,* August 20, 1878; Nashville *Banner,* June 7, 1882; Ball, "Public
Career of Colonel A. S. Colyar," 236.

he had studied law under Colyar in the 1850s, but Colyar certainly did not get Marks the nomination.

A lifelong Democrat, Marks had run as a Unionist candidate for the proposed secession convention in 1861, then, as a colonel in the Confederate army, lost a leg in the battle of Murfreesboro. He learned something of politics from his father-in-law, a state legislator.[13] In later years journalists were still arguing over just where Marks had stood on the state-debt question in 1878, and over which group in the convention had nominated him. A man of great caution, Marks was able to let both sides think he was friendly; the only defect of this policy was that eventually both sides tended to get disillusioned. His character was captured by a reporter writing of the intrigues of a legislative caucus a few years later. Marks was "discreetly noncommittal," even when a friend asked him for the time of day: after careful thought Marks took out his watch, peeked at it, then murmured, "You say first." [14]

The minority parties had trouble finding candidates to oppose Marks: the Republicans were turned down by one man, the Greenbackers by two.[15] The man the Greenbackers finally recruited was R. M. Edwards, who denounced "rings" in high places and invoked the memory of Andrew Johnson. But Johnson's old following failed to turn out for Edwards, whose votes tended to be highly concentrated by county and by district: 47 percent of the Greenback voters lived in five big counties, and in one of these, Shelby, over half the Edwards votes were in four rural districts which gave Marks less than 6 percent of his county total (see Map 2).[16] Greenback voters were likely to be former Confederates, especially in West Tennessee (see Appendix B, Table 3). The small party did not represent a farmers' revolt, particularly in Middle Tennessee, where it found support largely in the towns; the only social divisions clearly re-

13. Speer, *Sketches,* 74–77.

14. Memphis *Avalanche,* May 9, 1880; Knoxville *Chronicle,* August 7, 1880; Nashville *Banner,* January 10, 1885.

15. Verton M. Queener, "The East Tennessee Republicans as a Minority Party, 1870–1896," *East Tennessee Historical Society's Publications,* XV (1943), 54; Memphis *Avalanche,* August 30, November 5, 1878; Ashland City *Cheatham County Plaindealer,* October 10, 17, 1878; Lynn, "Tennessee's Public Debt," 46–47.

16. Memphis *Avalanche,* November 1, 6, 7, 1878.

34

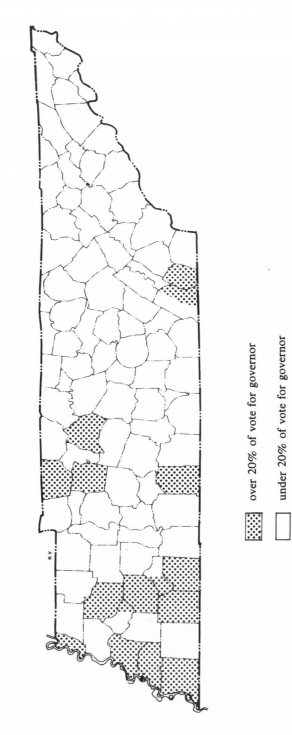

Map 2
GREENBACK PARTY STRENGTH, 1878

over 20% of vote for governor

under 20% of vote for governor

Source: *Tribune Almanac*, 1880, pp. 72–73.

flected in the Greenback party were those of region. Edwards received less than 11 percent of the vote, and Marks won easily after a campaign in which his party stressed the northern birth of the Republican nominee.[17]

Despite his lack of previous association with the Redeemer ruling group, Governor Marks did not try any big changes in politics. He reappointed at least two members of the Porter administration: the state school superintendent over at least five other applicants for the job, and the Memphis coal-oil inspector despite a "Cousin Albert" letter from Colyar urging another man.[18] These appointments made it possible for Senator Harris to overlook the sinecure Marks gave to a staff member of the Chattanooga *Times,* no friend of the senator. Marks's patronage policy, like his stand on the state debt, was one of appeasement rather than of independent leadership.

Governor Marks's message to the legislature, in January, 1879, declared that the state could not possibly pay its entire debt and recommended its adjustment.[19] A legislative committee investigated the state finances of 1866–1868, and the subsequent charges that the debt was based on "fraud and corruption and knavery" increased the pressure for repudiation. Moderate low-taxers were happy when the House passed a resolution for a settlement at fifty cents on the dollar and 4 percent interest (50–4), subject to approval by the voters in a referendum and by two-thirds of the bondholders. The state-credit men were pleased at the provision for submission to the bondholders, and the "irrepressible" low-taxers in the legislature could plan to take their case to the people. A committee composed of four Redeemers and one Republican went to New York and convinced a number of bondholders to accept a 50–4 settlement. Some of them objected, however, and state-credit men later denied that proper approval from the bondholders had been secured. But Governor Marks was persuaded and ordered a referendum. Now it remained

17. *Tribune Almanac and Political Register* (New York, 1838–1913, annual, title changes), 1880, pp. 72–73; Queener, "East Tennessee Republicans as a Minority Party," 54.

18. Nashville *Sun,* April 4, 1895; Colyar to Marks, January 14, 1879, W. H. Rhea to Marks, April 6, 1880, in CGO, TSLA.

19. White (ed.), *Messages,* VI, 566.

for the state-credit forces to overcome low-tax arguments and win the approval of the electorate.[20]

Public debate matched friend and foe of the 50–4 plan. Leading the dissenters, Colonel Savage insisted that it was better to say that the state owed nothing, but offer a 33 1/3-cent settlement for the sake of peace, than to say that the state rightfully owed its entire debt and then offer only half of it. His allies were Dorsey B. Thomas, state Senator S. F. Wilson, and other county-level politicians, mostly from Middle Tennessee, but their largest newspaper supporter was the Memphis *Avalanche*. A. J. Kellar's *Avalanche* urged its readers to vote down the proposal and let the bondholders and railroads settle the matter between themselves, a reference to a legal battle eventually won by the railroads. Opponents of the 50–4 settlement were relatively few and weak.[21]

Aligned in favor of 50–4 were Redeemers such as former governors John C. Brown and J. D. Porter and even some low-tax Democrats like A. S. Colyar. They were assisted by Governor Marks, two state supreme court judges, and Senator Bailey and Congressmen John F. House, G. G. Dibrell, and John D. C. Atkins, not to mention a host of state legislators. Senator Harris apparently stood aside from the controversy, but General Bate came out for acceptance. The press generally did too, including all major papers except the *Avalanche*. The Nashville *American* argued that a 50-cent settlement, for which the low-tax side had voted in the 1877 legislature, was all they had ever wanted, and that 4 percent interest on half the debt was the same as the 6 percent interest on 33 cents that Savage advocated. The *American* and the Memphis *Ledger* threatened that if the 50-cent proposal were defeated, the state might somehow be forced to pay the entire debt.[22] In case arguments based more or less on reason failed, an appeal was made to the emotions: "The bulk of the wealth and intelligence of the state is against, the most of the

20. Memphis *Weekly Public Ledger,* March 18, April 1, 22, 1879; Hamer (ed.), *Tennessee,* II, 685–86; Lynn, "Tennessee's Public Debt," 46–47.
21. [Savage], *Speech on the State Debt,* 14; Nashville *American,* June 3, 29, July 9, 19, 1879; Memphis *Avalanche,* August 1, 1879.
22. Nashville *American,* June 11, 19, 29, July 9, 17, 29, August 1, 1879; Memphis *Appeal,* July 5, 9, 16, August 7, 1879; Nashville *Banner,* May 19, 1880; Memphis *Public Ledger,* August 4, 1879.

taxpayers, and certainly the largest taxpayers are against [the non-paying party]. The commercial classes are almost a unit against them. The railroad interest, ramifying the entire state, is not only naturally against them on account of the high value they set . . . on credit, but also, in this case, on account of a substantial interest." The nonpayers' doctrines, shuddered the *American,* would disgrace even the Paris Commune. "Shade [*sic*] of Grundy, Polk, Bell, Nicholson, Johnson [!], what diminutive [things] crawl about in and squeak out from among the folds of your honorable gown? Are such men right, in moral or in political principles?" [23] The proponents of the 50–4 settlement were able to muster far more respectability and prestige than its enemies. Both sides relied more on feelings about whether paying the debt was basically right or wrong than on rational arguments over exactly where to compromise.

Despite the furor, the referendum brought a low voter turnout: compared to a total vote of nearly 200,000 for governor in 1876, the debt settlement was rejected by 46,310 votes to 76,232 (see Map 3).[24] The 50–4 proposal had determined enemies, and its appeal was too weak to conquer public apathy. Only those who questioned the legitimacy of the debt and disliked paying taxes to honor it had a clear, emotionally compelling position—which contributed to their victory.

Most voters against the 50–4 proposal lived in Middle and West Tennessee. The referendum majority there, which defied the nearly unanimous advice of the political elite, derived mostly from white, rural counties, perhaps with relatively poor farmland (see Appendix B, Table 5). Old friends of Andrew Johnson and, to a lesser extent, old Whigs, voted against the party leaders. The message should have been clear for politicians to read: a great many Democrats were so suspicious of their Redeemer leaders that they would not accept even a drastic concession by the state-credit side. Low-taxers like John H. Savage were encouraged by the result of the referendum, but the Redeemers were sufficiently blind, or overconfident, to proceed with their plans to regain full control of the Democratic party in 1880.

The 1879 referendum left the state-debt issue very much alive. But

23. Nashville *American,* July 12, 1879.
24. *Cumberland Almanac* (Nashville, 1877), 22; White (ed.), *Messages,* VI, 611.

38

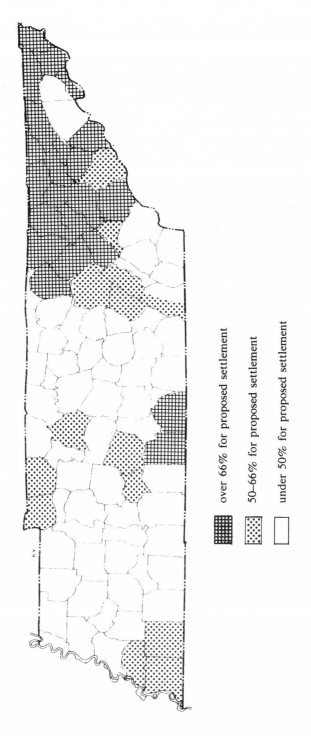

Map 3

STATE-DEBT REFERENDUM, 1879

over 66% for proposed settlement

50–66% for proposed settlement

under 50% for proposed settlement

Source: White (ed.), *Messages*, VI, 609–11.

that Tennesseeans had other public concerns was evident in the Shelby County local election of August, 1880. The central symbolic issue in that contest was the Republican nominee for sheriff, a black man named Ed Shaw. During the 1878 yellow fever epidemic he had received 1,677 votes for state senator, losing to a Democrat who won 2,247 votes. Shaw had a way of vexing white people. In 1868 he had been put off a train for refusing to leave a car reserved for whites. "Every time a wild-eyed urchin shouts . . . 'Ed Shaw' in the vicinity of the Appeal office, there is a prolonged spasm in the editorial department," chortled the rival *Avalanche* in 1878. The *Appeal,* still hysterical in 1880, labeled Shaw an "illiterate incompetent negro communist." The Memphis *Ledger* called him a "wild fanatic." The *Avalanche,* though under new state-credit, anti-Greenback management, frowned on such abusive language, remarking that Shaw was not the first bad candidate for office.[25] No white editor, of course, backed Shaw for sheriff.

By 1880 the Memphis epidemics had hastened a change in the electorate: the census of that year was the first to show a majority of Negroes in the county. Since 1870 the number of blacks in Shelby had increased from thirty-six thousand to forty-four thousand, while the number of whites had decreased from forty thousand to thirty-five thousand. Shaw could reasonably expect to do well and indeed carried ten country districts, some by landslide proportions, and captured two wards in Memphis. But the Democratic candidate not only carried the remaining six rural districts (one of them by a vote of 172 to 5 for Shaw), but took eight Memphis wards. In the first and third wards alone, he beat Shaw by a total of 2,183 to 220. The Democrat's county aggregate was 8,564, to 5,675 for Shaw and 1,740 for the Greenback candidate. Angry Greenback leaders charged that black voters had been intimidated or cheated. Black policemen, in a day before the secret ballot, were threatened with the loss of their jobs for having voted for Shaw. A white newspaper claimed that Negroes were cowed by the Republican party but failed to condemn white Democrats for their remarkable solidarity. Disheartened

25. Memphis *Appeal,* May 8, July 30, 1880; Memphis *Avalanche,* July 19, October 29, November 14, 1878, July 21, 22, 1880; Robert E. Corlew, "The Negro in Tennessee, 1870–1900" (Ph.D. dissertation, University of Alabama, 1954), 151; Memphis *Public Ledger,* July 2, 1880.

Shelby County blacks met and heard speakers tell them they could find a better life in Kansas, which many of them tried to do. In Nashville and in Haywood County, blacks scored minor victories in the 1880 local election; [26] but the defeat of Ed Shaw demonstrated that even with a strong candidate and a clear majority of the voters, black people had little hope for political power when white employers, landowners, public officials, newspapers, and ballot-counters united against them.

The major political battleground elsewhere in Tennessee in 1880 was the state debt. "Farmers are all laborers," cried a rural editor, "and they are not going to rely on the money kings of the East for relief from financial troubles any longer—but each says to the other—'Trust not for freedom to the banks;/In farmers' votes and farmers' ranks,/Our only safety lies!' " A city daily, not impressed, held firmly to its view that "a sound, debt-paying democratic platform, with a sound, debt-paying democratic candidate for governor, will win. No more compromise platforms or compromise candidates will be tolerated," it declared.[27] The Nashville *American,* the most fierce of state-credit newspapers, accused low-taxer J. H. Savage of trying to patch up a new party of men from both parties and both races. The conflict reverberated throughout the state. Wilson County Democrats split when low-taxers gained control of the county convention, provoking the outnumbered state-credit side to walk out and form their own convention. With the approach of the date for a special state convention for choosing delegates to the national Democratic convention, it appeared that the low-taxers might try to stage a revolt and even depose part of the state party committee. But the convention went smoothly and passed by state issues except for a fight over Wilson County credentials—a sign that the Redeemers could deny Marks a second term and write a state-credit platform in the August convention.[28]

26. Capers, *Biography of a River Town,* 164; Memphis *Public Ledger,* August 7, 9, 10, 25, 1880; Memphis *Avalanche,* August 10, 25, 1880; Memphis *Appeal,* August 3, 1880; Nashville *American,* August 7, 1880.

27. Humboldt *Argus,* quoted in Memphis *Avalanche,* April 6, 1880; Memphis *Avalanche,* April 7, 1880.

28. Memphis *Appeal,* May 11, June 6, 1880; Nashville *American,* June 8, 10, 1880; Memphis *Public Ledger,* June 9, 1880.

The low-tax forces were seriously weakened by the defection of A. S. Colyar. He gave a speech urging state credit as a matter of honor and self-respect, which the approving *American* printed in full. Later Colyar emphasized that he did not agree with what he described as the Republican position of paying whatever the creditors might ask, but that he only wanted to offer the bondholders what the state could pay. He admitted that he had once been called a low-taxer, but he explained lamely that those he had once associated with were now no-taxers.[29]

Another politician who spoke for state credit was John V. Wright. He had been elected to Congress as a Democrat for three consecutive terms in the 1850s and then to the Confederate Congress in 1861. After serving in the southern army, he lived in Columbia. Governor Porter, who had appointed Wright's cousin state school superintendent, placed Wright on a vacant circuit court bench. Now, in 1880, Wright said he felt compelled to speak out on the debt issue, proclaiming that Tennessee must be honest even if poor. He declared that some Democrats preferred to see their party defeated rather than their state dishonored. The skeptical Nashville *Banner* remarked that the poor-but-honest appeal sounded a bit demagogic,[30] and practical party man Isham Harris must have winced at Wright's intransigence.

Low-tax Democrats won the convention delegations from White, Warren, and Wilson counties, but it appeared that Davidson, Maury, Giles, and Montgomery would be held by the regulars. Increasing rancor made compromise ever more unlikely, as the low-taxers won some local victories but could not dislodge their foes from their powerful editorial positions or from the state Democratic machinery.[31]

When the second Democratic state convention met in August to nominate a candidate for governor, state-credit delegates caucused and decided to fight for agreement between the state and its creditors

29. Nashville *American,* June 9, July 27, 1880.
30. Hamer (ed.), *Tennessee,* II, 554; Speer, *Sketches,* 480, 524–26; Nashville *Banner,* July 7, 1880.
31. Nashville *Banner,* July 8, 1880; Knoxville *Chronicle,* July 11, 1880; Memphis *Avalanche,* July 21, 1880. Besides the Nashville *American,* the regulars were backed by the Memphis *Avalanche,* which Kellar had left, and by Adolph Ochs's Chattanooga *Times.*

as the basis for a debt settlement. They selected a committee of three, including Colyar, to negotiate with the low-taxers. The latter also organized a caucus, chaired by S. F. Wilson, and resolved not to support a candidate or platform not pledging to let the people vote on every aspect of the debt question.[32] The lines had hardened since 1878, and Tennessee Democrats were behaving almost as two separate parties.

With both sides organized, the first test vote would identify the masters of the convention. It came on the election of a temporary chairman, when thirty-year-old low-tax legislator David L. Snodgrass lost by the resounding total of 940 votes to 293. The same division persisted through the next day, when the convention's only harmonious action was to invite General Cheatham to sit on the dais. The report of the Redeemer majority of the platform committee, read by former governor Neill S. Brown, condemned all repudiation but called for the best settlement to which the creditors would agree. It also showed the Redeemers' independence of the railroads by proclaiming that the legislature should make them "do justice," "in view of the complaints coming up from every part of the State" about rate discrimination. The majority report was adopted over two dissenting planks. The convention was still under Redeemer control.[33]

The low-tax caucus, however, had bound itself not to support a platform not including a popular referendum, and now, by prearrangement, they walked out of the convention and immediately organized their own meeting. The remaining delegates nominated John V. Wright for governor while the low-taxers were choosing S. F. Wilson to run against him.[34] The Redeemers could not risk another referendum, but the low-taxers did not trust the old leaders with the people's taxes. This difference split the party.

Despite the result of the 1879 referendum, few well-known politicians backed Wilson: the safest position was quiet support for Wright on the grounds of party unity. John H. Savage, of course, was for Wilson, as was Dorsey B. Thomas, the bolter of 1876. But nearly all Democratic leaders stayed with Wright—as a Republican editor

32. Memphis *Appeal,* August 10, 1880.
33. *Ibid.,* August 11, 12, 1880; Memphis *Public Ledger,* August 12, 1880.
34. Memphis *Appeal,* August 12, 1880.

put it, the regular Democrats had the brains of the party. United States Senators Harris and Bailey, former senator Henry Cooper, a son of Whig leader John Bell, and one of President James K. Polk's nephews, who was regular Democratic state chairman, were the sort of people behind Wright. The Memphis *Ledger* was the only daily newspaper for Wilson, though he had several country weeklies.[35] Each side probably overestimated its strength: a low-taxer in a strong Wilson county could feel that the urban newspapers were simply out of touch, while an old-style politician who stayed in town could be confident that the people would follow their proper leaders as in the past.

The Nashville *Banner,* a moderate Wright paper, complained that Wilson was trying to pit the poor against the rich, and labor against capital, and cited Daniel Webster against political appeals to class. Perhaps Wilson was echoing his ally Colonel Savage, who accused capitalist V. K. Stevenson of getting rich from speculating in stock of the Nashville, Chattanooga, and St. Louis Railroad, to the injury of the people living along the line. Savage was making the point that the rich were in favor of paying the state debt, but the idea of a conflict of economic interest was not foremost in his mind. "Are men with salaries safe advisors for the humble?" he asked. "They may be wise in their way, but they know not the misfortune and misery of the poor." To show that he honored the common man as the clever rich did not, Savage declared that "a man who can make a Justice of the Peace, can discharge well the legal duties of Governor." The pro-Wilson Memphis *Ledger* charged that in the Confederate Congress, Wright had voted to exempt owners of twenty or more slaves from military service and that now he was trying to burden the poor man again, this time with the state debt;[36] though it is not clear why paying the debt through property taxes would hurt the poor more

35. Memphis *Public Ledger,* August 24, 26, September 8, October 6, 1880; Knoxville *Chronicle,* July 11, August 21, 22, 1880; Memphis *Appeal,* August 12, 1880; Nashville *American,* August 6, 19, 1880; Nashville *Banner,* August 26, September 25, 1880; Jackson *West Tennessee Whig,* October 1, 1880.

36. Nashville *Banner,* October 15, 1880; [John H. Savage], *Extracts from the Speeches of Col. John H. Savage, on the Fifty-and-Four Bill, Colyar, Bailey and Company: An Open Letter to the People: Read and Hand to Your Neighbor* (McMinnville, 1880), 4, 10 (quotes), 11–12; Memphis *Public Ledger,* October 26, 1880.

than the rich. Savage and the *Ledger* were both arguing that capitalists could not be trusted because they despised common men. Sensitivity of social status is a better key to understanding the politics of 1880 than economic class conflict.

Savage pointed to another difference between Wright and Wilson Democrats in saying that his own policy was favored by "two-thirds of the people, outside of the towns." [37] There is some evidence that his distinction, if not his statistic, was correct. The low-tax Jackson *Whig* threw fuel on the fire:

> Is it not high time that farmers should look more to their own interests and make their own selection for members of the legislature and of Congress? . . . when the party lash is applied, under the mandate of partisan commanders, it will be expected, I presume, that the farmers will submit, lamb-like, and be led to the slaughter of their political rights and personal liberties "for the good of our party." Farmers, will we do it, or will we, like men, claim our just rights and demand a voice in the legislation of our country? [38]

This rural hostility was reciprocated. Merchants were required to pay privilege taxes according to type of business and size of town, and a city paper raised that grievance in an inverted anticipation of William Jennings Bryan's assertion that urban prosperity rested on agriculture. "It has been the common practice of shallow-brained demagogues in Tennessee to array the country against the town," complained the Memphis *Avalanche.*

> These demagogues have even secured the passage of laws discriminating against the trade and industries of the cities, unmindful of the fact that the prosperity of the cities is the prosperity of the country. As the cities grow in wealth and population the country grows in wealth and population. The city furnishes a market for the country product, while the greater the concentration of merchandise and industries in the city the greater facilities for cheapness in buying is furnished the country. . . . The main strength of repudiation is among the rural population. While it is to their interest to maintain the public credit, they are not brought face to face with its necessity like the people of the city. [39]

Neither the *Whig* nor the *Avalanche* claimed that the economic

37. [Savage], *Extracts from the Speeches of Col. John H. Savage,* 4.
38. Jackson *West Tennessee Whig,* October 1, 1880.
39. Memphis *Avalanche,* October 24, 1880.

interests of the city and country were in conflict. What is clear is
that city and country distrusted each other.

Were these antagonisms imaginary, or were they manifested in the
behavior of the voters? Table 5 shows gubernatorial returns for

Table 5
TOWN–COUNTRY VOTING PATTERNS,
1880 GUBERNATORIAL ELECTION, SELECTED COUNTIES [40]

	Wright	Wilson	Hawkins	Wilson/ Wright
Memphis	3437	896	3471	.26
Shelby County outside Memphis	1828	754	4287	.41
Nashville	2693	1065	2758	.40
Davidson outside Nashville	2249	1906	3469	.85
Knoxville	993	31	1025	.03
Knox outside Knoxville	2077	33	3286	.02
Chattanooga	877	96	1687	.11
Hamilton outside Chattanooga	417	214	764	.51
Fayetteville district (#8)	310	103	198	.33
Lincoln except dist. 8	1270	1410	628	1.11
Clarksville districts (#12, 13)	834	69	481	.08
Montgomery except dists. 12, 13	1749	769	2102	.44
Bolivar district (#6)	99	118	178	1.20
Hardeman except dist. 6	321	1323	1103	4.1
McMinnville district (#1)	119	230	220	1.93
Warren except dist. 1	81	1210	239	15.0
Pulaski district (#7)	317	86	286	.27
Lynnville district (#15)	238	39	103	.16
Giles except dists. 7, 15	1828	578	1551	.32

several cities and towns and for their respective counties with town
totals subtracted. In East Tennessee, only Knoxville and Chattanooga are given, because Wilson received such a low vote in that
division of the state. In Knoxville, for example, Wilson did better

40. *Ibid.,* November 3, 4, 5, 1880; Nashville *American,* November 4, 6, 1880; Knoxville
Chronicle, November 4, 1880; Chattanooga *Times,* November 5, 1880; Fayetteville *Observer,*
November 4, 1880; Clarksville *Weekly Chronicle,* November 6, 1880; Bolivar *Bulletin,* November 11, 1880; McMinnville *Southern Standard,* November 6, 1880; Pulaski *Citizen,* November
4, 1880.

with respect to Wright than in rural Knox County, but his support was so slim that the figures mean little. In Giles, a state-credit county, the difference was very small, and in Shelby it was not overwhelming. Elsewhere, however, there was an unmistakable tendency for rural voters to favor Wilson much more than townspeople in the same county. The rhetoric of rural-urban conflict was paralleled in the election returns.

The 1880 gubernatorial election was a three-way contest; the fading Greenback party polled only 1.5 percent of the total.[41] With 24 percent, Wilson placed third but took enough votes from Wright to defeat him, as Andrew Johnson had done to Cheatham in 1872. Most Wilson supporters lived in Middle Tennessee and in the same rural counties which had backed Johnson and then defeated the 50–4 proposal in 1879 (see Map 4 and Appendix B, Table 6). These friends and neighbors of Colonel Savage had been the most reluctant supporters of a Democratic party controlled by Redeemers, and now their desertion brought it crashing down. Support for regular Democrat John V. Wright in West Tennessee correlates highly with prewar Whiggery, which fits Professor Woodward's view of the Redeemers as dominated by old Whigs, though Wright himself was an antebellum Democrat.[42] Perhaps the old issue of internal improvements lingered by association with the railroad debt. Throughout the state, though regional patterns differed, the low-tax rebellion of 1880 can be explained better by previous political behavior than by socioeconomic variables, urbanization excepted.

C. Vann Woodward has written that the Redeemers' fork of the road to reunion led to cooperation with the conservative East, but that it "took a lot of hallooing and heading off by the conservative leaders to keep the mass of Southerners herded up the right fork," since agrarians preferred the left fork leading to alliance with the West. In this view it was not until the Populist movement that the South failed to remain "fairly faithful to the Eastern alignment" established in 1877.[43] Aside from the difficulty that A. J. Kellar, a

41. Nashville *American,* November 6, 1882. The two Democratic parties backed a single ticket of presidential electors and saved the state for the national Democrats.
42. Woodward, *Origins of the New South,* 1–2.
43. *Ibid.,* 50.

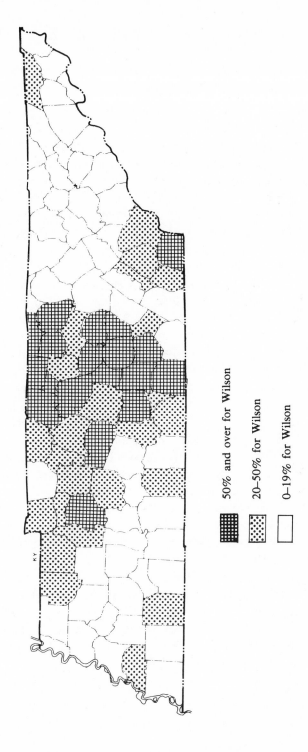

Map 4

VOTE FOR LOW-TAX DEMOCRAT S. F. WILSON FOR GOVERNOR, 1880

50% and over for Wilson

20–50% for Wilson

0–19% for Wilson

Source: *Cumberland Almanac*, 1881, p. 24.

key actor in the Compromise of 1877, was an inflationist and an enemy of the Tennessee Redeemers, the two-fork analogy does not work well for Tennessee. The low-tax Democrats stampeded from the Redeemer trail as early as 1880. If they found a left fork, more-over, they were not leftists in a twentieth-century sense, but wanted to limit concentrations of political and economic power. Some of the cowboys would soon ride away to catch up with the low-tax bolters.

A month after the election, Governor-elect Alvin Hawkins was in an optimistic mood. He wrote to another Republican, "I am gratified to know from many sources that the [Democratic] split continues to widen, what the result will be the Lord only knows." [44] The happy winner was a lawyer from Huntingdon, in Carroll County, which like Hawkins had been Whig before and Unionist during the war, and Republican ever after. A John Bell elector in 1860, Hawkins went to Congress in 1862 as a Unionist but was not admitted. However, Lincoln appointed him federal district attorney, and then Governor Brownlow placed him on the state supreme court. Hawkins was elected governor in 1880 on a platform denounc-ing any scaling of the debt as repudiation, but he was handicapped in fulfilling the pledge by the weakness of his office, by his minority victory, and by his lack of conspicuous ability. [45] His party was out-numbered in the legislature and dependent on cooperation from state-credit Democrats, who were torn between the memories of the 1860s and the compelling present necessity of a state-credit alliance with the Republicans. Ironically, it was thus the Democratic regulars of 1880 who found themselves the natural allies of Republicans in 1881. That is why the 1881 legislature was the most interesting and unpredictable one which met in Tennessee between the Civil War and perhaps 1911.

This fluid situation excited the political crystal-ball gazers. Sena-tor James E. Bailey, whose term expired in 1881, was a regular or state-credit Democrat, and so the other two groups had a common interest in blocking his reelection. The Washington, D.C., *Sun* re-ported the possibility of aid from low-tax Democrats for the election

44. Alvin Hawkins to W. B. Stokes, December 4, 1880, in W. B. Stokes Papers, TSLA.
45. Memphis *Appeal,* May 15, 1880; Queener, "East Tennessee Republicans as a Minority Party," 54; Nashville *Banner,* January 16, 1883.

of a Republican senator—a rumor the Memphis *Ledger* felt compelled to quash. But on the basis of the state-debt question, Republicans would join instead with the regular Democrats, one of whom thought he saw the dawning of a new era in which the South would be solid no longer but would divide on important issues if the Republicans were reasonable.[46] In 1881 there were not two major political parties in Tennessee, but three, and relations among them were a matter for conjecture.

Because Democratic voters in many counties split between regular and low-tax legislative candidates, the two factions together won only thirty-seven of the seventy-five seats in the House of Representatives. The Nashville *American* counted thirty-seven Republicans, leaving the balance of power to the one Greenback member. H. B. Ramsey, elected from Shelby County on a most anomalous Republican-Greenback fusion ticket, had sat in the 1879 House as a Greenbacker, but would be called a Republican in the 1883 House. Now in 1881 the Associated Press reported that Ramsey was "regarded as more of a greenbacker than republican," though the *American* put him in the GOP. His ambiguous status made him the ideal candidate for Speaker: he got the one Greenback vote needed for a majority over the Democrats. The Republican caucus choice for Speaker was appeased with the top committee chairmanship, and Speaker Ramsey appointed a black Republican chairman of the public roads committee. The sergeant-at-arms of the House was a white Republican, and his assistant was a black one. In the Senate the Democrats had a clear majority, but their division caused a deadlock in the election of a Speaker. The Republicans withdrew and decided to support a regular Democrat, but when they returned the Democrats were agreeing among themselves to vote for G. H. Morgan, a low-taxer. Hence the regular Democrats were excluded from the speakerships in both houses of the legislature, and they looked to the election of a United States senator with signs of alarm.[47]

46. Washington (D.C.) *Sun,* quoted in Nashville *American,* December 11, 1880; Memphis *Public Ledger,* quoted in Nashville *American,* December 17, 1880; Nashville *American,* November 21, 1880.
47. Nashville *American,* January 8, 1881; Knoxville *Chronicle,* January 5, 7, 1881; Nashville *Banner,* January 5, 1881.

Most Republican legislators were for Horace Maynard for the Senate. The Democratic aspirants included the incumbent Senator Bailey, General W. B. Bate, Congressman John M. Bright, and a stable of dark horses. The situation was so uncertain, chuckled a Republican, that it was "hard to discover a democrat of any prominence who is not expecting that lightening may strike him." The Democrats had such a thin margin in joint convention that the Nashville *Banner* insisted shrilly that any doubt over the election of a Democratic senator implied that a legislator of the party was willing to sell his honor and his vote. Soon there were signs that the Democrats would form a single caucus to maintain a solid front.[48]

Democrats who had just fought a hard campaign against each other, however, found sudden unity impossible, and personal ambition increased the friction. After Colonel Savage withdrew, his low-tax men split, many going to Bate. The friends of former congressman Robert L. Taylor of East Tennessee worked for him as a compromise candidate, though he was only six months over the constitutional age requirement. And regular Democratic state Representative Howell E. Jackson had "a bad case of the Senatorial itch, and live[d] in hourly expectation of being taken up as the only Democrat who [could] be elected." Low-tax Democrats agreed to stay with Bate, but Senator Bailey's regulars, including Jackson, remained loyal. Although Bate had voted for 50–4 in the 1879 referendum and for Wright in 1880, his lack of zeal had irritated the regulars. When General Bate finally withdrew, however, he could release his votes for IOUs against future campaigns.[49]

The twenty-eighth ballot for senator showed forty-three for Maynard and two for other Republicans, enough for election had the GOP united on Maynard. Only personal rivalry blocked the election of a Republican senator. The runner-up to Maynard was Taylor, whose tally was the most any Democrat had received up to that time. But if Taylor, who had antagonized neither faction, could not unite the Democrats, then very likely no one could, and party lines began to crack: a Democrat from a normally Republican district an-

48. Knoxville *Chronicle,* January 4, 1881; Nashville *Banner,* January 7, 11, 14, 1881.
49. Knoxville *Chronicle,* January 21, 1881; Memphis *Public Ledger,* January 24, 25, 1881.

nounced for Maynard. Nervous Democrats rallied to businessman Solon E. Rose of Pulaski, an old Whig and pre-Sumter Unionist. But before the vote was added up, Republican leader R. R. Butler, believing Rose would be elected, changed his vote to Howell E. Jackson, setting off a stampede which elected Jackson senator. He was, in the apt words of a Union veteran, "an unprovincial, unsectional, broad, liberal, Federal democrat, a worthy successor of the present Senator, who will represent us nationally, as well as locally, in these times of public progress." "[A]s it became evident that we could not succeed," a leading Republican wrote to Jackson, "it was the duty of our party to vote for the best man in your party." [50] The Republicans, ousted by the Redeemers a decade before, sent one of them to the Senate in 1881.

Howell E. Jackson was born in 1832, the son of a staunch Whig. Unlike his brother, General W. H. Jackson, he had no proud Civil War record. Leaving his Memphis law practice after the war, he moved to Jackson (named for Andrew, no relation) to divide his time between the law and the Jackson Cotton Mills. He was described as a "quiet and modest senator"; even a very friendly writer admitted that Jackson was not a good "mixer." Soon after going to Washington, the new senator wrote his wife that the deadlock over organizing the Senate was "enough to disgust a home body, like me, with public Life." [51] Significantly, he won a popular election only once: in 1880, he went to the state legislature, to find there more luck than he had any reason to expect. Jackson was a thoughtful, conscientious man, sympathetic with eastern Democrats like Grover Cleveland, and not inclined to use crowd-pleasing partisan rhetoric.

While public attention centered on the debt question and the senatorial election, a new issue was beginning to take form. Representative J. M. Coulter of Gibson County, a regular Democrat, introduced a bill that would outlaw unreasonable and discriminatory

50. Memphis *Public Ledger,* January 26, 1881; Knoxville *Chronicle,* January 26, 27, 30, February 22, 1881; Speer, *Sketches,* 204–208; H. H. Ingersoll to Jackson, January 27, 1881, O. P. Temple to Jackson, January 29, 1881 in Harding-Jackson Papers.

51. Nashville *Banner,* July 29, 1882, August 9, 1895; Jackson *West Tennessee Whig,* December 27, 1884; Speer, *Sketches,* 424–25; H. M. Doak sketch of H. E. Jackson, May, 1893, in Howell Edmunds Jackson Papers, TSLA; H. E. Jackson to wife, March 3, 1881, in H. E. Jackson Papers.

railroad rates and, most important, would establish a three-man commission with the power to set rates and examine the railroads' accounts. The Nashville *American* interviewed railroad men, but not merchants or farmers, to get their reactions and concluded that the Coulter bill would "put an end to all railroad extensions within the limits of the State . . . for it is hardly reasonable to expect that any company will expend $30,000 per mile in building railroads and then have a commission fix rates on such roads." The *American* granted the need for some form of legal control but marveled that the task of the proposed commission would be so complex that it seemed "almost to transcend the power of the human mind to grasp." These two arguments, that regulation would frighten away capital and that outsiders dare not meddle with the occult art of railroading, were heard many more times in the next few years. The Coulter bill, which was passed by the House but not by the Senate,[52] was the harbinger of a new issue which would become useful in reestablishing Democratic unity.

The state-debt question still overshadowed all else in the politics of 1881. As the session wore on without producing a solution, a state-credit editor warned darkly that low-taxers might be planning to choke the calendars with local bills. The Nashville *American* pleaded for a state-credit settlement: "Tennessee stands to-day upon the dividing line between—not credit and faith and dishonor alone— but between utter stagnation and progress. It is not a matter alone of just sentiment, of morality, but also of the highest interest." [53] Whether for morality, progress, or ready cash (as a low-tax skeptic charged),[54] the legislature enacted a law to fund the debt at full face value by 3 percent bonds (100–3), with interest coupons receivable for taxes. In thus making a debt settlement higher than those rejected by the legislature and the people during the previous four years, the Republican–state-credit alliance demonstrated their own lack of political realism and provoked the low-taxers to angry intransigence.

Tabulation of the roll-call votes on the Coulter railroad bill and

52. Nashville *American,* February 8, 9, 1881; *House Journal,* 1881, p. 804; *Senate Journal,* 1881, p. 697.
53. Nashville *American,* March 13, 31, 1881.
54. Murfreesboro *Free Press,* April 8, 1881.

on the 100–3 debt settlement reveal the two basic divisions in the legislature: roughly speaking, Republicans were located in the lower left quarter of the matrix in Table 6, regular Democrats in the upper

Table 6
VOTES OF HOUSE AND SENATE COMBINED ON
H.B. 200 (COULTER RAILROAD BILL) AND H.B. 600
(100–3 DEBT SETTLEMENT) [55]

| | | 100–3 Settlement | |
		Yes	No
Railroad	yes	23	29
bill	no	23	4

$$\phi = -.43 *$$

* For explanation of ϕ (phi), see Appendix A.

left quarter, and low-tax Democrats in the upper right quarter. Would a new majority coalition be formed against the low-tax Democrats, as Governor Hawkins hoped, or would the Democrats pull together against the Republicans? Astute Democratic politicians realized that the future of their party depended on an early end to debt discord and emphasis of an issue like railroad regulation which could unite regular and low-tax Democrats.

Strong discontent with the new 100–3 settlement made itself felt immediately. Rutherford County Democrats held an indignation meeting, chaired by a thirty-four-year-old farmer named John P. Buchanan, to resolve that the law was a step toward serfdom. Powerful men took action, too. John Savage remembered many years later that Colonel W. H. Cherry, who was deeply involved in leasing convicts from the state, offered him a thousand dollars to start a low-tax newspaper, which Savage turned down.[56] This is plausible, because in 1881 Cherry helped provide over thirteen thousand dollars for capital expenditures and initial operating losses of the new Nashville *Morning World,* which was considered an enemy "organ" by state-credit men. Savage recalled a strategy meeting involving

55. *House Journal,* 1881, pp. 699, 804; *Senate Journal,* 1881, pp. 679, 697.
56. Gallatin *Tennessean,* quoted in Ashland City *Cheatham County New Era,* May 5, 1881; Murfreesboro *Free Press,* May 6, 1881; W. H. Cherry to S. A. Champion, March 16, 1882, in S. A. Champion Papers, TSLA; Jackson *West Tennessee Whig,* September 9, 1885; [Savage], *Life,* 168.

himself, S. F. Wilson, former governor Marks, and some powerful back-stage politicians including friends of Senator Harris, who was using his influence to bring some Redeemers around into opposition to the 100–3 law.[57] The politicians had various motives: Cherry wanted to save the convict lease; Harris needed a united party to reelect him in 1883; Savage and Wilson feared exclusion from a ruling alliance of Republicans and state-credit Democrats. Some key regulars began working with the low-taxers, because while the 100–3 law stood, it would keep Democrats divided and let the Republicans share power. The old Redeemer group now divided, some following Harris and others remaining loyal to the ideal of state credit.

The new coalition of Democrats filed suit against the 100–3 law. The case of *Lynn et al.* v. *Polk et al.* went to the Tennessee supreme court, where the legal issue was whether the provision making coupons acceptable for taxes bound the freedom of future legislatures in an unconstitutional manner. Chief Justice J. W. Deaderick and a special substitute judge appointed by Governor Hawkins wanted to uphold the law, but a three-man majority, including Peter Turney, struck down the 100–3 funding act as unconstitutional. The day before the decision, Tennessee bonds fell sharply on the New York market, and some thought it very strange that low-tax men and bond speculators seemed to know of the decision in advance. The first step in rebuilding the Democratic party, the destruction of the 100–3 law, was accomplished. The Republican Knoxville *Chronicle* feared the approach of political pandemonium, and the state-credit Nashville *American* cried, "We shall have no freedom from agitation, no political peace, no progress, no full prosperity until we meet our obligations and restore our credit." Several days later this voice was silenced: the *American,* probably the largest newspaper in the state, changed owners, and H. M. Doak resigned as editor. A. S. Colyar, his successor, replaced Doak's state-credit line with a soothing song of compromise and harmony. The Memphis *Avalanche* remarked that now Senator Harris and his friends could lead their party to a new debt settlement and unity, which is what they meant to do.[58]

57. Report on expenses of Nashville *World,* December 23, 1881, in Champion Papers; Cole to H. E. Jackson, January 14, 1882, in Harding-Jackson Papers; [Savage], *Life,* 170.
58. Nashville *American,* February 11, 12, 13, 14, 26, March 5, 1882.

Isham G. Harris was a remarkably skillful politician. A Democratic state chairman called him "a very great campaigner, and the best organizer I know." In 1861 opponents of Governor Harris' secessionist policy bitterly denounced him as "King Harris," a "dictator." After the war the Republicans delighted in sustaining this image by using the epithet "Boss" with his name. His reputation, and that of his party, have suffered distortion ever since.[59] His prestige as a former governor who had stood up to Lincoln was great, and he was, from 1870 till his death, always among the most influential men in his state. But only after 1881–1882 did he attain his position of clear preeminence, partly because of Democratic patronage flowing anew from Washington and partly because he shrewdly sensed the kind of coalition his party needed. Even then, however, Harris was not "boss" of his party, or even of a monolithic faction of it: he used issues and status-group identifications to secure his own personal position. Within this narrow sphere, he was very adept indeed.

During the 1870s Harris was one of the Redeemers, though he was not an old Whig, not an industrialist, and not even much interested in commercial growth and urban "progress." Like other party leaders, Harris took a firm state-credit position on the debt and went along at first with the 100–3 settlement of 1881.[60] Although he was not identified with the rebellious and slightly disrespectable low-tax bolters, he was not known as an extreme state-credit man either—so was able to apply the lessons of the 1879 referendum and of the fifty-seven thousand votes cast for S. F. Wilson. If any one man saved the Democratic party in 1882, it was Senator Harris.

59. W. H. Carroll to W. F. Harrity, September 5, [1892], in Grover Cleveland Papers, Library of Congress. A recent example of the exaggeration of Harris' influence is David M. Abshire, *The South Rejects a Prophet: The Life of Senator D. M. Key, 1824–1900* (New York, 1967).
60. [Savage], *Life,* 163–64; Ashland City *Cheatham County New Era,* August 24, 1882; I. G. Harris to W. H. Carroll (undated copy, telegram), in notebook, Harding-Jackson Papers; Knoxville *Chronicle,* October 7, 1880; Washington (D.C.) *Republican,* quoted in Nashville *American,* January 29, 1881.

3

Bourbon Control
1882–1886

The word *Bourbon* has become threadbare and ambiguous, but it can hardly be avoided in description of the dominant Tennessee Democrats of the early 1880s because contemporaries used it that way and because there is no better substitute.[1] The term is used here, therefore, in the same sense in which it was used then: to denote ingrained conservatism. Horace S. Merrill has applied the name *Bourbon Democrats* to Grover Cleveland and such "conservative spokesmen of business in their party." The group known as Bourbons in Tennessee, though they agreed with Cleveland on limited government and a low tariff, detested the businessmen who applauded Henry Grady's New South and who wanted clean, nonpartisan government. "Your very proper reference to the hordes of office seekers," wrote business-minded editor Adolph S. Ochs to Cleveland, "especially meets with favor with those who view with alarm the unsightly scramble for office. . . . Qualification for office and not reward for political work should be measure of a man's fitness." [2]

These New-South men, despite the tariff issue, tended increasingly to support Cleveland more than the Tennessee Bourbons did. In many ways the most progressive group in their party in Tennessee, these business and professional men were regarded by the Bourbons

1. See Dewey W. Grantham, Jr., "The Southern Bourbons Revisited," *South Atlantic Quarterly,* LX (1961), 286–95. Grantham rightly notes that the word is hard to define. Perhaps the meaning varied from state to state.
2. Horace S. Merrill, *Bourbon Leader: Grover Cleveland and the Democratic Party* (Boston, 1957), 44; A. S. Ochs to Grover Cleveland, March 5, [1893], in Cleveland Papers. See Paul M. Gaston, *The New South Creed: A Study in Southern Mythmaking* (New York, 1970). It is in regard to the New-South men of the 1880s that Dan M. Robison's concept of "Whig-industrialist" Democrats is most appropriate; Robison, *Bob Taylor and the Agrarian Revolt in Tennessee* (Chapel Hill, 1935).

as traitors to Jeffersonian democracy and fellow-travelers with the Republicans, who did not like them either. Thus mugwump Democrats were caught in the partisan crossfire. A Redeemer squirmed because "everything that is not Republican is [called] Bourbon." [3] These New-South spokesmen had no mass following. Bourbonism was more powerful because it combined postwar sectional resentment with the ancient Democratic suspicion of industry and eastern cities, and because both these sentiments could be directed against a single target. The enemy, of course, was a caricatured Republican party and everything it was supposed to stand for: fiscal extravagance, governmental centralization, favoritism toward eastern corporations and banks, and racial equality.

Some Bourbon rhetoric might be cited against their characterization as conservatives. "Can it be that corporations created by the will of the people, through legislation, become invested with rights beyond the reach and control of the power that gave them being?" asked Governor Bate in support of the railroad commission. "Such an assumption undermines the axioms which underlie free institutions," he continued, "and is a denial to the people of the inalienable right of supreme control in governmental affairs." The Democratic state convention of 1882 declared itself "unalterably opposed to every species of monopoly as destructive of liberty and the best interest of the people." To the Bourbons' enemies, however, the old Jacksonian crusade against monopoly and privilege seemed a dangerous anachronism. Supporters of federal aid for the Southern Pacific Railroad, for example, censured dogmatic Bourbons for clinging to the old principle of Democratic opposition to internal improvements.[4]

The Bourbons thought of themselves as heirs of the old Jefferson-Jackson tradition, but they had lost the hopefulness of earlier days. The decades of vigilance against abolitionists and Radicals had cramped their spirit, and economic forces had transformed the political context. "The Southern Bourbons have learned nothing since 1860," said a Redeemer critic. In 1894 a minor politician could

3. Nashville *American,* December 3, 1880.
4. Robert H. White (ed.), *Messages of the Governors of Tennessee,* VII (Nashville, 1967), 149, 8; Memphis *Avalanche,* February 10, 1871.

testify proudly and with no intended irony, "I am a Bourbon, moss-back Democrat," and Isham Harris praised a man "chiefly because he belongs to that class of old fashion hard shelled, strict construction democracy for which I have always fought." The Bourbons, then, appear paradoxical within the interpretive framework of Charles A. Beard, who would have expected advocates of railroad regulation and later followers of William Jennings Bryan to be for progress and against the status quo. But kinship to Jefferson, Jackson, and Bryan was no embarrassment to the Bourbons. A perceptive recent scholar has written that the Jacksonians felt that the "job of government was negative in the sense that it need not act to create the good society; it needed only to keep a sharp eye on and check those who might corrupt the good society." [5] The Bourbons feared social change and tried to stop it.

It was crafty Senator Harris who rebuilt the Tennessee Democratic party on a Bourbon foundation, amidst the wreckage of the Redeemer coalition. His desire for reelection in 1883 lent urgency to his task. Harris' influence undoubtedly encouraged the request by the low-tax Democratic State Committee for a united state party convention in 1882. The bolters explained that the supreme court decision against the 100–3 law made compromise possible. On cue, Gibson County Democrats met to resolve for party unity, and nine small-town newspapers chimed in. The regular Democratic state committee met to hear General Bate and Colonel Colyar argue for union with the low-taxers; despite opposition, the unifiers carried the day, and the committee proposed that both Democratic state chairmen jointly call together the state convention. The willingness of the regular Democrats to merge on equal terms with the bolters who had ruined their last campaign was tribute to the large impact of the Wilson vote on the politicians' idea of public opinion. Colyar's Nashville *American* chided those who dragged their feet with the reminder that beating the Republicans was of first importance. Soon the me-

5. Memphis *Avalanche* October 23, 1870; *Contest for Governor in Tennessee: Complete Proceedings of the Joint Convention and Investigating Committee, the Evidence in Full and Arguments of Counsel* (Nashville, 1895), I, 511; Isham G. Harris to Cleveland, May 2, 1893, in Cleveland Papers; John W. Ward, "Jacksonian Democratic Thought: 'A Natural Charter of Privilege,' " in A. F. Davis and H. D. Woodman (eds.), *Conflict and Consensus in Early American History* (3rd ed.; Lexington, Mass., 1972), 308.

chanical details were settled, and the two state committees issued a call for one convention.[6]

However avidly many Democrats hoped to unify their party, others did what they could to interfere. Governor Hawkins called a special session of the legislature for late April, for the purpose of replacing the defunct 100–3 funding law with another. The Democratic press quickly denounced the extra session as a device for splitting their party by continuing the Republican–state-credit legislative alliance of 1881. Colyar warned that if a proposed 60–6 bill was passed during the extra session, and if a Democratic convention refused to approve it, a state-credit ticket would be fielded to keep the Republicans in power. Eight low-tax Democratic senators— nearly a third of the Senate—felt so strongly about blocking the 60–6 bill that they considered filibustering or even resigning. The 60–6 bill, providing for interest beginning at 3 percent and rising 1 percent every two years to a level of 6 percent, was enacted by almost the identical forces which had passed the 100–3 bill in 1881.[7] The three cheers given by the state Republican convention for the "state credit Democracy" probably backfired: by boasting of their intention to divide the opposition, the GOP gave ammunition to the Democratic unifiers, and helped the Bourbons make stubborn state-credit men seem to be mere accessories of the Republicans. The passage of the 60–6 bill in the spring of 1882 turned out to be the last gasp of the Republican–state-credit alliance, because Senator Harris was detaching big chunks of the Democratic party from the old regulars.

The state-credit Nashville *Banner* supported the 60–6 settlement and charged that Senator Harris, Colonel Colyar, and former governor Marks were forming a cabal to divide the spoils, which was not far from the truth. More irrelevantly, the *Banner* attacked black Republican leader Ed Shaw, who had broken with the Hawkins administration, and criticized the Bourbons for cooperating with Shaw and "his communist Memphis mob." The paper dismissed the low-tax Democrats as an "obstinate and implacable" minority who

6. Nashville *American,* March 25, April 3, 4, 5, 12, 16, 1882.
7. *Ibid.,* April 25, May 5, 16, 1882; Nashville *World,* April 25, 1882; Nashville *American,* May 28, 1882; *House Journal,* 1881, p. 699; *House Journal,* 1881 3rd extra session, p. 113; *Senate Journal,* 1881, p. 679; *Senate Journal,* 1881 3rd extra session, p. 57.

could be disregarded, and encouraged the gubernatorial candidacies of Redeemers W. M. Daniel and W. B. Bate. But the 60–6 law was a convenient target for the rival Nashville *American,* which insisted illogically that any debt settlement involving the Republicans was unsound because of the horrors of Reconstruction. Democratic meetings in Gibson, Madison, Giles, Coffee, and several more counties passed resolutions condemning the 60–6 law, but few such county meetings backed the weakened state-credit cause, which was in trouble on the eve of the June Democratic convention.[8]

The state convention was confronted by six candidates for governor. John R. Neal had been Speaker of the Senate in 1879, when he represented the Chattanooga district. Robert L. Taylor reportedly advocated "honest and just principles," though he did not announce them. Convict lessee W. H. Cherry's Nashville *World* supported Congressman John D. C. Atkins, a Democratic legislator before the war, then a Confederate colonel and member of the Confederate congress. His wife was James D. Porter's first cousin, and Atkins' daughter had married Porter's son. Another candidate was W. L. Ledgerwood, a Tennessee native and Union veteran who had helped organize the first postwar Democratic party in Knox County. The strongest candidate was General W. B. Bate, who had run well in the 1881 Senate race, and who had considerable support among the low-taxers—a big advantage, since no low-tax leader was among the candidates.[9]

John H. Savage said in his memoirs that he had approached Bate in 1882 and told him that he could be governor, but Bate did not seem interested. Savage then wrote to his friends in support of Taylor: "I did not know what his position was upon the State debt question, but he could be controlled and would adopt our policy and we would elect him. So the low tax party was organized on Bob Taylor as its candidate." However, a journalist, remembering 1882 after a shorter length of time, recalled that Bate had been nominated

    8. Nashville *American,* April 27, 30, May 22, 29, 30, June 6, 9, 10, 12, 20, 1882; Nashville *Banner,* June 2, 3, 5, 6, 1882.
    9. Nashville *Banner,* June 20, 1882; Nashville *World,* June 9, 1882; *Biographical Directory of the American Congress,* 654; Speer, *Sketches,* 35–40; Knoxville *Journal,* November 18, 1890.

by low-tax delegates.[10] Savage probably exaggerated his own role, tempted by Taylor's later fame. In any case, Bate's views were ambiguous enough to permit both the Nashville *Banner* and Savage to like him.

Before the convention opened, a group of delegates gathered to hear harmony speeches by Colyar, Savage, former governor Marks, H. E. Jackson, and Isham Harris, who took a state-credit position but said he would compromise for unity's sake.[11] If all these speakers could agree on a platform and a candidate, the Democratic party would be invincible. Just as in 1880, however, the platform proved to be a source of discord. But this time the low-taxers were on the winning side and rejoiced at the endorsement of a plank calling for a fifty-cent debt settlement, with 3 percent interest for ten years, then 4 percent. The platform also condemned monopolies and railroad rate discrimination.

The disgruntled *Banner* attributed the change since 1880 to manipulation at the county level to exclude state-credit men from the convention. Two years before, the adoption of a state-credit platform had prompted a walkout by low-taxers, and now the irreconcilable defenders of Tennessee's honor had their turn. Many of them, though supporters of a fifty-cent settlement in 1879, signed protests against the platform. Duncan B. Cooper led a walkout by approximately one-fifth of the delegates, who met under the gavel of General W. H. Jackson to make plans but not a nomination.[12] This action, while similar to the low-tax bolt of 1880, was much more logical because it supported the alliance of state-credit Democrats and Republicans in the legislature: a Democratic split would help Governor Hawkins win reelection.

In the regular convention Bate led on the first ballot. Although Atkins' withdrawal allowed Taylor almost to pull even with the general, Bate grew stronger on each vote and won on the fifth. The *Banner,* his strong friend before the nomination, denounced Bate now that his Bourbon ties were clear, and began giving favorable publicity to the activities of the state-credit bolters. They met in the

10. [Savage], *Life,* 191; Knoxville *Journal,* August 11, 1886.
11. Nashville *World,* June 22, 1882.
12. Nashville *American,* June 22, 1882; Nashville *Banner,* June 29, 1882.

counties to choose delegates for an anti-Bate convention.[13] The general faced a mutiny in his party's ranks.

Who were the state-credit bolters? The Nashville *American* admitted that they were "among the very best [men] in the state." But the Jackson *Tribune and Sun* poured its scorn on them and on "the aerial blue that surrounds the Alpine heights of political purity where the calm serenity of the railroad attorney, the innocent boldholder, is never disturbed by the odorous sweat of the toiling millions and the agonized groans of oppressed labor." The *Tribune and Sun* used, and may have coined, the phrase "Sky Blue Democrats," a name the bolters were proud to wear for years afterward. Forty-four sky-blue leaders who can be positively identified include a former governor, five current or former members of the United States Congress, fourteen veterans of the legislature, and two future members of the United States Supreme Court.[14]

The twenty-five whose occupations are known include sixteen lawyers, one editor who was probably a lawyer, two farmers, two publishers, a banker, a doctor, a realtor, a merchant, and a railroad president. In addition, one of the unknowns held stock in a railroad construction company, and of those counted as lawyers two were also bank presidents and two were railroad directors. Of the unknowns, at least half were very likely lawyers, since many were professional politicians.[15] These sky-blues were educated, genteel

13. Nashville *American,* June 22, 1882; Nashville *Banner,* June 22, July 1, 1882.

14. Nashville *American,* July 7, September 18, 1882. Following is a list of the forty-four sky-blue leaders mentioned in the text: Matt W. Allen, J. E. Bailey, J. R. Bond, Campbell Brown, W. H. Carroll, Frank Cheatham, J. W. Childress, Jr., Thomas Claiborne, R. P. Cole, W. A. Collier, D. B. Cooper, Edmund Cooper, Holmes Cummings, S. E. Cunningham, J. M. Dickinson, J. A. Fite, J. H. Fussell, A. E. Garrett, J. H. Holman, W. H. Hyronemus, H. E. Jackson, W. H. Jackson, E. A. James, D. N. Kennedy, H. H. Lurton, J. C. Luster, A. B. Martin, D. D. Maney, R. L. Morris, A. S. Ochs, H. K. Plummer, M. T. Polk, J. D. Porter, D. H. Poston, P. D. Sims, E. Story, J. J. Turner, Fount Wade, J. E. Washington, J. E. Wells, Archibald Wright, J. V. Wright, Luke Wright, and Casey Young.

15. Nashville *Banner,* June 22, 27, 1882, August 1, 1895; Nashville *Weekly Toiler,* November 2, 1892; Nashville *American,* June 24, July 12, 26, 1882, March 1, 1884, August 28, 1885, April 13, 1886, September 3, 1887, April 22, 1891; clipping in scrapbook, in J. H. Fussell Papers, TSLA; A. Wright to [B. F. Cheatham], October 7, 1878, A. S. Marks to W. B. Bate, February 2, 1886, in CGO, TSLA; Memphis *Public Ledger,* July 2, 1880; Memphis *Commercial,* February 9, March 24, September 1, 1893; E. F. Cheatham to S. A. Champion, May 25, 1882, in Champion Papers; Speer, *Sketches,* 429, 445, 524; P. D. Sims to H. E. Jackson, July

professional men, who lived in large towns. Some had cooperated politically with local Republicans, and financially with eastern ones. They approved the social order because they enjoyed high positions in it; unity of economic interest is not apparent, though many of them stood to gain from increasing urban prosperity. The Redeemers most dependent on their political careers went along with the Bourbon coalition, but these sky-blues refused to acquiesce in conceding political recognition to rough-hewn country politicians like Colonel Savage, whose narrow negativism they could not share.

Another aspect of the sky-blues was their genealogical relationship to each other, to other prestigious persons, and to leaders of previous generations. Chart 1 shows the relation of J. W. Childress, Jr., to President Polk, of Duncan B. Cooper to Governor John C. Brown, of D. D. Maney to John Bell, as well as the relation of all these to each other and to sky-blues Marshall T. Polk, Campbell Brown, and Edmund Cooper. Childress and D. B. Cooper were sky-blue leaders of the first rank: the former had been chairman of the Democratic state committee in 1880, and the latter published the Nashville *American* for a time in 1882 on behalf of the sky-blue cause.

Chart 2 shows the kinship of Senator James E. Bailey, banker D. N. Kennedy, and J. W. Clapp; and also that J. M. Dickinson, chairman of the State-Credit Democratic state committee, was a distant kinsman of the wives of both General W. H. Jackson and Senator Howell E. Jackson, prominent spokesman for the sky-blue campaign. These men were variously related to Judge John Overton of the Tennessee Supreme Court, Senator and Attorney-General Felix Grundy, and Judge John McNairy, all three of whom had been personal friends of Andrew Jackson. W. H. Carroll, a prominent Memphis Democrat and sky-blue not shown on a chart, was the grandson of Governor William Carroll. If the sky-blue men named above had been merely quiet supporters of the state-credit bolt, their significance would be less, but they included captains of the move-

3, 1884, in Harding-Jackson Papers; *Poor's Manual of the Railroads of the United States for 1885* (New York, 1868–1924, annual), 480, 489; *Who's Who in Tennessee: A Biographical Reference Book of Notable Tennesseans of Today* (Memphis, 1911), 89; A. S. Colyar to Andrew Johnson, August 28, 1871, in Johnson Papers; Sparta *Expositor*, August 9, 1889.

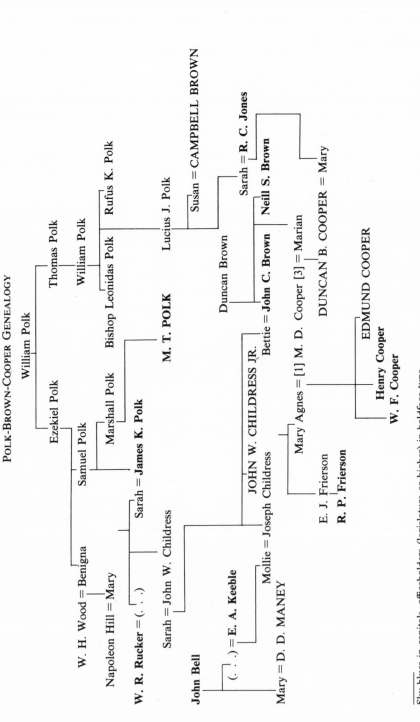

Chart 1
POLK-BROWN-COOPER GENEALOGY

Sky-blues in capitals, officeholders (legislature or higher) in boldface type.

Sources: Polk chart and genealogy, and genealogies in Cooper and Dudley Gale papers, TSLA; Speer, *Sketches,* 7–10, 26–27, 43; S. J. Folmsbee, R. E. Corlew, and E. L. Mitchell, *History of Tennessee* (New York, 1960), II, 132; TSLA, *Biographical Directory, Tennessee General Assembly: 1796–1967: (Preliminary, No. 6) Rutherford County* (Nashville, 1968), 33, 39; *Nashville American,* January 4, 1887.

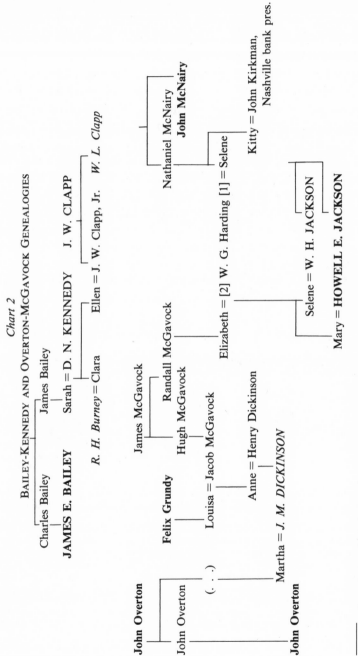

Chart 2

BAILEY-KENNEDY AND OVERTON-MCGAVOCK GENEALOGIES

Sky-blues in capitals; officeholders before 1882 in boldface type, after 1882 in italics.

Sources: Speer, *Sketches*, 3–5, 429–31; genealogy in J. M. Dickinson papers, TSLA.

ment. To the extent that there was an oligarchy of old families active in Tennessee politics, they were sky-blues.[16]

Despite this collection of talent, however, the state-credit bolters had some difficulty in finding a gubernatorial candidate. Some thought that Howell E. Jackson would run: W. A. Collier of Memphis wrote to the senator that the sky-blue nomination was his for the taking, mentioning the possibility that Jackson resign from the Senate on becoming governor, then have the legislature send him back to the Senate. But, Collier, continued, "To be frank with you we cannot hope to elect our candidate & you would be saved the necessity of resigning your position." He tactfully suggested that Jackson might best serve the cause by securing another man to make the race. Collier optimistically predicted that Senator Harris would be defeated for reelection, and that a sky-blue gubernatorial candidate could replace him.[17] The sky-blues knew they could not win, but hoped to sabotage the Bourbon coalition with a suicidal campaign.

Three weeks after their walkout, the sky-blue delegates assembled

16. More information about some notable sky-blues will help give a further impression of the sort of men they were. Campbell Brown, a Confederate major and a former legislator from Maury County, reputedly owned one of the most beautiful farms in the state, and was famed as a breeder of blooded horses. Archibald Wright was a former member of the state supreme court, a bank director, and father-in-law and law partner of future supreme court judge W. C. Fowlkes. His son, General Luke E. Wright, also a sky-blue, was chairman of the state-credit Shelby County delegation to the 1880 Democratic convention. Holmes Cummings, an attorney, bank director, railroad director, and former legislator, had been the state-credit forces' successful candidate for chairman of the 1878 state Democratic convention. J. W. Childress, Jr., was a director of the Nashville, Chattanooga, and St. Louis Railroad. Joseph E. Washington's father was, at one time or another, charter stockholder and director of the N C & St. L, large stockholder and third vice-president of the L & N, and director of the Tennessee Coal, Iron, and Railroad Company. John V. Wright had served in the United States and Confederate congresses, and received a state judgeship from Governor Porter; he was a cousin of state school superintendent Leon Trousdale.

By contrast to the sky-blues, the Bourbon (regular) Democratic state committee chosen in 1882 consisted of A. T. McNeal, a relative of the Polk family and thus of several sky-blues; D. D. Anderson, son of a California supreme court justice; two former legislators, D. L. Snodgrass and W. A. Quarles; two incumbent legislators, W. C. Houston and J. M. Head, who was also a journalist, businessman, and lawyer; at least two more active politician-lawyers, J. J. Vertrees and S. A. Champion; and five others of whom nothing is known before 1882: J. T. Hillsman, John Allison, Jr., John McGrath, J. L. Pearcy, and T. J. Edwards. Of these, only McNeal, Quarles, and perhaps Anderson and Champion had a social status comparable to nearly all the forty-four sky-blues.

17. W. A. Collier to H. E. Jackson, July 4, 1882, in Harding-Jackson Papers; J. A. Trousdale to C. W. Trousdale, September 21, 1882, in Trousdale Papers, TSLA.

again. Their platform opposed all repudiation and backed the 60–6 settlement of 1882. It also, like the regular Democratic platform, asked for railroad regulation, though in mild terms. The convention reportedly gave its greatest applause to a plank opposing repeal of the Four Mile Law, which prohibited the sale of liquor within four miles of a chartered school outside an incorporated town. Originally this law had been intended to apply only to the University of the South at Sewanee, but was redrafted in general terms. Prohibitionists began getting town charters annulled, however, and used the law as an entering wedge for statewide prohibition.[18] It is significant that the sky-blues, who were last-ditch Redeemers, were distinguished from the Bourbons by their defense not of railroad interests but of middle-class respectability.

As their nominee for governor, the state-credit Democrats settled on forty-six-year-old Joseph H. Fussell of Columbia. A graduate of Jackson College in that town, he had worked as a carpenter, fought in the Confederate army where he rose to the rank of captain, gained admission to the bar, and become attorney-general for the ninth judicial circuit of Tennessee. Joe Fussell was a godly man who saw himself as the servant not only of Tennessee's honor but of an even higher purpose. "I was nominated by acclamation," he wrote from the Nashville train station. "My best friends here were most anxious that I should accept, [and] I did so. . . . Tell Mother I trust as she said that the Lord is directing this whole affair. I will have a hard canvass but hope to be able to make it. The cause is just." Fussell believed that "the highest civilization is a result of the purest Christianity," [19] in pursuit of which he would be elected moderator of the Cumberland Presbyterian Church. Captain Fussell was pushed forward by the experienced politicians who wanted not office for themselves but defeat for Bate.

Several days after the sky-blue meeting, a state prohibition convention met in Nashville, where they read and debated a letter from Emerson Etheridge urging them to nominate Fussell for governor.

18. Nashville *American,* July 12, 1882; Paul E. Isaac, *Prohibition and Politics: Turbulent Decades in Tennessee, 1885–1920* (Knoxville, 1965), 10–11.

19. Nashville *American,* July 12, 1882; *Who's Who in Tennessee,* 89; Joe [Fussell] to Thomas, July 12, 1882, undated speech in Fussell's handwriting, both in Fussell Papers.

The convention adjourned without naming anyone, but Fussell's own interests may have inclined more to prohibition than to the state-debt issue: he carefully clipped an item from the Memphis *Avalanche* about his strength among prohibitionists and Bate's popularity with liquor dealers who wanted the Four Mile Law repealed. Very likely in Fussell's mind the two causes of prohibition and state credit were joined by their righteousness. State-credit leaders expected this visionary to attract city and town voters, but prohibition brought him even less mass support than his state-credit stand.[20]

On the opposite end of the political spectrum, forty-six Greenbackers met in convention and declared that the state bonds were void. They also endorsed the National Greenback Labor platform and proclaimed their enmity to monopolies and national banks. John R. Beasley, a low-tax Democrat who refused to follow Savage into the Bourbon coalition, was nominated for governor. Elected to the 1881 legislature from Franklin County, Beasley was recognized as a leader of the low-tax faction in the House of Representatives. A country weekly had praised his vigilance against monopoly on behalf of the people, and sadly noted that he was one of the most abused men in the legislature. He did not seek acceptance through conformity: in 1886 he published a booklet advocating equality for women, stating that the federal government did not deserve allegiance because of its policy of contracting the currency, and asserting that crime resulted from poverty not liquor. During the 1882 campaign his foes even charged that he did not believe in the immortality of the soul.[21] Beasley differed with Captain Fussell over much more than the validity of the state debt, but was no more capable of beating Bate than was Fussell.

Candidates Fussell and Beasley campaigned hard, touring the state with Governor Hawkins, the Republican nominee. Bate's strategy was to remain aloof, allowing one of his supporters to denounce

20. Nashville *American*, July 21, September 30, 1882; clipping from Memphis *Avalanche*, July 23, 1882, in scrapbook in Fussell Papers.
21. Nashville *American*, November 4, 1880, June 13, July 24, 1882; Knoxville *Chronicle*, January 7, 1881; Murfreesboro *Free Press*, April 8, 1881. J. R. Beasley, *The Conflict Between Liberty and Prohibition: An Inquiry into the Most Practicable Method of Reforming the World: With Other Essays on Political Subjects* (Chattanooga, 1886).

"the common interest and joint labors of Hawkins, Fussell, and Beasley to deceive Democratic voters, and perpetuate Republican rule in Tennessee." General Bate, an old-fashioned orator, treated the National Association of Veterans of the Mexican War to some patriotic reminiscences. As for the issues, the Bourbons played down the state debt. Senator Harris, for example, claimed to be for state credit, but dwelt on the dangers of federal centralization, tariff protection, and rampant monopolies, all lurking in Republican policy. Sky-blue Duncan Cooper charged the Bourbons with trying to rouse prejudice against the railroads, which were convenient symbols of alien, arbitrary power.[22]

A Democratic farmer of Madison County recorded in his diary his response to the Bourbon strategy: "Genl Bate—Democratic candidate for Governor spoke today—invited—on the occasion of Ratification [of the state convention]—very good crowd present —don't think there will be any bolting to amount to anything—it is best to support Bate and defeat Hawkins the Republican—it's the only way to do it." [23] Most Democrats agreed in November, and it was fortunate for Cooper that he believed truth superior to victory, for the latter belonged to Bate. The general's 119,000 votes gave him a comfortable margin over Hawkins, at 92,000. Joe Fussell, with the Lord's help or without it, received fewer than 5,000 votes. Greenbacker Beasley's 9,500 votes were more than Edwards got in 1880, but not enough to pose a threat to Bate.[24] The Bourbon strategy worked beautifully.

The sky-blue bolt of 1882 looks especially ineffectual compared to the low-tax Democratic party of 1880. The low-taxers had a mere handful of prominent party leaders, and only one daily newspaper; Fussell was backed by the cream of the state's social elite, and by half the daily Democratic press.[25] Yet S. F. Wilson received 44

22. Bolivar *Bulletin,* October 12, 1882; Clarksville *Chronicle,* quoted in Nashville *American,* October 20, 1882; Nashville *American,* August 26, September 12, 15, 17, 1882.
23. Cartmell Diary, July 4, 1882 (TSLA).
24. Nashville *American,* August 20, November 6, 1882; *Tribune Almanac,* 1883, pp. 72–73.
25. In August, 1882, the Chattanooga *Times* surveyed the press of Tennessee. Of ninety newspapers in the state, nine were dailies. The Republican Knoxville *Chronicle,* of course, was for Hawkins. The rest were evenly split: the Nashville *World,* Memphis *Appeal,* Memphis

percent of the Democratic vote in 1880, eleven times Fussell's share, and remains the most successful third-party gubernatorial candidate in Tennessee history. A sky-blue voter more likely lived in a town or a relatively black county than a Wilson supporter, and was less likely to have been for Andrew Johnson a decade earlier. The group of forty-four sky-blue leaders discussed above contained seven known old Whigs and only three known antebellum Democrats, an inconclusive number. In any case, Fussell voters were not drawn from the old Whig ranks (see Appendix B, Tables 6 and 7). The low-tax party had been a powerful forerunner of the Bourbonism against which the sky-blues registered their futile protest.

The weakness of the sky-blues compared to the low-taxers of 1880 revealed the astuteness of the Bourbon strategy, which placed a higher priority on placating the low-taxers than on satisfying those at the other extreme. This policy resulted in a shift in the center of gravity in the Democratic party, which after 1882 was more agreeable to certain dissenters of the 1870s than to some of the Redeemer leaders. The price for the support of John Savage and Dorsey Thomas was to drive away General W. H. Jackson and former governor Porter, but it was a good bargain. Sky-blue patricians would be uncomfortable on the fringe of a Bourbon-oriented party, but they could not destroy it. Nor could they prevent its formation, a change exceeding in depth and permanence the farmers' revolt of the 1890s, which Bourbonism partly anticipated and which, ironically, would drive sky-blues back into the mainstream of their party.

Weeks after the 1882 election the defeated sky-blues were even further humiliated. A shortage of $400,000 was discovered in the state accounts, and Treasurer Marshall T. Polk, an old-line Redeemer and nephew of a president, was out of town. He was intercepted in Texas on the way to Mexico, but not before the Bourbons had charged the Republican–state-credit coalition with having failed to prevent the scandal. "[T]he curses of the Democracy are long and bitter against the whole crew," wrote a man in Paris, Henry County.

Public Ledger, and Knoxville *Tribune* were for Bate, and the Nashville *American,* Nashville *Banner,* Memphis *Avalanche,* and the *Times* itself were for Fussell. Of about sixty country weeklies which were political, the *Times* credited ten, twenty, and thirty to Hawkins, Fussell, and Bate, respectively. Chattanooga *Times,* quoted in Nashville *American,* August 15, 1882.

"The only friends the . . . treasurer has here is [*sic*] among the Skye [*sic*] Blues. . . . I feel very much like the entire S B crew ought to be tried for treason against the state." Appropriately, the legislature elected in Polk's place a brother of Dorsey B. Thomas, who had challenged Redeemer Governor Porter at the polls in 1876.[26] The whole episode revealed the transformation of the Democratic party since then.

The greatest danger to the Bourbon coalition lay in the conflicting personal ambitions of its members. Democrats in the House of Representatives divided in the election of a Speaker, allowing the Republicans to decide the vote in favor of the aspirant more independent of Governor Bate. There were so many candidates for comptroller that thirty-five ballots were required for a majority in joint convention. The most important election pitted two of Governor Bate's top supporters against each other: John H. Savage was trying to unseat his old enemy, Senator Harris. Colonel Savage shrilly accused him of having used state funds illegally while wartime governor—of having taken $3,750 in gold, for example, which Savage equated with M. T. Polk's huge theft. Savage attributed Harris' lasting popularity to hundreds of appointments he had made during the war. Senator Harris calmly brushed these charges aside, and won easily over Savage and a Republican candidate. The legislators voting for Savage nearly all lived in counties clustered around Warren, the colonel's home.[27] The Bourbon coalition worked more smoothly in the senatorial election than in any other matter before the 1883 legislature, an indication that the most important purpose of the Bourbons in the legislature was to reelect Senator Harris.

If the Bourbons were to stay in power by shifting political debate to the dangers of centralization by Republicans, financiers, and cor-

26. Polk chart, TSLA; M. T. Polk to H. E. Jackson, July 16, 1882, in Harding-Jackson Papers; Nashville *Banner*, June 15, 1880; Nashville *American*, January 6, 8, 1883; Nashville *World*, January 6, 1883; A. G. Trevathan to Champion, January 9, 1883, in Champion Papers; Charles A. Miller, *Official and Political Manual of Tennessee* (Nashville, 1890), 173; Speer, *Sketches*, 563.
27. *House Journal*, 1883, pp. 13, 194, 217–75; Nashville *Banner*, June 22, 1882, January 13, 1883; Nashville *American*, June 22, September 27, December 15, 24, 1882; *Senate Journal*, 1883, p. 190.

porations, they had to dispose of the state-debt problem immediately. Under the Republican–state-credit settlement of 1882, $9 million worth of state bonds had already been funded at sixty cents by September 1 of that year. Almost as soon as they arrived in Nashville the next January, the Bourbons passed resolutions directing state officers to stop the funding process and the payment of interest on the new bonds. Enacting another debt settlement was more difficult, however; the Democratic caucus argued for weeks over interest rates and other details. "[T]he unity of the party is worth all the money in the world," said the Bourbon Nashville *World* with unintentional humor, as low-taxers showed signs of militancy. Senator Harris reminded his men of the 1882 platform which they were pledged to uphold. Finally the Democratic caucus reached agreement and got a bill enacted funding most of the debt at fifty cents and 3 percent interest.[28] The state-debt question, a largely symbolic issue of little or no substance for most Tennesseeans, was finally buried in favor of other symbols, mostly more vague and tractable.

An exceptionally concrete issue used by the Bourbons in 1883 to unite their party and to distinguish it clearly from the Republicans was railroad regulation. The subject was not a new one in Tennessee: as early as 1877 an act forbade rates higher for the short than for the long haul, required rates to be posted publicly, and barred excessive rates—but in terms so cloudy as to make evasion easy. The 1880 regular Democratic platform included a demand that the railroads be compelled to "do justice," and in the following session the legislature debated the Coulter regulation bill, which was killed in the Senate. Nor was railroad regulation limited to Tennessee: Virginia had created an advisory commission on the Massachusetts model in 1877; South Carolina, Kentucky, and Alabama followed in 1878, 1880, and 1881. The stronger type of commission, originating in the Midwest and holding power to set and enforce rates, came to Georgia in 1879 and South Carolina three years later. By 1882, public interest

---

28. Nashville *American,* September 1, 1882, January 4, February 17, 21, March 7, 1883; *House Journal,* 1883, pp. 51, 604; *Senate Journal,* 1883, pp. 67, 576; Nashville *World,* February 15, 16, 17, 21, 22, 23, 1883.

in Tennessee was sufficient to cause even the Republicans to pay lip service to regulation in their platform.[29]

Feeling against railroads was not based on imaginary grievances. Competing lines were consolidated, as at Nashville, where the six roads originally built into the city were all controlled by the Louisville and Nashville in 1882. But it was the smaller towns, and the farmers dependent on them, who especially suffered. The charge for shipping flour from Franklin or Pulaski to Montgomery, Alabama, was 58 cents per barrel; but a barrel of flour shipped from Nashville, through Franklin and Pulaski, to Montgomery was charged 43 cents. A Nashville man could send grain to Atlanta for 20 cents per hundred pounds, but his competitor in Shelbyville or Murfreesboro, though closer to Georgia, paid 4 cents more. The rate on a barrel of flour from Nashville to Charleston, South Carolina, was 38 cents, but to ship the same item to landlocked Charleston, Tennessee, cost 48 cents. Some rate schedules were even more grossly disproportionate to distance. Dried fruit was charged 24 cents per hundred pounds for the fifty-six miles from Rogersville to Knoxville, and then was sent from Knoxville to Cincinnati, over three hundred miles, for 25 cents. Three and a half barrels of whiskey were charged $4.05 for the eleven miles from Bradford to Milan, and then were taken over four hundred miles to Cincinnati for $3.60. Merchants in Paris complained that certain goods were shipped from Louisville at 60 cents per hundred pounds, but that the same goods sent from Louisville via Paris to Murray, Kentucky, were charged only 35 cents.[30] These were some of the more outrageous cases, but it is easy to see why farmers and merchants alike resented railroad policies, and listened when John Savage said, "The history of railroad building and management in Tennessee shows violated laws and charters, rebates, special rates to favorites, discriminations against persons and places, the ruin of stockholders, and immense fortunes for a few high offi-

29. Edward Cameron Duggins, "The Background for Regulation of the Railroads in Tennessee" (M.A. thesis, University of Tennessee, 1939), 50–51; Maxwell Ferguson, *State Regulation of Railroads in the South* (New York, 1916), 43, 44, 141.

30. *First and Second Annual Reports of the Railroad Commissioners for the State of Tennessee* (Nashville, 1884), 27, 28, 70.

cials." [31] The railroads thus appeared to be agents of unwelcome change, of injustice and corruption. Regulation, the Bourbons' response, was a good political issue partly because the Republicans always obligingly voted against it.

Unhappily for the Bourbons, the railroads had friends in Tennessee mightier than the Republicans. Former governor James D. Porter was president of the Nashville, Chattanooga, and St. Louis line, a subsidiary of the Louisville and Nashville; railroad boards of directors included men with connections in newspaper publishing and politics. A. S. Colyar's Nashville *American* urged extreme caution in starting a railroad commission. The Nashville *Banner* held up a carrot, reminding its readers to be grateful for railroad aid during floods and epidemics; and a stick, mentioning that the Nashville, Chattanooga, and St. Louis was threatening not to extend its line from Sparta to Livingston if a railroad commission was created. The Knoxville *Chronicle* wanted a national commission, or perhaps a state commission with advisory powers only, if it included men of integrity and not fanatics like Savage and S. F. Wilson. The railroads had great influence over the country weekly press by their power to adjust rates, or give free shipment, according to newspapers' editorial views.[32]

A leading argument of opponents of a railroad commission was that it would frighten away capital, retard construction of new lines, and hurt the general prosperity of the state. Many business-minded Tennesseeans agreed with Colyar that the interests of railroads and of the public were "largely identical." On the other hand, a well-informed advocate of regulation could point to neighboring Georgia, comparable to Tennessee in wealth and population. During 1882 Georgia, with a railroad commission, built over twice the new railroad mileage of Tennessee, with no commission.[33]

31. John H. Savage, "Railroads in Tennessee: Their War upon the People!" undated speech in Harding-Jackson Papers.
32. *Poor's Manual of the Railroads,* 1885, pp. 489, 490; *ibid.,* 1890, pp. 462, 470; Memphis *Public Ledger,* July 2, 1880; Nashville *American,* June 23, 1882; Nashville *Banner,* January 31, 1883; Knoxville *Chronicle,* January 16, 1883; *Reports of the Railroad Commissioners,* 1884, p. 75.
33. Nashville *American,* December 1, 1882; Duggins, "Background for Regulation of the Railroads," 81.

Another antiregulation argument was that any limitation placed on private corporations by the state would threaten to undermine the basic principles of laissez-faire capitalism. But proponents of regulation replied that when a railroad used the power of eminent domain, it forfeited its private character and came under the public jurisdiction. In the House of Representatives, J. M. Head of Sumner County stated that railroads were not private property, but public highways, and thus subject to state authority.[34]

Representative Head and his Bourbon allies in the 1883 House, whom the Chattanooga *Times* described as "a herd of roaring lunatics," got the Democratic caucus to agree to two strong regulation bills and make them party measures. The first bill would forbid rebates, discrimination against localities, and higher rates for shorter distances; it covered freight or passengers entering or leaving the state, if starting or stopping in it. Heavy fines were specified for violators. The second caucus bill would establish a regulatory commission, composed of one member from each division of the state, first appointed by the governor and then elected every two years. The commission would have the power to investigate railroad finances and to set freight and passenger rates.[35]

Opponents of regulation sprang into action. The commission bill was "little short of autocratic," warned the Nashville *American,* and the Memphis *Avalanche* was horrified by the "communistic bill to destroy railway property." Nashville merchants organized a petition campaign against the bills. Representative Fletcher R. Burrus of Rutherford County, a lawyer, part owner of an Arkansas cotton plantation, and member of an old, prominent family, introduced a substitute for the caucus report. Burrus said he regretted that his bill was construed as a merely advisory commission, but admitted some months later that railroads had been in on its drafting. Bourbon leaders attacked the weak Burrus bill, declaring that lobbyists and other opponents of regulation were not members of the producing classes which paid the unfair rates, and accusing the lobbyists of

34. Duggins, "Background for Regulation of the Railroads," 78–79; Nashville *American,* March 18, 1883.
35. Chattanooga *Times,* quoted in Knoxville *Chronicle,* March 21, 1883; Nashville *American,* March 12, 1883.

threatening reprisals against recalcitrant legislators' home counties. A Bourbon motion to table the Burrus substitute carried by a vote of forty-nine to forty-four, all the Republicans voting with the minority. Party discipline then prevailed; the Democrats ran over every Republican roadblock, including an anti-Jim-Crow amendment offered by a black representative. The caucus bills were passed and sent over to the Senate.[36]

The upper chamber passed a weaker bill in place of the House measures: Republican and cooperative Democratic senators made huge loopholes for new railroads, existing rate contracts, special treatment to encourage industry, and any discrimination needed by the roads to secure a "fair and just return." House Democrats used parliamentary sleight of hand to get the mild Senate bill past filibustering Republicans—a move justified by a Bourbon editor on the grounds that the railroads had treacherously pretended to favor the Senate bill to kill the strong House version, then turned against the Senate bill when it reached the House. John Savage charged that the Louisville and Nashville paid lobbyists $8,400 to defeat the House caucus bill, and sarcastically likened the new law to "sending boys with pop-guns to fight against an army with rifle cannons." [37]

The commission, headed by Colonel Savage, found little success in its attempts to change railroad policies. President J. D. Porter of the Nashville, Chattanooga, and St. Louis answered an inquiry about rates by stating that his company's charter, which set maximum fares, was plenty of protection for the public, and that he would therefore not send a rate schedule to the commission. Requests for lower local rates on cotton were made to five lines, but only the Chesapeake, Ohio, and Southwestern complied. This line also acted on a suggestion that it build a terminal at Covington. The commission reported that of the many complaints of rate discrimination and overcharges, only a few could be accepted, because the law required

36. Nashville *American,* March 10, 16, 20, 21, 1883; Memphis *Avalanche,* quoted in Knoxville *Chronicle,* March 20, 1883; Nashville *Banner,* quoted in Knoxville *Chronicle,* March 16, 1883; Speer, *Sketches,* 103–105; Nashville *World,* September 17, 1884; *House Journal,* 1883, pp. 750–51, 755–62, 764–65, 777–78.

37. *Tennessee Acts,* 1883, pp. 271–79; *Senate Journal,* 1883, pp. 724–25, 740; Nashville *American,* March 30, 31, 1883; Knoxville *Tribune,* April 5, 1883; Savage, "Railroads in Tennessee."

them to be in writing, and many people were afraid of going on record against the railroads. Before the frustrated commission could issue any binding orders or decrees, it was slapped with a temporary restraining injunction from a United States Circuit Court. Attorneys for the two largest railroads in Tennessee had told the court that the regulatory law was unconstitutional because it violated corporate charters and trespassed in the federal jurisdiction of interstate commerce. Poor old Colonel Savage, his agency crippled by the Senate and handcuffed by the court, cried that he had "no apology to make, or pardon to ask from ambitious, time-serving politicians, from bondholders, or greedy monopolies," that he "regret[ted] nothing that he ha[d] done to protect the people against their wrongs." [38] But the railroads and their allies were not through with him yet.

Railroad regulation was a major issue in 1884, when Governor Bate and the commissioners faced the electorate. Some county Democratic conventions were strongly in favor of trying again with another railroad law. The Bourbon Nashville *World* hammered at the sins of the roads and urged the election of the incumbent commissioners, nominees of the state Democratic party. But the prorailroad Nashville *American,* edited by A. S. Colyar, printed special supplements distributed with the Clarksville *Chronicle,* the *Smith County Record,* the Pulaski *Citizen,* and nine other small-town weeklies. This propaganda, probably paid for by the Louisville and Nashville, was sugar-coated with praise for the national Democratic ticket, but also clearly conveyed the message that the railroad-commission law was unwise and unpopular. Commissioner Savage was a "communist crank," according to one editor. "Democrats, scratch the Railroad Commission," exhorted Adolph Ochs's Chattanooga *Times;* the Republican nominees were "pledged not to serve." Railroad Democrats distributed fake party ballots with the commissioners' names missing.[39] The battle was over the few thousand Democratic voters

38. Savage, "Railroads in Tennessee"; *Reports of the Railroad Commissioners,* 1884, pp. 20, 26, 29, 79, 114; Nashville *American,* November 6, 1883.
39. Nashville *American,* June 12, 1884; Nashville *World,* September 1, October 31, 1884; Pulaski *Citizen,* August 28, 1884; Covington *Tipton Record,* quoted in Nashville *Banner,* October 29, 1884; Chattanooga *Times,* November 2, 1884; Jackson *Forked Deer Blade,* November 1, 1884.

who could kill the commission by abstaining and permitting the election of Republican commissioners opposed to regulation.

Colonel Savage and his colleagues were defeated in 1884, scratched from the Democratic ballot by sky-blues in the towns, who could be expected to register dissatisfaction with the Bourbons (see Appendix B, Table 8). In Middle Tennessee, where the commissioners fared the worst, the urban sky-blues were joined by hill-country whites living in counties falling behind in population growth and agricultural prosperity. For some reason farmers chose the politicians for scapegoats rather than the railroads. The Bourbon strategy of using railroad regulation to help build a new majority was a good one, except for one important flaw: their strong anti-Republican rhetoric denied them any access to GOP votes, so that relatively few railroad Democrats could tip the balance of power merely by abstaining. The result of the 1884 election buried railroad regulation in Tennessee for several years.

The 1885 legislature only conducted the railroad commission's funeral. The House of Representatives rejected, in rapid order, four weak railroad bills; some said that a free excursion to New Orleans in the middle of the session helped legislators see the cogency of the railroads' arguments. Then the legislature enacted a bill by Democratic Senator W. B. Lamb of Lincoln County abolishing the moribund existing commission. Not a single Republican in either house opposed the Lamb bill, which passed because Bourbon leaders failed to hold all the Democrats in line. Men from cities and white counties tended to desert to the Republicans more than Democrats from rural black counties.[40] The known hostility of United States Circuit Judge John Baxter made retention of the old commission seem pointless, and new laws risky—an easy excuse for Democrats wishing to break with the party leadership.

A. S. Colyar, Adolph Ochs, and some of the other anti-Bourbon

---

40. Nashville *American,* March 27, 28, 29, 1885; Jackson *West Tennessee Whig,* May 20, 1885; *House Journal,* 1885, p. 666; *Senate Journal,* 1885, pp. 334–35. If the race-urban index of a county is its percentage black population in 1890 minus its percentage in towns over 2,000, then the average race-urban index of home counties of House Democrats voting for the Lamb bill was 6.5, and of House Democrats voting against the bill, 21.5.

Democrats who wrecked the Railroad Commission also made a strong fight for protection against the Bourbons' law-tariff doctrine. At the state Democratic convention of 1884, Colyar debated S. F. Wilson on the subject, but the Bourbon tariff-for-revenue-only plank won by a vote of 794 to 535.[41] The protariff minority represented counties more white, urban, and prosperous than the Bourbon majority (see Appendix B, Table 9). Relatively black counties in Middle Tennessee, which had supported the Redeemer Porter administration in the 1878 convention, now backed the Bourbons in 1884, having made the transition with Isham Harris. The 1884 convention division did not resemble that of 1878, nor the sky-blue bolt of 1882, nor the scratching of the railroad commissioners in 1884. Clearly there were no continuing, stable opposing factions in the Democratic party, but shifting alignments over changing issues. There were mixtures of class and status motivations in these divisions, but only on the tariff issue were economic considerations of more than minor importance.

Democratic businessmen caught up in the contemporary American fascination with rapid economic growth were impatient with the Bourbons and their old-fashioned, rural attitudes. "This class of men," wrote industrial promoter Colyar, "of which we have quite a number in the south, are a great drawback. They don't want any manufacturing done in the south, because it will put up the price of farm labor. They believe the south ought to have the ways of an aristocracy, money or no money; that the improvement of the rivers is an officious interference with the laws of navigation and the rights of the catfish." [42]

Such feelings were exacerbated, in some cases, by resentment toward the Bourbons for deposing the uncompromising Redeemers of the 1870s. Some Democrats from booming Chattanooga urged the appointment of James D. Porter to the federal cabinet on the grounds that the sky-blues were sulking in their tents and needed to be appeased: "It is needless to disguise the fact, that further ostracism of the best element of the party for holding their own honest views

41. Nashville *American,* June 19, 20, 1884.
42. Nashville *Union,* February 22, 1886.

will work disaster to it." [43] A third factor working against the Bourbons was the memory of the old Whig party. Colyar implied that "those of the South who ha[d] not always been Democrats, but who ha[d] voted with the party in recent years" were "disgusted with the ignorant and offensively arrogant Democratic leadership." [44] Possibly only the dismal failure of the sky-blue bolt in 1882 prevented a similar attempt two years later.

The Republican party was well aware of the Bourbons' difficulties, and sought to increase them by nominating a Confederate veteran from one of Tennessee's old Whig families to run against Governor Bate in 1884. The very opposite of a carpetbagger, Frank T. Reid was received in the best homes of Nashville. After his nomination, a sky-blue Democrat revealed his doubts to Senator Howell Jackson. "Should the democracy—I mean the real, the honest democracy of Tenn. vote for Reed [sic] as against Bate the representative of repudiation and a hurtful tariff meddling?" he asked, and then concluded: "The best thing that can befall the Tennessee democracy in my opinion is for Reed to beat Bate, not by democrats voting for Reed, but simply refusing to vote for Bate." The Nashville *Banner* did not hide its hope that Bate would lose. Colyar's Nashville *American,* however, little as it loved the Bourbons, supported Bate: Reid was pledging to try to end the convict-lease system. A handful of Democrats voted for Cleveland and for Reid, who ran a thousand votes ahead of his national ticket. Bate won by a margin of less than 3 percent of the total number of votes cast. [45]

Despite the precariousness of their position in 1884, the Bourbons can be credited with some positive achievements. Out of the wreckage which was the Democratic party in 1881, they made a new coalition which took account of the thousands of voters who insisted that the Redeemers' state-credit principles showed no understanding

43. E. A. James, R. M. Barton, Jr., Creed F. Bates, Adolph Ochs, *et al.* to H. E. Jackson, December 8, 1884, in Grover Cleveland Papers, Library of Congress.

44. Nashville *American,* August 29, 1884. Colyar's actions did not match his rhetoric: he had run against old Whig John C. Brown for governor in 1870 and 1872, but backed the Bourbon Bate, an old Democrat, in both 1882 and 1884.

45. Speer, *Sketches,* 113–19; Nashville *World,* September 13, 1884; P. D. Sims to H. E. Jackson, July 3, 1884, in Harding-Jackson Papers; Nashville *Banner,* October 1, 3, 1884; *Tribune Almanac,* 1885, p. 81; White (ed.), *Messages,* VII, 97.

of the common man's burdens. Then, after years in which gradations on the scale of debt compromise had become lines for battle, the Bourbons quickly settled the matter once and for all. What had been lacking was merely the will to cooperate: the low-tax majority against 50–4 in 1879 agreed quite readily to the Bourbon 50–3 law, except a Greenback fringe. The most astute part of the Bourbons' strategy was to shift political discussion to new issues, so that quibbling over exactly how much to scale the debt became pointless. The new issues were based directly on the popular attitude which had given the low-tax revolt its strength: a suspicion that alien men or institutions would somehow take the destinies of ordinary citizens out of their own hands. "The aim of Government should be to distribute wealth, not concentrate it," explained a small-town banker,[46] who might have summed up the Bourbon philosophy in a nutshell by adding "power" to "wealth." Such a viewpoint was more representative of rank-and-file Democrats than was the Redeemer confidence of the 1870s; and lest Bourbon Jeffersonianism seem purely reactionary, let us recall that the Railroad Commission of 1883 was Tennessee's first serious effort to deal with the new corporate concentrations of economic power.

One aspect of the Bourbon coalition was increased discipline of the Democratic party in the legislature. A major weakness of the party during the Redeemer decade was that they often divided on important roll calls and allowed the Republican minority a decisive role. It was in 1881, when this tendency became an explicit liaison, that Democratic leaders were forced to reorganize their party. In elections, Democratic legislators had customarily taken their differences onto the floor, assuming that since none of the majority party would vote for a Republican, it would be safe to thrash around for several ballots until some Democrat came up with a majority of votes. This system had one defect: as in the election of Senators Andrew Johnson and Howell Jackson, it permitted the Republicans to elect the Democrats they liked best, regardless of the wishes of most Democrats. An important exception to this pattern was the election of Senator Isham Harris in 1877, when the Democrats bloc-

---

46. A. T. McNeal to Grover Cleveland, September 10, 1887, in Cleveland Papers.

voted for him on the first ballot. The old system prevailed in 1883 (except for Harris' reelection), but in 1885 it began to change. The Senate fumbled chaotically through thirty-seven ballots for Speaker, with as many as fifteen of the thirty-three members receiving votes at once; then the Democrats caucused, composed their differences, came in the next morning, and elected a speaker immediately. The more efficient House Democrats caucused in 1887 before the first ballot, when they elected a Bourbon Speaker. In 1883 the party relapsed into the old system, again allowing the Republicans to choose the Democratic House Speaker; but after 1887 the caucus system stuck in both houses.[47]

Table 7
RISE OF THE DEMOCRATIC CAUCUS, 1871–1895 [48]

		House	Senate
Number of ballots needed			
to elect speaker in:	1871	9	2
	1873	24	44
	1875	10	13
	1877	9	4
	1879	12	16
	1881	5	99
	1883	7	16
	1885	1	38
	1887	10	18
	1889	1	1
	1891	1	1
	1893	1	1
	1895	1	1

Significantly, the caucus very rarely laid down a party line on legislation, as it did on the railroad commission, but the years of the Bourbon coalition saw the rise of a new and permanent sense of Democratic unity in the legislature.

Most Bourbons, steadfast opponents of governmental paternalism, were practitioners of racial paternalism; in this respect there is no

47. *House Journal,* 1877, p. 67; *Senate Journal,* 1885, pp. 6–48; Nashville *American,* January 7, 1885; *House Journal,* 1885, p. 7, also 1887, pp. 24–25.
48. *House Journal,* 1871–95; *Senate Journal,* 1871–95.

evidence that they differed significantly from their Redeemer predecessors. Leading Bourbons, with a few exceptions, did not use the distinctively virulent racist rhetoric that came into vogue in the South of the 1890s. In one notable instance, moreover, they welcomed an important black politician into their coalition—none other than Ed Shaw, denounced as a "wild fanatic" in the Memphis press when he ran for sheriff in 1880. Two years later some very prominent white Memphians told General Bate that Shaw, who had broken with Governor Hawkins, had carried Shelby County for the Democrats and should be rewarded generously. In 1884 Shaw stumped for the Bourbons and helped give Bate official notice of his renomination. Blacks voted quite freely: eleven of the seventeen legislative elections won by Negroes in Tennessee before 1964 were in the years 1882 through 1886.[49] This is not to say that the Bourbons were liberal, for they certainly were not. They were secure enough in their white supremacist ideology to violate it for tactical advantage.

Bourbon leaders may well have looked forward to 1886 with confident assurance that their party would continue to govern Tennessee, and that troublemakers like Howell Jackson and A. S. Colyar lacked the popularity to disturb the hegemony of the Bourbons within the party. They did not reckon on Bob Taylor.

49. Memphis *Public Ledger,* July 2, 1880; Nashville *American,* April 28, 1882, June 20, 1884; G. W. Gordon *et al.* to W. B. Bate, November 9, 1882, in CGO, TSLA; Nashville *Banner,* October 22, 1884; list of black legislators in Tennessee, obtained from Dan M. Robison, Nashville.

4

Bob Taylor and
the Politics of
Style

The Bourbons remained the strongest group in the Tennessee Democratic party after 1885, but they lost control of the office of governor. After the popular Robert L. Taylor won the nomination, they were prepared to accept him into their coalition despite his reluctance to use their Jeffersonian-Confederate rhetoric. But once in office, Taylor angered the Bourbons by giving patronage to New South men. He received a second nomination in 1888 only after a bitter fight, and failed to build, or perhaps even to imagine, a lasting coalition with Republicans or town Democrats to supplant the Bourbons. They were able to elect former governor Bate to the United States Senate, where he would be, in the words of a sky-blue, "a mere continuation of Harris." [1] Bob Taylor's principal, though unintended, achievement was to weaken the Bourbons enough to smooth the way for an entirely new group to rise to sudden dominance in the Democratic party.

It has been suggested that "the factions [*i.e.* the Bourbons and their industrialist opponents] effected a working arrangement" in 1886 whereby the Bourbons would relinquish the governorship in exchange for control of both Senate seats. There is insufficient evidence for this view, and two arguments against it. First, the opposing groups in the Democratic party were not well-disciplined factions, but loose and shifting coalitions. No factional leaders had the power to rein in the ambitions of all their followers, nor did these coalitions include everyone. Second, the party was not notably harmonious in

---

1. R. L. Lightfoot to H. E. Jackson, April 13, 1886, in Harding-Jackson Papers. Senator Jackson's seat became vacant when Cleveland appointed him to replace Circuit Judge John Baxter.

84

1886–1887: the legislative caucus took sixty-eight ballots to nominate Bate for the Senate in 1887, and the state convention of 1886 needed fifteen ballots to choose among four contenders for governor.[2] Such wrangling does not point to a "working arrangement" but does suggest that the Bourbons lost the governorship partly through disorganization.

Very early in the campaign it seemed that the two important candidates would be Bourbon banker Albert T. McNeal of Bolivar and General George G. Dibrell of Sparta, part owner of a coal mine, former railroad president, and five-term Redeemer congressman. McNeal did not run, but Dibrell did, attracting New South men— railroad capitalists and sky-blues, in the hostile eyes of a Bourbon editor. Bourbons of the Memphis area supported National Democratic Committeeman Robert F. Looney, who had once backed Colyar for governor and who, like Dibrell, was an old Whig and coal-mine investor. Looney was hurt by his association with the Pan-Electric Telephone Company, which appeared in a congressional investigation to have had improper influence on a federal suit against the rival Bell Company. Senator Harris' embarrassing position as a major Pan-Electric stockholder may help explain the Bourbons' relative weakness in 1886.[3]

In East Tennessee, Harris apparently backed one of the three politicians who tried to exploit the feeling that it was high time for an East Tennessee governor. Sectional feeling was increased in June when a special Democratic convention for state supreme court nominations chose a newcomer to the area to represent the eastern division, which was constitutionally entitled to at least one justice. Robert L. Taylor, another East Tennessean, formally entered the crowded gubernatorial field at the end of June. A. S. Colyar and the Nashville *Banner* said they wondered whether Taylor was favored

2. Robison, *Bob Taylor*, 47; Nashville *American*, August 13, 1886, January 25, 1887.

3. W. B. Bate to Albert McNeal, February 13, 1885 (copy), in CGO, TSLA; Nashville *Union*, June 25, 1886; Bolivar *Bulletin*, November 7, 1890; Jackson *West Tennessee Whig*, September 5, 1885, February 27, 1886, January 1, 1887; Speer, *Sketches*, 121–23, 226–30; *Biographical Directory of the American Congress*, 903; Memphis *Appeal*, July 16, 1886; Nashville *American*, August 12, 1886; Memphis *Avalanche*, August 16, 1878; Davis, "Arthur S. Colyar," 250; Knoxville *Journal*, May 28, July 3, 1886; New York *Times*, April 1, 3, 6, 7, May 1, 1886.

by the Bourbons as a dark horse to stop Dibrell, but they doubtless knew better, for Taylor was free of factional ties. Indeed, as in 1878, the wide-open scramble for the nomination revealed the absence of any well-organized factions within the Democratic party.[4]

Born in 1850 in a county of extreme East Tennessee named for one of his ancestors, Bob Taylor could count many other illustrious men among his kinfolk: Whig Unionist Congressman Nathaniel G. Taylor (Bob's father), Confederate Senator Landon C. Haynes (maternal uncle), United States Senator Zebulon Vance of North Carolina (wife's first cousin), a cofounder of a major railroad (great-uncle), and a number of other congressmen, state legislators, and lesser officeholders.[5] Bob's family differed from the patrician Redeemer and sky-blue families in two important ways: it was mostly from East Tennessee, and it was sharply divided by the Civil War. But he was not a commoner like Andrew Johnson. Taylor's antecedents were less humble than those of Isham Harris or A. S. Colyar.

Young Taylor entered politics in 1878 when his brother Alfred lost the First District Republican congressional nomination, and the underdog Democrats turned to Bob as a way of attracting Alf's disgruntled friends. Bob's upset victory owed much to his brother's supporters, but 1878 was a good year for Tennessee Democrats, who won every congressional seat in the state but one. As a freshman congressman Taylor made little impact, but he did speak out on the inflationist side of the money question, and introduced an unsuccessful income-tax bill. These positions have been cited as evidence that Taylor used "the basic reasoning" later employed by the Populists. But in 1878 A. J. Kellar and A. S. Colyar, who were not farmers and never sympathized with Populism, also took the inflationist view; and in 1891 the income tax was advocated not only by the Populists but also by Congressman Josiah Patterson of Memphis, a bitter enemy of Populism.[6] If Bob Taylor was an agrarian spokes-

4. Nashville *American,* June 12, 29, July 22, August 12, 1886; Knoxville *Journal,* June 11, 19, July 9, 1886; Greeneville *Bulletin,* quoted in Nashville *American,* October 15, 1885; Memphis *Appeal,* June 5, 9, 1886; Nashville *Banner,* June 10, 11, July 19, 1886; Jackson *West Tennessee Whig,* June 12, 1886; Nashville *Union,* July 22, 1886.

5. Speer, *Sketches,* 212–14, 462–63, 564–66; Nashville *Union,* January 18, 1887; Robison, *Bob Taylor,* 50, also 49–53 for more on Taylor's early background.

6. Robison, *Bob Taylor,* 54–55; Memphis *Appeal-Avalanche,* May 7, 1891.

man in Congress, then the term *agrarian* must be broad enough to include many Tennessee conservatives.

Ambitious young Bob was a strong contender for James E. Bailey's United States Senate seat in 1881. The next year he and General Bate were rivals again, this time for the Democratic gubernatorial nomination, but Bate won without much trouble. In 1884 Taylor was one of the Democratic presidential electors for the state at large, which gave him a chance to travel around and show himself to the voters while speaking for Cleveland. Another reward for this service to the party was a new job. "Mr. Cleveland impressed me as a wise man when I learned that he had appointed me Pension Agent," said Bob with tongue in cheek. "I was really struck with his good judgment." Taylor resigned as editor of the Johnson City *Comet* with his typical extravagance: "Today I bid farewell to the Comet, and wipe my weeping eyes." [7] He was now in a good position for another crack at the gubernatorial nomination in 1886.

Taylor was a great entertainer on the stump, but his political competitors were not laughing. When the state Democratic convention met, he led the three men who were still in the field against him: Dibrell, Looney, and T. M. McConnell of Chattanooga. Taylor's able managers gradually increased his strength over fifteen ballots for the required two-thirds, despite an effort by his foes to unite on McConnell.[8] Bob won in part because he overcame the sectionalism which limited the appeal of the others.

Table 8

FIRST BALLOT, GUBERNATORIAL NOMINATION,
1886 DEMOCRATIC STATE CONVENTION, BY DIVISION OF STATE [9]

Candidate—Division	West	Middle	East
G. G. Dibrell—M	66½	284	46½
R. F. Looney—W	136½	65½	2
T. M. McConnell—E	3	43½	153
R. L. Taylor—E	170	221	115

7. Robert L. Taylor to H. E. Jackson, April 21, 1886, in Harding-Jackson Papers; Johnson City *Comet,* quoted in Jackson *West Tennessee Whig,* July 1, 1885.
8. Nashville *American,* August 12, 13, 1886.
9. *Ibid.,* August 12, 1886.

The Bourbons' failure to keep the party committed to railroad regulation was signaled by the defeat of a proregulation plank by a two-to-one vote in the convention. A hot issue in the previous campaign, railroad policy split Taylor's delegates in about the same proportion as the whole convention (see Table 9). Businessman Di-

Table 9
FIRST BALLOT, GUBERNATORIAL NOMINATION,
1886 DEMOCRATIC STATE CONVENTION; VOTE TO TABLE
PLANK FOR RAILROAD REGULATION; COUNTY TOTALS
ESTIMATED PROPORTIONATELY [10]

Delegates of:	Table	Not Table
Dibrell	284	89
Looney	79½	106½
McConnell	143½	55½
Taylor	315	175

brell's supporters were heavily against regulation, and only Looney's Bourbons favored it. The finished platform ritually endorsed Cleveland, Bate, and such party doctrines as states' rights, Irish independence, and reductions in tariffs, taxes, and the national debt. The disagreement over federal aid for education was evaded in a platitude opposing unconstitutional federal appropriations. After the defeat of the railroad plank, not a glimmer of agrarian protest remained in the platform Bob Taylor would run on. It is true that Taylor's convention support was overwhelmingly rural in character: only 9 percent of his votes came from counties with over a fifth of their people in towns over two thousand, compared to corresponding figures of 23 percent, 42 percent, and 60 percent for Dibrell, Looney, and McConnell. But ruralism is not agrarianism, and Table 9 suggests that the Bourbons were more agrarian, in the sense of resisting unfettered capitalism, than were Taylor's men.[11]

Bob's humorous style, his most salient characteristic, was more widely noticed at first than his views on public issues. "[Bob] will doubtless make a breezy canvass and the boys may rally around him enthusiastically," the Nashville *Banner* predicted, "but there will be

10. *Ibid.*
11. *Ibid.*, August 12, 14, 1886; 1890 Census, *Population,* 317–28.

something lacking in the campaign which should be there." Earlier the *Banner* had warned that Bob did not have "the qualities needed in the coming canvass, when a dignified conservatism and solidity of personal character will be more effective in securing public confidence and support than the more factitious methods and tricks and antics of the hustings." "After all," sourly conceded a Memphis editor, "while Bob was not our choice, his fiddling is good. There isn't too much of his political career and record, but what there is of it was brilliantly executed, animated, and spirituelle. In anecdotal transfixion of Republican foes he is unsurpassed." Taylor was master of florid rhetoric, but did not take it too seriously. In a debate of the 1884 presidential campaign, Bob's opponent portrayed the Republican party as an eagle, soaring aloft with free schools and free homesteads in his talons. Taylor quipped that the eagle really carried "forty acres of land" in one claw and "that mule" in the other.[12] The genteel were embarrassed at the prospect of a comedian in the capitol, but Taylor's effective stump style was the basis for his career.

Taylor's youth also drew attention. A Republican welcomed the thirty-six-year-old nominee as a leader of young Democrats who would replace old men like Harris and Dibrell. "The young men of Tennessee nominated Bob Taylor," said the Nashville *Union,* but then *Union* editor A. S. Colyar was sixty-eight. The Memphis *Avalanche* saw in Taylor reason to hope that war nostalgia was fading enough to let young men move up in politics; but then the owner of the *Avalanche,* who was younger than Bob, was running for Congress in 1886. The idea of youth, little noted before the convention, now began to echo as editors read each other. The highly partisan Nashville *American* reported early in the race that the crowd in Bob's hotel room "was distinctly youthful," that of his company "scarcely a member had passed forty years if appearances were not deceptive." According to historian Dan M. Robison, part of the "secret of 'Bob' Taylor's strength" in 1886 lay in his appeal to the younger generation.[13]

12. Nashville *Banner,* November 1, 1884, July 8, August 13, 1886; Memphis *Avalanche,* August 14, 1886.

13. Knoxville *Journal,* August 17, 1886; Nashville *Union,* August 20, 1886; Memphis *Avalanche,* August 20, 21, 1886; *DAB,* XIV, 523; Nashville *American,* August 13, September 10, 1886; Robison, *Bob Taylor,* 43.

The strongest evidence that Taylor especially attracted youth, however, consists in vague, partisan claims without empirical foundation. Some comments resulted mainly from the force of the realization of Taylor's own age: when he was born, Isham Harris and John H. Savage were already sitting in Congress. But young men were not new to Tennessee politics. In the current legislature, Senate Speaker C. R. Berry was only two years older than Taylor; three members of the legislature were twenty-one, twenty-three, and twenty-four when sworn in in 1885. The average age of thirty-one of the thirty-three state senators elected in 1886 was forty-four, and nine of them were under thirty-eight.[14] While it is true that before Bob no Tennessean was elected governor or United States senator who was too young to have fought in the Civil War, his appeal to youth is unsupported except by those with an interest in stressing the vigor and confidence of his campaign.

If there was real significance in Taylor's youth, it lay in his lack of association with the war, not in his appeal to young men. Bob did not use Bourbon rhetoric. Furthermore, he was not on the best of terms with those who did, having locked horns with General Bate twice. Taylor's opponents for the nomination circulated a statement he had made as a legislative candidate that he stood against Senator Harris. Someone wrote a letter to the New York *Times,* signed "Tennessee Democrat," calling Taylor an ally of sky-blues James D. Porter and Howell E. Jackson against "repudiationists" Harris and Bate. The Nashville *American* countered that it mattered not who were Taylor's past associates, then added inconsistently that he never had opposed Harris and Bate.[15] Anyway, the very existence of such a popular, independent figure, who could enthrall a Democratic crowd without using the Jeffersonian-Confederate themes, was a threat to the ruling coalition.

Another favorite topic of the press and later historians was the unusual situation of an interfraternal campaign. The Republicans had nominated Bob's brother Alfred A. Taylor, at least partly to discourage the Democrats from nominating Bob. Now a Bourbon

14. Jackson *West Tennessee Whig,* January 10, 1885; Nashville *American,* January 2, 1885, February 21, 1887.

15. Knoxville *Journal,* August 15, 1886; Nashville *American,* August 21, 1886.

editor squirmed at the "repulsive" sight of two brothers running against each other, using the term *war of the roses* to show his distaste. But Bob cleverly picked up the term, likening Alf and himself to two roses, and managed to catch the voters' imagination by making the "war of the roses" a festive affair. The Democratic candidate had the advantage over his brother, who was more elegant and argumentative but less fluent and polished on the stump. A Tennessee writer in a national magazine made Bob out as something of a clown who spoke in an Appalachian dialect and wooed the voters by fiddling their troubles away. Far from resenting this public image, Bob encouraged it. After his death, three of his brothers published a book about him in which they recalled hilarious practical jokes the candidates had played on each other in 1886. In one town Bob spoke first, and his brother quickly realized that he was solemnly delivering Alf's speech verbatim. When Alf rushed back to his hotel room, he found his speech text gone and Bob's friends convulsed with laughter. Alf tasted revenge in Lincoln County, famous for its whiskey. Some local Democrats burst in looking for Bob, mistook Alf for his brother, and asked him for a friendly drink. Alf sternly lectured them on the evils of whiskey until they had all quietly slipped away, but the reddest face belonged to Bob, who had to track down each thirsty Democrat and explain the prank. All this adolescent fun hurt neither candidate. A recent student concluded rightly that much of Bob's popularity was based on his successful projection of a naïve-but-honest "mountain boy" image.[16]

Only pages before recounting the whiskey episode, the Taylor brothers soberly declared that the 1886 campaign had avoided personal slander and invective, since Bob and Alf had kept "the discussion upon a high plane of the political issues involved." But the campaign, even more than most American political races after 1840, consisted of personalities and slogans rather than substantive issues. Towns competed in their lavish welcomes for Bob and Alf. Follow-

---

16. Memphis *Appeal,* June 19, August 13, 1886; Nashville *American,* August 15, September 10, 1886; Nashville *Banner,* September 16, 1886; William Allen Dromgoole, "Fiddling His Way to Fame," *Arena,* II (1890), 728–29; James P., Alf A., and Hugh L. Taylor, *Life and Career of Senator Robert Love Taylor* (Nashville, 1913), 172–76; Robert L. Taylor, Jr., "Apprenticeship in the First District: Bob and Alf Taylor's Early Congressional Races," *Tennessee Historical Quarterly,* XXVIII (1969), 24–41.

ing the theme of the War of the Roses, Republicans organized parades decked in red ribbons and banners, while the Democrats appropriately used white. Frequent features along the way were pretty girls in the parades, fervent admirers breaking down in tears, and sentimental old people recalling the campaign of 1844 and blessing Bob the "mountain boy." In this feverish atmosphere, Bob's train was forced to stop near Knoxville, in Republican territory, for a piece of wood on the track. Although the railroad insisted that the object was there by accident, the Nashville *American* angrily charged that the stopped train had been stoned by restless local Republicans, and added that Bob had been jeered and his banners torn down.[17] Such was the "high plane of the political issues involved."

Issues entered the campaign mainly because Bob Taylor's position on them was disputed. The Nashville *Union* protested that the *American* was trying to get Taylor to advocate free trade and that his past positions could not be so construed. Colyar's *Union* quoted Bob as saying he wanted the tariff to account for differences in American and foreign wages, and pronounced him in harmony with the 1884 national Democratic platform, which confidently demanded that while "all taxation shall be limited to the requirements of economical government," tax cuts must not put American labor at a disadvantage. This plank was endorsed in the state platform Taylor was running on. Bob himself said "I am not a free trader, but I am not for the tariff of the Republican party."[18] This empty banality, like the national tariff plank, was designed to offend the fewest number: Taylor could pronounce it and then let his followers fight each other over the correct exegesis.

The tariff and all other issues were eclipsed in Tennessee by a bill introduced in Congress in December, 1883, by Senator Henry W. Blair of New Hampshire which provided for federal aid for education. The bill would appropriate $15 million for the first year and nine more annual grants decreasing by a million dollars a year. Since

17. James P., Alf A., and Hugh L. Taylor, *Life and Career of Senator Robert Love Taylor,* 170–71; Nashville *American,* October 1, 2, 16, 24, 29, 1886.
18. Nashville *Union,* August 18, September 13, 1886; Thomas Hudson McKee (ed.), *The National Conventions and Platforms of All Political Parties, 1789–1901: Convention, Popular, and Electoral Vote: Also the Political Complexion of Both Houses of Congress at Each Biennial Period* (Baltimore, 1901), 205; Nashville *American,* August 14, September 14, 1886.

the money would be distributed according to illiteracy, the South would receive a greatly disproportionate share. This proposal had a great appeal to those interested in education in Tennessee, which spent an average of 72 cents per pupil per month for public schools in 1885, most of which went to pay a teacher's salary which averaged $28.52 per month. But some southern Democrats opposed the bill because they saw in it not only an excuse to spend the revenues of a high protective tariff, but also a threat to the Bourbon limited-construction theory of the constitution.[19]

The Blair bill had come before the Tennessee legislature in 1885 in the form of a resolution calling on the state's congressmen to vote for it. In the lower house, a motion to table this resolution failed because enough Democrats joined the united Republicans to outvote the Bourbons. Table 10 shows that this division was similar to the

Table 10

ROLL-CALL VOTES, 1885 HOUSE OF REPRESENTATIVES, ON
BLAIR BILL AND ON REPEAL OF RAILROAD COMMISSION [20]

		To Table Resolution Supporting Blair Bill	
		Yes	No
To repeal RR	yes	10	41
commission	no	28	6

$$\phi = -.62 *$$

* For explanation of ϕ (phi), see Appendix A.

vote for repeal of the railroad-commission law of 1883. The twenty-eight men taking the Bourbon position against the Blair bill and for the railroad commission tended to be from rural, relatively black counties: the average race-urban index for these twenty-eight is twenty-one, while the average index for the forty-one voting the opposite way is four.[21] Clearly, the Blair bill was an issue that could

19. Woodward, *Origins of the New South*, 53, 64; "Annual Report of the State Superintendent of Public Instruction," *House Journal Appendix*, 1889, p. 218. For the Blair bill in national politics, see Allen J. Going, "The South and the Blair Education Bill," *Mississippi Valley Historical Review*, XLIV (1957), 267–90.

20. See also *House Journal*, 1885, pp. 121–22, 665–66.

21. The race-urban index for a constituency is the percentage of blacks in the population in 1890 minus the percentage of the population in towns over two thousand in 1890. 1890 Census, *Population*, 317–28, 428–29.

hurt the Bourbons by driving away business-progressive Democrats in white and/or urban counties.

Senator Howell Jackson increased this possibility by continuing to advocate the Blair bill. At a teachers' convention at Jonesboro, he argued for a loose construction of the Constitution, recalling that the states had not been demoralized by the distribution in 1836 of surplus federal funds. Jackson declared that only about one-third of the state's school-age children attended school on an average day, and that the average term was seventy-eight days long, paid for by an expenditure per pupil only one-tenth the Massachusetts rate. More money for schools, he told the underpaid teachers, would raise the level of the electorate and make workers more productive. The convention promptly endorsed the Blair bill. Senator Isham Harris, not impressed by these facts and figures, held his ground against both the Blair bill and tariff protection.[22] By 1886 opposition to the Blair bill had become a litmus test of Bourbonism, and Bob Taylor was closely watched for signs of his intentions.

After the state party convention, Bourbon spokesmen claimed that Taylor opposed the Blair bill because the platform did, but others retorted that he had been a "pronounced advocate" of the bill before his nomination. In an attempt to clear up the confusion, or perhaps to maintain it, Taylor issued a statement on federal aid: "I favor the application of the surplus fund now in the national treasury to the reduction of the national debt. I favor most positively and earnestly a system of universal free education, and believe that such a system can be best established and carried out through the sale of our immense public domain." This proclamation was hailed by both sides. One skeptic tersely remarked, "[I]n attempting to straddle the educational question Mr. Taylor makes a mess of it."[23] Candidate Taylor's quandary was that he could afford to alienate neither the Bourbons, who could sway the bulk of his party, nor the progressive Democrats, who might be attracted by Alf Taylor's forthright stand in favor of federal aid.

22. Jackson speech in Jackson *West Tennessee Whig,* October 28, 1885; Nashville *American,* September 11, 1885.
23. Nashville *Banner,* August 19, 30, September 3, 6, 1886; Nashville *Union,* August 22, September 1, 1886; Knoxville *Journal,* August 31, 1886.

Partly because of the Blair-bill problem, Bob's campaign speech relied on his personal style and avoided thorny issues. First he dazzled his listeners with oratorical pyrotechnics: "As God has diversified his creation and made the moon and planets, stars and sun of heaven to differ from each other in glory, in movement and position, and sent them all circling in space in perfect harmony, so in politics he ha[s] diversified our people in thought and opinion, yet harmonized all on the one great principle of free government." Then he reviewed the sins of the Republicans, and proceeded to dodge the Blair-bill question by a piece of pure sophistry. "I declare to you," he said, "that there is not a dollar of surplus in the United States Treasury. I declare to you that there is no such thing in existence as the Blair bill." He reasoned that since the Republicans in Congress had passed a resolution that the Treasury surplus be applied to the national debt, the surplus was not available for any other purpose and therefore did not exist, and neither did the bill, which depended on it. Bob's inspirational, if vague, peroration anticipated Henry Grady. After the war, he said, the returning veterans were not overcome by their loss and grief.

> Farmers, mechanics, engineers, artisans, manufacturers, statesmen, lawyers, teachers, physicians and divines, they [began] the grand structure of the New South. The debris and wreckage of the war's destruction [were] cleared away and the foundations [were] built upon the enduring principles of free thought, free action, free labor, a free ballot, justice, law, order, the education of the masses, the autonomy of the States, constitutional government, one flag and a reunited republic. These, my countrymen, are the principles of the progressive Democracy of the New South. They inspire the energy, the push, the grit and snap which are rapidly rearing the southern half of the grandest structure of advanced civilization the world ever saw.[24]

In its emphasis on a new beginning, its expansive confidence, and its implicit materialism, this statement is one of the best expressions by a Tennessean of the New-South "booster" progressivism of the 1880s, which derived partly from the Redeemers but more clearly from A. J. Kellar and A. S. Colyar, dissenters of the 1870s. This one statement by Taylor should have warned the Bourbons that Taylor, once in office, would be dangerous to their coalition.

24. Nashville *American,* September 10, 1886.

The ingredients for Democratic victory were present in 1886: party unity, the blurring of important issues, and a highly entertaining candidate who was determined, as he put it, to go into the "back counties" and "seek the people who have not been aroused yet." [25] These things combined with voters' Democratic habits to give Bob Taylor more votes than any other man had ever received for governor of Tennessee in a nonpresidential election. But the significance of Taylor's vote has been exaggerated in the standard account of the election, which includes the data given in Table 11: "From a study

Table 11
FIGURES USED BY D. M. ROBISON TO SHOW
BOB TAYLOR'S POPULARITY

Presidential Years	Dem. Vote, Governor	Off Years	Dem. Vote, Governor
1876	123,740	1878	89,018
1880	136,615 *	1882	118,821
1884	132,201	1886	126,628 **
1888	156,699 **	1890	113,549
1892	126,348	1894	104,356
1896	156,228 **		

* Split between J. V. Wright and S. F. Wilson.
** Years when Bob Taylor was Democratic nominee.

of [this] table," Robison observed, "it would appear that Robert L. Taylor strengthened the Democratic ticket in Tennessee from between eight to twenty-four thousand votes whenever he headed it." [26] Table 11 fails to show, however, that the vote of both parties tended to fluctuate together, depending on the general level of political interest. It is illuminating to see these figures expressed as percentages of the two-party vote:

The percentages for presidential years represent a convergence of many factors, but clearly they will not support the contention that Bob Taylor produced unusually large Democratic victories. The

25. *Ibid.*, August 18, 1886.
26. Robison, *Bob Taylor*, 71.

Table 12
DEMOCRATIC PERCENTAGE OF DEMOCRATIC AND
REPUBLICAN VOTE FOR GOVERNOR, 1876–96 [27]

Presidential Years	Democratic Percentage	Off Years	Democratic Percentage
1876	63 *	1878	68
1880	55	1882	56
1884	52	1886	53 **
1888	53 **	1890	60
1892	56	1894	50
1896	51 **		

* No Republican candidate; independent Democrat substituted.
** Years when Bob Taylor was Democratic nominee.

off-years column indicates that the famous campaign of 1886, far from causing a huge Democratic landslide, as Robison's table implies, actually yielded a reduced Democratic share of a larger total vote. If Bob Taylor's campaigns got out the Democratic vote, they aroused the Republicans against him too.

Analysis of the election of 1886 by counties reveals that the partisan division among the electorate was very similar to those of previous years, continuing to reflect the Confederate-Unionist distinction and, to some extent, the earlier Whig-Democratic one (see Appendix B, Table 10). Insofar as Bob's support differed from the combined Bate-Fussell percentage of 1882, Taylor gained most in Republican counties and non-cotton-producing areas, and generally among former secessionists (see Appendix B, Table 11); these increases probably resulted from greater voter turnout. Among the regional differences across the state, West Tennessee registered accessions for Taylor in urban counties and on valuable farmland. This election, unlike the preceding Democratic convention, does not support the view that Taylor had a great attraction for farmers: the partial correlations for the state as a whole for urbanization are zero in Tables 10 and 11 of Appendix B. Bob Taylor was elected governor in 1886 by force of party tradition.

27. *Cumberland Almanac* (Nashville, 1877), 22; *Tribune Almanac,* 1880, p. 73, 1883, p. 73, 1897, p. 260; White (ed.), *Messages,* VII, 97, 234, 283, 364, 471, 557.

The differences within the Democratic party, somewhat repressed during the campaign and hidden by the election returns, soon flared into open conflict. The occasion for dispute was Governor Taylor's principal message to the legislature, delivered on February 10, 1887. After extolling Tennessee's rich resources and potential for economic growth, Taylor urged reform of taxation to relieve owners of real estate. Then he turned to the subject of education, shifting to more emphatic language:

> Of all the interests of the State, that which relates to the education of her people is the most important. . . . Of all the enemies to a republican form of government, *popular ignorance* is the most dangerous; of all its most reliable safeguards, popular *intelligence* is the best. . . . this question . . . imposes upon us a duty more imperative than all others—that of devising more adequate ways and means for the education of the children of Tennessee. . . .
> My sense of duty to the children of the State compels me to say that if there is a surplus of money in the National Treasury not applicable to the payment of the national debt, the appropriation of the same for this purpose, stripped of the conditions of Federal supervision, would be an inestimable blessing to them.[28]

The Nashville *American* reported that when this section was read to the lawmakers, "significant nods were exchanged on the Republican side while Democratic members, as a rule, seemed surprised." Several of the latter responded by opposing Senate confirmation of Taylor's nominee for state school superintendent, who favored the Blair bill. "In Tennessee we made a square fight in the last canvass against the idea underlying the Blair bill & *crushed it,*" reported a disgusted Bourbon, "but it rises again . . . & our Governor was captured by the advocates of a High Tariff & *charity* to the *states* & the '*Poor Children*[.]'" The Bourbon press, backed up by the Louisville *Courier-Journal,* dusted off the familiar states' rights doctrines and denounced Taylor for reversing his position.[29]

28. White (ed.), *Messages,* VII, 245, emphasis original.
29. McNeal to D. S. Lamont, May 5, 1887, in Cleveland Papers, emphasis original; Nashville *American,* February 11, 12, 13, 1887; Knoxville *Tribune,* February 15, 1887; Knoxville *Journal,* February 12, 1887.

Members of an aroused public wrote Taylor, threatening to turn against him if he was really for federal aid, or, in one case, reassuring him that his friends were truer, though less numerous.[30] But seven urban dailies praised the governor for both wisdom and consistency. Colonel Colyar welcomed the message, declaring that it helped put the governor "in the front rank in the onward march of the new south." [31] Two weekly papers that had earlier helped Colyar sabotage the railroad commission now, under practically the same ownership, jumped to Taylor's defense. "You are in the right," wrote an East Tennesseean. "Your fight is on the side of Democracy Progress Right and the People, and against machinism Bourbonism Damfoolism and disappointed office seekers." [32]

As the cracks in the party widened to a chasm separating Taylor and the Bourbons, a small but significant voice was calmly neutral. The *State Wheel,* official organ of several county chapters of the Agricultural Wheel, casually remarked that the governor "seem[ed] to be a kind of political acrobat or prestidigitator—now you see it, now you don't. In the campaign last fall he opposed [federal aid to education], and now the papers of his party are reading him free lectures on political integrity. It is no fight of ours, and we mention it merely as news." [33]

Another, and perhaps more important, Bourbon complaint against Taylor was his delivery of patronage to their enemies. "The cause of the trouble against Governor Taylor," claimed an anti-Bourbon newspaper, "had its origins in his appointing the best men for the positions in his gift, without regard to party service." One of the few Bourbons who was offered a job rejected it because, he said, the governor had "surrounded himself with mugwumps." Once

30. John W. Bayliss to R. L. Taylor, March 7, 1887, John T. Allen to R. L. Taylor, April 14, 1887, in CGO, TSLA.

31. Knoxville *Journal,* February 12, 1887; Memphis *Appeal,* February 12, 1887; Memphis *Avalanche,* quoted in Knoxville *Tribune,* February 15, 1887; Nashville *Banner,* February 14, 1887; Memphis *Scimitar* and Chattanooga *Times,* quoted in Nashville *Union,* February 19, 1887; Colyar quote from Nashville *Union,* February 11, 1887.

32. Carthage *Record* and Pulaski *Citizen,* quoted in Nashville *Union,* February 19, 1887; S. J. Kirkpatrick to R. L. Taylor, February 22, 1887, in CGO, TSLA.

33. Jackson *State Wheel,* quoted in Nashville *American,* February 21, 1887.

safely in office, Bob Taylor not only refused to join the Bourbons, but openly defied them.[34]

A year after the uproar over the Blair bill, a Bourbon editor claimed that the governor was under the influence of A. S. Colyar. "Our Governor was weak and easily led astray," charged the Knoxville *Tribune;* "Colyar was his seducer." The *Weekly Toiler,* state organ of the Farmers' Alliance, agreed: "The Farmers don't want R. L. Taylor any more, simply because he has no head of his own, but is supposed to wear the head of a certain fine old gentleman who heads the tariff monopoly and has a hand in all the combinations and speculative booms in Tennessee." [35]

Although Taylor was too ambitious to become the mere puppet of Colyar or anyone else, the governor and the colonel struck up a personal friendship which lasted from 1887, when Taylor recommended Colyar for a foreign embassy; through 1892, when Colyar was press agent for Bob's tour as a fiddling performer; at least until 1897, when Colyar's intoxicated son boasted that his father "stood right in with Bob Taylor" and could fix up a pardon right away. The governor not only praised the spirit of New South capitalism, but practiced it: he owned stock in the Nashville Iron, Steel, and Charcoal Company worth over a third of his annual salary, and after his second term formed a law partnership in Chattanooga with a Republican railroad attorney.[36] To the extent that Robert L. Taylor was identified with a group within the Democratic party after he became

34. Nashville *Banner,* February 14, 1887; J. B. Fort to Glidwell, February 25, 1887, in CGO, TSLA; Jackson *West Tennessee Whig,* February 23, 1887; unidentified, undated newspaper clipping in CGO, TSLA. A list of some of Taylor's appointments follows: as state superintendent of education, Frank M. Smith, president of the state teachers' association; as chancery judge in Memphis, Bedford M. Estes, an old friend of Howell E. Jackson, a former temporary judge by appointment of Governor Porter, and a stockholder in a bank and in an insurance company; to the University of Tennessee Board of Visitors, Jesse W. Sparks, a lawyer and gentleman farmer who was a director of a railroad and of a bank; as Chattanooga police commissioner, George W. Ochs, brother of newspaper publisher Adolph S. Ochs.

35. Knoxville *Tribune,* April 8, 1888; Nashville *Weekly Toiler,* quoted in Knoxville *Tribune,* May 6, 1888.

36. D. S. Lamont to R. L. Taylor, December 13, 1887, W. O. Mims to Peter Turney, February 18, 1897, M. Aspun to R. L. Taylor, April 13, 1887, all in CGO, TSLA; Knoxville *Journal,* March 26, 1892; Nashville *American,* August 14, 1890; Nashville *Banner,* March 15, 1890.

governor, he was the ally of A. S. Colyar and other proponents of New South capitalism.

Governor Taylor's Bourbon enemies, determined to deny him a second term, entered the state Democratic convention of 1888 with a majority of the delegates. They elected an "oldfashioned, mossback, caucus Democrat" as temporary chairman, and Bourbon W. C. Houston of Cannon County as permanent chairman. On the first ballot Taylor received 649½ votes, a minority, but the Bourbons were badly split among regional candidates. East Tennesseean T. M. McConnell drew over half his 241 votes from that region, though it had only about a quarter of the convention votes. W. M. Daniel got only 65 of his 226 votes from counties more than fifty miles from Clarksville, his home town; and J. A. Trousdale, with 100 votes, found a scant dozen over fifty miles from his home at Gallatin. W. P. Caldwell received every one of his 114 votes from West Tennessee.[37]

This pattern suggests that local candidates were most effective in beating the governor in county conventions and primaries. Once the state convention delegates were chosen and under control, they could be used to elect an anti-Taylor keynote speaker and perhaps to unite on an opposition candidate. The plan did not work, however, because nomination required a two-thirds majority and because Taylor's delegates were loyal to him. After thirty-six ballots the governor's strength remained unbroken, and a Bourbon attempt to enter Congressman Benton McMillin as a dark horse only lost more votes to Taylor. Finally, the governor was renominated on the fortieth ballot by the exhausted convention, but about a sixth of the delegate votes were still bitterly withheld from him. "Never in the political history of Tennessee," ventured the pro-Taylor Memphis *Avalanche,* "has there been so bitter a fight among Democrats as that made against Governor Taylor." The unhappy Clarksville *Chronicle* expected Colonel Colyar to support Taylor "heartily . . . as the nominee is

---

37. Knoxville *Tribune,* May 9, 1888; Nashville *Banner,* May 9, 1888; Memphis *Avalanche,* May 10, 1888; Nashville *American,* May 10, 11, 1888; quote from J. L. Stark to R. L. Taylor, April 17, 1888, in CGO, TSLA.

not only to his liking, but of his own making." [38] The Bourbons had received a setback in 1886 when they failed to control the nomination for governor; the defeat of their determined effort to stop Taylor in 1888 was a catastrophe.

On the first ballot in the 1888 convention, Taylor's strength was based on white, cotton-growing, and to some extent urban, counties (see Appendix B, Table 13). The Bourbons tended to be stronger where population was increasing—which is surprising, in the light of their relative skepticism about progress. Delegates for Taylor were not protesting poor land, or economic hardship as shown by a decrease in the number of farms. The lack of clear continuity of factions in the party is demonstrated by the low Pearsonian correlations between Taylor's support in 1888 and the counties voting for the tariff in the 1884 convention (see Table 16). The 1888 convention yields no evidence that Bob Taylor was leading a revolt, agrarian or otherwise. If there was a revolt, he was fending it off.

The standard historical work on Bob Taylor concluded that his contribution to Tennessee politics was that of a "master conciliator" who avoided identification with any faction in his party, yet won the loyalty of the supposed small-farmer followers of Jackson and Johnson so that their agrarian discontent was channeled within the Democratic party. This interpretation not only fails to resolve its own contradiction between Taylor's alleged leadership of discontented agrarians and his advocacy of industrial development to "keep Tennessee abreast of the more advanced states." [39] The standard view is based on a fundamentally mistaken reading of the evidence. Taylor's popularity did not end bitter controversy within the party, nor was he the leader of an agrarian revolt. He resembled Andrew Johnson, moreover, not so much by the nature of his mass support as by his political friendship with industrialist A. S. Colyar. Bob Taylor won votes not by rallying discontent, but by ignoring it.

---

38. Nashville *American,* May 11, 12, 13, 15, 16, 1888; Nashville *Banner,* May 12, 14, 15, 16, 1888; Knoxville *Tribune,* May 12, 16, 1888; Memphis *Avalanche,* May 16, 1888; Clarksville *Chronicle,* quoted in Nashville *Banner,* May 19, 1888.

39. Robison, *Bob Taylor,* 204–18. The notion that Tennessee Jacksonians were characteristically small farmers is refuted for one key county in Burton W. Folsom II, "The Politics of

Table 13

ROLL-CALL VOTES, 1885 HOUSE OF REPRESENTATIVES,
ON REPEAL OF RAILROAD-COMMISSION LAW,
AND ON RESOLUTION PROPOSING CONSTITUTIONAL PROHIBITION
(DEMOCRATS ONLY) [40]

		Repeal RR Commission	
		Yes	No
Prohibition	yes	30	25
	no	13	5

$$\phi = -.15 *$$

* For explanation of ϕ (phi), see Appendix A.

Table 14

ROLL-CALL VOTES, 1885 HOUSE OF REPRESENTATIVES,
ON RESOLUTION PROPOSING CONSTITUTIONAL PROHIBITION,
AND ON RESOLUTION SUPPORTING BLAIR BILL
(DEMOCRATS ONLY) [41]

		Prohibition	
		Yes	No
Blair	yes	27	9
bill	no	27	9

$$\phi = 0 *$$

* For explanation of ϕ (phi), see Appendix A.

Table 15

SIMPLE CORRELATIONS BETWEEN SUPPORT FOR
PROHIBITION IN 1887 REFERENDUM AND FIRST-BALLOT VOTE
FOR TAYLOR IN 1888 STATE DEMOCRATIC CONVENTION [42]

	Tenn.	E. Tenn.	M. Tenn.	W. Tenn.
Number of counties	94	36	38	20
Simple correlations	+.25	+.32	−.10	+.05

Elites: Prominence and Party in Davidson County, Tennessee, 1835–1861," *Journal of Southern History,* XXXLX (1973), 359–78.

40. *House Journal,* 1885, pp. 666, 688–89.

41. *Ibid.,* 121–22, 688–89.

42. *Tribune Almanac,* 1888, pp. 78–79; Nashville *American,* May 11, 1888. For other correlations for 1887 referendum, see Appendix B, Table 12.

Table 16
SIMPLE CORRELATIONS BETWEEN FIRST-BALLOT VOTE
FOR TAYLOR IN 1888 DEMOCRATIC STATE CONVENTION
AND SUPPORT FOR TARIFF PROTECTION IN 1884
DEMOCRATIC STATE CONVENTION [43]

	Tenn.	E. Tenn.	M. Tenn.	W. Tenn.
Number of counties	78	29	32	17
Simple correlations	+.05	—.09	+.16	+.28

Taylor succeeded in defying the Bourbon coalition and in establishing himself as a formidable public figure able to win elections on the appeal of his personal style. But he failed to replace the Bourbons with an enduring new political majority, either within the Democratic party or across the old party lines. The structure of the Tennessee political environment prevented such political realignment.

A stable anti-Bourbon majority within the Democratic party, though perhaps superficially plausible because of Taylor's renomination, was out of the question. No lasting coalition could be built on the shifting sands of one man's popularity. Pro-Taylor New South men like A. S. Colyar, moreover, could not convert a majority of Democrats to their view. They defeated the railroad commission, at the polls and in the legislature, only through Republican help. New South men could not win secure control of the Democratic party because most Democrats were farmers with Bourbon attitudes.

But if some Democrats agreed with the Republicans on the tariff, on railroad regulation, and on the Blair bill, a new Taylor majority based on these issues and cutting across old party lines is conceivable. Such a possibility is enhanced by Bob's East Tennessee background and by the fact that part of Democratic West Tennessee voted with Republicans in favor of prohibition in an 1887 referendum (see Map 5). But a new party composed of Republicans and rebellious Democrats was impractical because the constituencies of the issues dividing Democrats overlapped each other only partially (see Tables 13–16). Dissenting Democrats did not split off and join the Republicans partly because various issues split the majority party in different ways.

43. Nashville *American*, May 11, 1888, June 20, 1884.

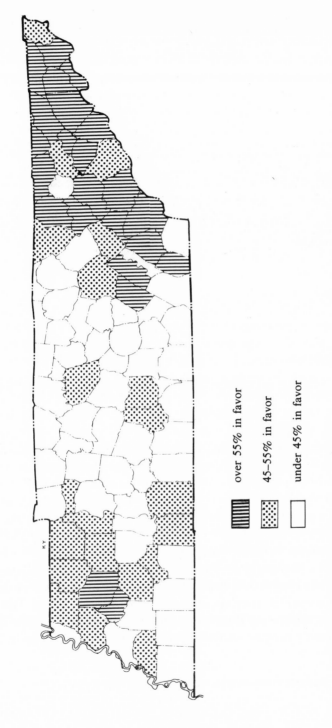

Map 5
REFERENDUM ON PROHIBITION, 1887

over 55% in favor

45–55% in favor

under 45% in favor

Source: *Tribune Almanac*, 1888, pp. 78–79.

Even if Taylor could have found issues, like opposition to railroad regulation and support for the Blair bill,[44] which would tend to pull the same Democrats over to the Republicans, he could not have made such an alliance permanent. Temporary cooperation was possible across party lines in the legislature or among the voters on a nonpartisan issue like prohibition. But the memory of the old Unionist-Confederate division was so strong, not least in Bob's own East Tennessee, that no transient issues could supersede it. Taylor won the voters' confidence by his appealing style and established himself as a relatively independent politician. He could do no more, given his reluctance to speak for the class and status grievances which fed both Bourbonism and the Farmers' Alliance.

44. ϕ (phi) $= +.62$ for whole House of Representatives (for explanation of ϕ see Appendix A). *House Journal,* 1885, pp. 121–22, 666.

5

The Rise of the Farmers' Alliance

During the late 1880s a mass movement arose among Tennessee farmers without assistance from Bob Taylor or other established politicians. Previous farmers' groups and other voluntary associations had tended to overlap and interlock with local ruling elites. The Farmers' Alliance tried to change that pattern by drawing a firm line excluding the merchants and professional men of the towns. This policy was not entirely successful, because occupational distinctions were often ambiguous and because the Alliance shared the national attitude of respect for business and professional accomplishments. But it was the effort which was new and significant. The Alliance attempted to carry the ancient prejudice of country against city into effect, and to lift the economic and psychological burdens of the farmers by striking at those who obviously held power, and who seemed to be responsible for the helplessness of individual farmers. This ambivalence in the Alliance—respect for the social order and resentment toward those who headed it—would later become a serious internal contradiction.

Before the Alliance, agricultural organizations in Tennessee were not troubled by this ambivalence, because they did not try to oppose the power of the towns. Earlier groups both served their stated purpose, the improvement of agriculture, and also helped give their members a sense of community. A monthly agricultural paper at Nashville commented in 1840 on the second aspect of farmer organizations. "These assemblies," it said, "are well calculated to unite their members in the strongest bonds of affection as friends and brothers in the great cause of improvement. Their moral influence and tendency are to raise the humble and bring down the high and opulent to sit at the feet of the poor man and receive wholesome lessons from his lips." [1] During the 1850s Tennessee farmers joined a national trend in organizing agricultural societies, especially to hold county fairs. By 1859 there were at least forty county societies, encouraged by the state Agricultural Bureau as one of its main activities.[2] Although these associations no doubt ranged in their interests from improving crop yields to holding picnics, they were not involved in politics or public controversy.

After the Civil War the tradition of the prewar county associations was carried on, especially by the annual East Tennessee Farmers' Convention, founded in 1875. This group went so far as to advocate the passage of a railroad-commission law in 1883, but it stayed clear of partisan politics and gained a reputation for informing farmers about better agricultural methods. It continued meeting through the years when the Farmers' Alliance made the headlines, and the East Tennessee Convention could not remain fully insulated from the Alliance. In 1890 the secretary of the Convention was a prominent Allianceman, and L. L. Polk of North Carolina spoke on "the duties of the hour." But more attention was given to the reading of papers on agricultural methods, including one by the state commissioner of agriculture and another by Major Campbell Brown of Maury County, a patrician sky-blue leader. The next year the state president of the Farmers' Alliance spoke to the East Tennessee Convention about farmer politics, but more typical were the 1892 appearances of the president of the University of Tennessee and a representative of the United States Department of Agriculture.[3] Such activity did not annoy merchants or politicians.

With the example of the East Tennessee Farmers' Convention before them, a group of farmers from other parts of the state met in March, 1883, to hear convention president J. A. Turley explain how his group met and heard papers on agriculture. In the spirit of

---

1. Quoted in Blanche Henry Clark, *The Tennessee Yeomen, 1840–1860* (Nashville, 1942), 74.

2. *Ibid.,* 72–73, 83–84.

3. Knoxville *Journal,* May 18, 1886, March 26, 1887, May 18, 1892; Knoxville *Chronicle,* January 18, 1883; Nashville *Weekly Toiler,* July 24, 1889; Nashville *American,* May 22, 1890; Nashville *Banner,* May 20, 1891. Polk was a prominent North Carolina Alliance leader.

the East Tennessee organization, this meeting petitioned Congress to give the federal Department of Agriculture cabinet status and asked that American consuls abroad gather agricultural information. The meeting was dominated by men who may have been farmers but who were primarily politicians: state Senator E. Edmundson, sponsor of the watered-down railroad-commission law of 1883, was chairman, and state Representative John H. McDowell was secretary. This March meeting led to the first convention of the Middle Tennessee Agricultural Association, which heard speeches by United States Senator Howell Jackson and newly appointed Railroad Commissioner J. A. Turley. The not-so-plain farmers in the audience included General B. F. Cheatham, General W. H. Jackson, Major Campbell Brown, state Representative W. J. Hale, and Senator Edmundson.[4] The Middle Tennessee Agricultural Association and its East Tennessee counterpart were not vehicles for the expression of economic grievances or social discontents, but were part of a broad current of improvement and uplift.

A few weeks after the Middle Tennessee Association's meeting, farmers of Rutherford County organized in Murfreesboro, where they were told that their purpose was not religious or political. Rather, the new statewide county groups "were intended for the advancement of the farmer and his elevation above the simple, plodding plowman, by contact and interchange of views." To this end, committees were appointed on "the general state of agriculture, statistics, public roads improvement, [and] condition and diseases of domestic animals," and delegates were selected for a statewide association. Of twenty men listed as serving on the four Rutherford County committees, twelve were located in the tax rolls of a few years later. Of the dozen, eleven owned an average of 453 acres of rural land apiece; the other owned town property assessed for taxation at $3,500, and one of the eleven owned town property assessed at $3,200. President of the Rutherford County organization was Major C. F. Vanderford, whose 449 acres composed the fifth-largest landholding in his civil district. The remaining eight of these twenty included a former legislator and two attorneys. In the confident

4. Nashville *American*, March 24, June 10, 1883.

words of Major Vanderford, "This [is] a progressive age and the farmer must think more, and read more, write more about his business." [5]

The state farmer conventions had their counterpart organizations not only below, at the county level, but also above. Tennessee was represented in Louisville at an 1883 national Farmers' Congress, which cited the lobbies maintained by bankers, railroads, and industry, and implied that a farm lobby was needed to counterbalance them. One of the delegates sent to Louisville by Governor Bate was secretary and general agent of the East Tennessee Land Agency and Emigration Bureau of Knoxville, and no doubt found many potential customers among the delegates. The interests of farmers, real estate promoters, and other boosters were not always clearly distinguished by the sponsors of these meetings. Thus the Tennessee assistant commissioner of agriculture, statistics, mines, and immigration urged the governor to attend an Interstate Agricultural and Industrial Convention in Jackson. Former governor Alvin Hawkins, General W. H. Jackson, and former Congressman John M. Bright were among those asked by Governor Bate to attend such meetings. [6] During the early 1880s prosperous Tennessee farmers formed organizations not to protest the Gilded Age, but to join it.

The Patrons of Husbandry in Tennessee resembled these farmer-promoter conventions in leadership. The realtor sent by Governor Bate to the Louisville meeting was a former state officer of the Grange. Another officer in the 1870s was J. M. Head of Sumner County, a lawyer who later became quite prominent as a legislator, state Democratic committeeman, journalist, and small-time capitalist. An active Grange organizer rivaled A. J. Kellar for the Memphis postmastership after the Compromise of 1877, but soon was running for criminal court clerk on Kellar's Greenback ticket. [7] These men

5. *Ibid.,* June 10, August 12, 1883, February 2, 1890; Rutherford County tax books, 1889–90, film, TSLA; Murfreesboro *Free Press,* August 17, 1883.

6. Nashville *American,* December 6, 1883; Thomas J. Hudson to Bate, October 19, 1883, C. W. Charlton to Bate, November 30, 1883, Robert Gates to Bate, January 19, 1886, A. G. Hawkins to Bate, November 17, 1883, W. H. Jackson to Bate, November 30, 1883, J. M. Bright to Bate, November 16, 1883, all in CGO, TSLA.

7. Nashville *American,* November 4, 1880, January 6, May 13, 1887; Nashville *Banner,* April 17, 1895; Memphis *Avalanche,* March 22, 1877, July 14, 1878.

and others like them did not enter politics as Grangers, but joined the Grange as politicians.

The Grange had little or no impact on politics in Tennessee. During the 1870s General W. H. Jackson urged his fellow Grangers to work for the creation of a state agricultural commissioner, on the model of the state's antebellum banking commissioner, with power to revoke railroad charters; but the organization did not press the issue. The Tennessee Grange faded quickly: from 19,780 families (third highest in the South) in 1875 and 10,216 in 1876, membership unaccountably plummeted to 1,474 in 1877 and none in 1880. Though the society flickered briefly back into life while the Farmers' Alliance was strong, it remained obscure and insignificant after 1880.[8]

Evidence on Granger leaders is slim, and on rank-and-file members there is no information at all. It is very likely, however, that ordinary members and politicians alike regarded the Grange in much the same way as the orders, brotherhoods, and churches known to every county and especially to the county-seat towns. Leadership in various aspects of community life did not require special skills, and so devolved upon one elite. Thus, of the two joint superintendents of the Methodist Sunday School at Ashland City in 1878, one was an attorney who later went to the state Senate, and the other attended several Democratic state conventions, ran for the legislature, and edited a weekly newspaper, where he took the opportunity to write of Christ's second coming. The mayor of Murfreesboro was also Worshipful Master of his Masonic lodge. Other lodge officers included a former county court clerk who served on a charity concert committee; a onetime general-store and hotel manager who had been mayor and then county Democratic chairman; a governor's grandson who was Murfreesboro city marshal; a town alderman and former legislator who was secretary of the Rutherford County Farmers' Association; a former chairman of the Democratic caucus in the legislature; and a former legislative candidate who was also an officer

---

8. Speech of W. H. Jackson to Patrons of Husbandry at Bell Buckle, n.d., in Harding-Jackson Papers; Robert L. Tontz, "Memberships of General Farmers' Organizations, United States, 1874–1960," *Agricultural History,* XXXVIII (1964), 154; Nashville *American,* March 21, 1891.

in the Rutherford County Fair Association and whose 750 acres made him the tenth-largest landowner in a county of 35,000 people.[9] In the absence of a traditional social hierarchy, voluntary organizations like the Masons served to indicate a man's standing in his community.

Local bar associations were normally tied by interlocking membership to other elites, especially through politics. Including both past and present officeholders, the Murfreesboro Bar Association of the early 1890s could count among its twenty-three members two congressmen, five successful and two unsuccessful legislative candidates, three judges, two mayors, a state Democratic convention temporary chairman, and numerous state and county Democratic party officials and delegates.[10] As in Murfreesboro, lawyers typically had no monopoly of political power, but certainly held more offices per capita than any other occupational group.

A single family could claim a disproportionate share of local power. General G. G. Dibrell of Sparta was a five-term congressman and successful capitalist, and the son of a state official. The general's own son Frank was by turns deputy sheriff, chairman of the county Democratic committee, chairman of the White County court, and state senator. Six other Dibrells of George's or Frank's generation in White County were sheriff, postmaster, circuit court clerk, candidate for alderman, and two were delegates to a Democratic state convention.[11] In effect, the Dibrell family itself was one of White County's ruling groups.

9. Pleasant Valley *News,* February 21, 1889; Nashville *American,* February 13, August 12, 1883, May 17, June 19, August 29, September 4, 1884, February 16, April 2, June 10, July 8, August 28, November 13, 1886; Ashland City *Cheatham County Plaindealer,* July 18, 1878; Ashland City *Cheatham County New Era,* October 13, 1881; Murfreesboro *Free Press,* July 7, 1882, November 21, 1891; *History of Tennessee, from the Earliest Time to the Present: Together with an Historical and a Biographical Sketch of Maury, Williamson, Rutherford, Wilson, Bedford, and Marshall Counties, Beside a Valuable Fund of Notes, Original Observations, Reminiscences, etc. etc.* (Nashville, 1886), 826; *Who's Who in Tennessee,* 393; Rutherford County tax book, 1889, film, TSLA.

10. Speer, *Sketches,* 138–41; Nashville *American,* February 2, October 13, 1890, May 23, October 2, 1892; Nashville *Banner,* October 3, 1892, August 15, 1894; *History of Tennessee: Maury, Williamson, Rutherford, Wilson, Bedford, and Marshall Counties,* 812; Miller, *Official and Political Manual,* 186.

11. Speer, *Sketches,* 226–30; Sparta *Expositor,* August 9, 1889, September 12, 1890; Nashville *Banner,* January 3, 1893; Nashville *American,* August 12, 1886, March 24, 1888; Sparta *Index,* March 17, 1876.

Thus in most Tennessee county-seat towns in the last quarter of the nineteenth century, community structure was characterized by a number of groups which served to define status and, in some cases to hold power: fraternal organizations, families, churches, professional groups (including prosperous farmers), Democratic (sometimes Republican) party organizations, and property owners. Two aspects of these local groups should be emphasized. First, they were composed of interlocking memberships, which meant that a single elite, rather than competing ones, was politically, economically, and socially dominant. Second, this elite, from which women and black people were entirely excluded, was composed mostly of business and professional men who may have owned rural land but did not draw their livelihood from working on it. Farmers who did share political power were generally substantial landowners whose attitudes did not clash with those of their friends from town. The reticular local power-status-property relationships were centered in the towns.

It is very significant, therefore, that the twin farmer organizations of the late 1880s, the Agricultural Wheel and the Farmers' Alliance, deliberately tried to cut themselves off from the towns rather than become one of the interlocking local groups as previous agricultural societies had done. When the Wheel and Alliance merged in 1889, the resulting Farmers' and Laborers' Union (often referred to by contemporaries, and herein, as "the Alliance") specifically barred from membership anyone connected by ownership or employment with a mercantile business of any kind, except Alliance cooperatives; anyone with a license to practice law; and any stockholder in a bank. The postmaster of Murfreesboro, a member of the Wheel, was excluded from the united Alliance because the membership clause admitted only "farmers, farm laborers, country school teachers, country ministers of the gospel, country doctors and country mechanics." [12] The normal web of power relationships was a form of community integration, and the attempt to segregate the Alliance from the towns indicated alienation of some farmers from local elites.

The conception of the interests of farmers as an occupational group, which lay behind the membership requirements excluding

12. Nashville *Weekly Toiler,* October 30, December 4, 1889.

Table 17
LANDHOLDINGS OF KNOWN ALLIANCE MEMBERS
IN RUTHERFORD, LAUDERDALE, AND WHITE COUNTIES,
EXCLUDING TOWN RESIDENTS OWNING NO FARMLAND [13]

County	Rutherford	Lauderdale	White
Mean size of farms	112 Acres	79 Acres	122 Acres
Mean value/acre of farmland	$19	$11	$9
Taxpaying Alliancemen	7	7	11
Median Landholding of Alliance Group	132 acres	287 acres	70 acres
Mean Landholding of Alliance Group	182 acres	342 acres	272 acres

town people, did not discriminate among white farmers themselves. Therefore, men in the fringes of the county-seat elites could join the Alliance because they were technically farmers.

Table 17 shows the mean and median landholdings for all known Alliancemen who could be located in the tax rolls of three counties. Table 17 does not give a random cross-section of Alliance landholdings: leaders' names tend to survive most, and probably several of those not located in the tax rolls were absent because they owned no property and paid no poll tax. But while the Alliance was not dominated by big landholders as much as the agricultural societies of the early 1880s, it did include some rather well-to-do farmers. The single Rutherford County delegate to the state Wheel convention of 1889 not only owned 455 acres of farmland, but had five town lots, and paid taxes on a very high total property assessment of $18,400. This Wheeler was the fourth-largest landowner in his civil district, and the value given his property by the tax assessor was over eighteen

13. *Ibid.*, September 5, November 21, 1888, January 30, February 20, May 15, June 3, July 24, August 7, 1889, February 5, 12, 19, July 30, 1890, May 13, June 3, 1891, January 27, 1892; Nashville *Banner*, August 11, 1891; S. E. Cunningham to R. L. Taylor, June 15, 1890, in CGO, TSLA; Nashville *American*, September 15, 1891; Memphis *Appeal-Avalanche*, March 1, 1892; Rutherford County tax book, 1889, film, TSLA; Lauderdale County tax book, 1893, courthouse, Ripley; White County tax books, 1889–90, film, TSLA; Thomas J. Pressly and William H. Scofield (eds.), *Farm Real Estate Values in the United States by Counties, 1850–1959* (Seattle, 1965), 52–53; U.S. Census Office, *Report on the Statistics of Agriculture in the United States at the Eleventh Census: 1890* (Washington, D.C., 1895), 180–83.

times the average assessment per family in the county. A congressman who lived in Murfreesboro found that his total property assessment of $21,200 was no barrier to Alliance membership.[14]

The president of the Lauderdale County Alliance had a farm of 111 acres, not much larger than the county average, but one of his Alliance neighbors owned 897 acres. In White County, though two Alliancemen owned 405 and 343 acres, respectively, and a third owned 1,798 acres of largely uncultivated land, a fourth had only three acres and two more paid no property taxes, only the poll tax.[15] These three counties in diverse regions show that large farmers became members of the Farmers' Alliance, but also that farmers owning little or no land joined the movement. However the membership was distributed between these extremes, the criterion for admission did not differentiate among farmers by wealth as it did against town people by occupation. In Max Weber's terms, the Alliance defined its membership not by economic class, but by social status.

The main root of the farmers' alienation was their feeling that they were not given the respect they deserved. The Alliance, said the official *Weekly Toiler,* not only brought cooperation but made the world "respect us and honor our calling as they [had] not done before." In the same spirit, the *Toiler* reported that national Alliance president Evan Jones was treated with great respect when he rode the train. The *Toiler* was "proud to know that sensible people of other avocations are beginning to recognize our calling as on a level in the scale of honor with any other profession." An exemplar of the scornful attitude farmers hoped to overcome was the Chattanooga *Times.* "The great drawback on our farming," the *Times* declared, "is that our white proprietors are indifferent, lazy, and ignorant of their calling. They spend too much time around the village stores and grogshops, and revenge themselves for the failure their stupidity and neglect bring, by 'damning the lazy nigger.' " With no sympathy for rural life, the *Times* was not surprised that

14. Nashville *Weekly Toiler,* July 24, 1889; Rutherford County tax books, 1889–90, film, TSLA; 1890 Census, *Population,* 928; Knoxville *Journal,* July 22, 1890.
15. Nashville *Weekly Toiler,* January 27, 1892; Lauderdale County tax book, 1893, courthouse, Ripley; Memphis *Appeal-Avalanche,* March 1, 1892; White County tax books, 1889-90, film, TSLA.

the 1890 census showed migration to the cities. The "most apparent" reason for urbanization was a surplus of agricultural products, and, by implication, of farmers.[16] Many *Times* readers and other city people shared these negative attitudes toward farmers. A common stereotype was the inarticulate, gaunt-faced "hayseed" wearing a straggly beard and a faded pair of overalls.

A West Tennessee Allianceman, although sympathetic with his fellow farmers, tended to agree with the *Times* that farmers' problems were at least partly their own fault. Despite a diversity of crops, excellent soil and a favorable climate, "the business of the agriculturist [was] the poorest, most slavish, drudging business that is followed in Lauderdale county." He complained that farmers were so unsystematic in accounting that they did not know what was profitable and what was not, and contended that the custom of importing grain and fruit, instead of growing them, was inefficient. He urged farmers to wake from their lethargy and not let their elected officials permit trusts and monopolies to oppress them.[17] Another contemporary analyst of the South's problems drew a bleak picture of farm life: "Men who can not see afar off, moving in a narrow circle, toiling hard, discouraged, despondent, in debt, the farm under mortgage, ruin and poverty staring them in the face, are easily led into desperate measures, and that to their own undoing. . . . The situation in the country, view it as we may, is serious."[18]

A publicist of the Wheel and Alliance, whose work appeared in Arkansas in 1889, stressed the "monotony of the farmer's life."

> Day after day he and his family pursue the same appointed round of toil. . . . He usually lives a lonely and secluded life, rarely going beyond the limits of his farm, except to town, the country store or post-office on business. . . . No wonder, then, that with constant toil and unbroken solitude as his only companions, the farmer should be a careworn, prematurely old man. . . . In the monthly meetings of the subordinate Wheels . . . [a]cquaintances are made, new friendships are formed, and old ones strengthened. The farmer is taught that the world does not end

16. Nashville *Weekly Toiler,* May 1, October 30, 1889; Chattanooga *Times,* January 22, July 6, 1890.
17. Nashville *Weekly Toiler,* January 30, 1889.
18. Charles H. Otken, *The Ills of the South; or Related Causes Hostile to the General Prosperity of the Southern People* (New York, 1894), 31.

for him at the boundaries of his farm; that there are hopes, fears, joys and sorrows beyond his domain in which it [is] his duty to take an interest; that the fields for the cultivation of the intellect are broader than his acres of wheat[.] [19]

In terms reminiscent of the Agricultural Society he had joined in 1883, Governor J. P. Buchanan told his fellow Alliancemen that if the order did nothing more than get farmers to read, think for themselves, and be proud of their occupation, it would be worthwhile.[20] A crucial function of Alliance activities, even when ostensibly economic or political in nature, was to bolster morale.

An important aspect of the Alliance which combined economic and social purposes was its attempt to lessen farmers' dependence on merchants. Alliancemen consistently worked to undermine retail merchants, while securing cheaper goods for themselves, by establishing cooperative stores. The Wheelers planned a system of co-ops as early as 1886. In several counties, warehouses were built by the Wheel for crop storage, and in the peanut region of the western Tennessee River counties, Wheelers had a Peanut Association which hoped to control the state crop. A tobacco warehouse was maintained for members' use at Clarksville, the nation's second leaf-tobacco marketing center. One of the most popular efforts, measured by the frequency of endorsement by local Alliances, was a boycott of Oliver plows. Through their Wheel cooperatives, farmers could buy wagons, reapers, buggies, grain drills, plows, and other supplies at a discount of up to 40 percent.[21]

Potentially the most effective buying and marketing cooperation was that of individual farmers, and many county Wheels and Alliances tried it. Weakley County Wheelers planned a store in the county seat, and the Coffee County Wheel reported that it would establish a co-op and also encourage better stock-raising methods. Knox County Alliancemen built a flour mill and then voted to organize their own beef-cattle market. A "mercantile business" in Franklin

19. W. Scott Morgan, *History of the Wheel and Alliance, and the Impending Revolution* (Hardy, Ark., 1889), 197–200.
20. Nashville *American,* June 10, 1883, August 12, 1891.
21. Morgan, *History of the Wheel and Alliance,* 110, 112, 113–14; Jackson *State Wheel,* February 18, 1887; Nashville *Weekly Toiler,* January–March, *passim,* May 15, 1889; Theodore Saloutos, *Farmer Movements in the South, 1865–1933* (Berkeley, 1960), 66.

County was backed by four thousand dollars in Alliance capital.[22] The secretary of a local Wheel in Lauderdale County on the Mississippi River mailed a report to the state headquarters describing cooperative activity and giving an insight into the relations between farmers and the merchants whom they were trying to render obselete.

> Ashport wheel is moving off right although we are a young wheel and few in numbers, we are making things hum down here on the riverfront, we now have a steamboat landing and have now put up our freight house 16 X 20 feet in size; so now we are in better shape to transact business with the Memphis agency. The local merchant[s] here are straining every nerve against us, but it has only served to unite us more strongly and work for our common interests. We are proud of our freight house; we have worked hard to get it; we have endured sneers, jeers, and persecutions in every shape and form, but we have moved steadily on, working our passage, slow but sure, and victory is ours.[23]

The Memphis agency was manned by a full-time Wheel-Alliance agent, who did fifteen to twenty thousand dollars of business per month in 1889 as a distributor to locals like the one at Ashport.[24] Wholesale merchants and rural retailers might well have seen the Alliance as a threat to their very livelihoods.

Alliance farmers were vying with businessmen in a commercial market, but the farmers did not consider themselves as merchants. Alliance ideology held that mercantile enterprise was nonproductive and hence less legitimate than agriculture. The Alliance therefore claimed that its business agents were not merchants and so were not subject to the state's fixed privilege tax levied according to type of business and size of town. In 1888 the city of Nashville sued the Alliance agent there to collect a $102 privilege tax, but the Alliance won a judgment which saved its agents an estimated $50,000. For added safety, Alliance legislators obtained passage of a bill to exempt the business agents of agricultural organizations from taxation. Tennessee became the only state with such a law, a reflection of the

22. Nashville *American,* April 28, 1888; Nashville *Weekly Toiler,* April 10, 1889; Knoxville *Journal,* October 18, 1890; J. Knox Moore to J. P. Buchanan, November 24, 1890, in CGO, TSLA.
23. Report of S. C. Barnes, Lauderdale County, in Nashville *Weekly Toiler,* April 10, 1889.
24. Nashville *Weekly Toiler,* December 4, 1889.

degree of Alliance strength in the legislature, and of the sort of purpose for which this strength was effective.[25]

In seeking to "crush the hydra-headed monster monopoly," as its state president phrased it, the Alliance went beyond the building of channels to divert trade from retailers. In some cases it raised dams to block business from merchants who offended them. Two Alliance papers warned farmers to boycott merchants even if they met Alliance agency prices, because prices would go up again if the agents were put out of business. Alliancemen were warned to "steer clear" of a farmers' exchange tied to the Memphis business community, but the new counter-Alliance enterprise soon had 251 members and facilitated the sale of $4,000 worth of land and $6,000 or $7,000 worth of livestock. A more successful Alliance action was taken in White County, where the farmers boycotted a Nashville wholesale shoe firm, which sent one of its partners to plead for mercy. In East Tennessee, the Washington County Alliance resented the action of Knoxville merchants who all refused to do business with farm organizations. The county's Alliancemen decided to boycott the whole city of Knoxville. What a city editor deplored as a "State and local policy of competition and antagonism to established commercial interests" provoked hostility to the Alliance in the towns, whose elites faced an unprecedented economic threat.[26]

Local Alliances, composed of neighbors who knew each other well, concerned themselves easily with the institutions of family and religion. A Humphreys County man was turned down for Wheel membership because he reportedly mistreated his wife. A local Alliance in Wilson County heard Miss Evie Hall read a paper on the question of whether girls should marry before the age of eighteen, but the farmers avoided taking a stand. If these matters seem to be the sort one would expect to find discussed in Sunday school, perhaps the distinction between church and Alliance was not quite clear. When a member wrote the *Weekly Toiler* to ask whether there were

25. *Ibid.,* October 17, 24, 1888, February 27, April 17, 1889; *Senate Journal,* 1889, p. 480; *House Journal,* 1889, p. 690.

26. Nashville *Weekly Toiler,* August 29, 1888, April 24, May 8, 15, 1889, January 29, 1890; Jackson *State Wheel,* February 18, 1887; Memphis *Appeal,* May 14, 1890; Nashville *Banner,* August 12, 1890 (quote).

prescribed prayers for opening and closing meetings, editor J. H.
McDowell answered, "No. There are no printed forms. Just ask
God's divine blessing upon our work for poor down trodden, oppressed humanity. Ask wisdom to guide and direct our deliberations,
and let it come from the heart, not mere lip service." [27] Rural life
was not readily compartmentalized.

The best testimony that the Farmers' Alliance and the Agricultural Wheel offered real hope to Tennessee farmers is their rapid
growth in membership. The Wheel was the first to reach Tennessee,
and it remained larger in the state than the Alliance until their
merger in 1889. Founded in 1882 in Arkansas as a seven-man debating club, the Agricultural Wheel spread from there into neighboring
states. The first Wheel in Tennessee was organized on February 1,
1884, in a log school near Ralston, in Weakley County. Five more
local groups were added during the next month, but a year followed
in which expansion halted. Then came a year of explosive growth,
perhaps aided by organizers from Arkansas, when 113 Wheels were
started in Weakley, Henry, Obion, Carroll, and Gibson counties, all
in West Tennessee. A Tennessee Wheel was organized on July 10,
1885, including 154 local and 5 county Wheels. A few weeks later
a Nashville *American* reporter stopped at the state agriculture commissioner's office, where the assistant commissioner for West
Tennessee was talking about the Wheel. It had 500 members, he said,
centered in Weakley County, and seemed progressive and prosperous, with all the advantages and none of the objectionable features
(unspecified) of the Grange.[28] Late in 1885 the *American* noticed the
order again.

> [The Wheel] has a membership, in Weakley County alone, of about
> twenty-five hundred, and is increasing rapidly. The farmers of that re-
> gion seem to realize that the monetary and manufacturing interests have
> formed combinations and associations, and influenced legislation in a
> way which has resulted to [*sic*] the detriment of the laboring man, and
> particularly, the agriculturist. To countervail this influence, by . . .

27. Nashville *Weekly Toiler,* June 27, September 26, 1888, December 4, 1889.
28. John D. Hicks, *The Populist Revolt: A History of the Farmers' Alliance and the People's
Party* (Minneapolis, 1931), 111; Morgan, *History of the Wheel and Alliance,* 108–109; Nashville
Weekly Toiler, August 1, 1888; Nashville *American,* August 5, 1885.

organization and by the dissemination of sound doctrines, the Wheel has been organized.[29]

Editor J. J. Vertrees of the *American,* who two years later was a leader of Bourbon forces opposing the renomination of Bob Taylor for governor, saw in the Wheel an impulse akin to his own suspicion of trusts and "combinations." A Memphis paper described the Arkansas Wheel as a "conspiracy" to injure the Democratic party, but the press generally accepted the organization without hostility before 1890.[30]

A nonpolitical order, the early Wheel played no part in the first nomination of Bob Taylor, remaining concerned more with co-ops and internal problems. Wheel President J. R. Miles urged his brothers to end a "division along the line" and warned of bribes from capitalists. "We are now in the midst of a powerful revolution of some kind, it is evident," he observed, though he did not identify its nature or causes. Miles recommended the adoption of a newspaper as state organ, and the Wheel selected the *Toiler* of Fulton, Kentucky, later of Nashville. Of the 243 local Wheels, 129 were represented at another meeting called a few weeks later to respond to the organization of a national Wheel. The Tennesseeans agreed to accept the national constitution provided that the word *white* was inserted in the membership clause, and that the top two officers would receive nominal salaries. Evidently any serious internal divisions were mended, for by the next summer 700 new local Wheels were organized.[31] Accurate membership figures were unavailable even to Wheel officers, but the order was larger than any previous secular mass movement in Tennessee.

Virtually indistinguishable from the Wheel was the Tennessee Farmers' Alliance. The Alliance in the South originated in Texas in the mid-1870s, nearly died out from internal dissension, but revived by 1880. In the spring of 1887, when the Wheel was already established in Tennessee, Alliance organizers fanned out over the South in an ambitious missionary effort. At that time the first suballiance,

29. Nashville *American,* December 7, 1885.
30. Memphis *Appeal,* June 3, 12, 1886.
31. Nashville *American,* July 13, September 9, 1886; Morgan, *History of the Wheel and Alliance,* 110.

or chapter, was started in Tennessee. A year later J. H. McDowell, southern Alliance vice-president for the state, convened a meeting of Alliancemen at Nashville. Although expecting union with the Wheel, they modeled a state-level constitution after that of the Texas Alliance, and chose state officers from counties scattered from Sullivan to Shelby. In the summer of 1888, when Tennessee's 308 local Alliances accounted for about 3 percent of those in the whole southern Alliance, the state organization held its first regular session in the state Senate chamber. The earlier provisional selection of John P. Buchanan as president and McDowell as secretary was ratified. Buchanan reassured the delegates that although Alliance growth was not as fast as had been hoped, it was sure and steady. He urged the delegates to improve their farms, to recruit more members, and especially to trade only with Alliance co-ops, warning, "We cannot escape the influence of the pools, trusts, corners, and a thousand other rings that have been formed to catch every dollar we raise." The president closed with a promise that right would finally triumph over wrong, but he and the young Alliance were more earnest than confident.[32]

At the time of its first regular state meeting the Tennessee Alliance claimed twenty thousand members, of whom about one-eighth were women. The seventeen county-level Alliances concentrated in Middle Tennessee did not conflict with the Wheel's original five-county base area. Buchanan estimated that the Wheelers numbered 130,000 in Tennessee, though several weeks later the *Toiler* gave a state Wheel total of 78,000, still the highest Wheel membership of any state. The official paper reported 1,575 local Wheels at the end of 1888, compared to 360 suballiances. Sometimes the Alliance claimed spectacular success in organizing: in White County, for example, there were 5 Alliancemen on September 1, 1888, who expanded to 145 men in five suballiances by the middle of November and to 300 by Christmas, when merchants were forced by the farmers to cut prices. In Cannon County, Alliance strength in the spring of 1889 jumped in three months from zero to seventeen suballiances, of 10

32. Hicks, *Populist Revolt,* 104, 110; Morgan, *History of the Wheel and Alliance,* 295; Nashville *Weekly Toiler,* July 25, December 5, 1888; Nashville *American,* March 2, 3, August 15 (quote), 1888.

to 75 men each. There were problems, too. A letter to the *Toiler,* or perhaps an editorial disguised as a letter, complained of frustration among Rutherford Wheelers because of a lack of enthusiasm and dedication. Miner Thomas F. Carrick, a leader of the Knights of Labor, urged Alliancemen to overcome discord and attack the enemy, not each other.[33] Rapid growth was accompanied by lack of cohesion and discipline.

Internal stress did not emerge as rivalry between the Wheel and the Alliance at the state level. When the state Alliance was formed, it decided to work through the Wheel business agent rather than choose its own, and a joint Wheel-Alliance state executive committee was soon created. When the national Wheel and Alliance conventions, both meeting in Meridian, Mississippi, in December, 1888, agreed to unite, their respective Tennessee branches were ready. They met together the following July to agree on a joint constitution and elect officers of the new Farmers' and Laborers' Union. Buchanan was elected president without dissent, and a man from Henry, a strong Wheel county, became vice-president. The key office of lecturer, or traveling speaker, was given to a twenty-four-year-old. The only sour note was the appearance of the state secretary of the old Wheel, who was sent to prison for five years for embezzling Wheel funds. Otherwise, the farmer organization was approaching the peak of its size, influence, and prestige in Tennessee.[34]

One man present at the state Farmers' and Laborers' Union meeting was representing the state Colored Alliance, but his presence was accepted calmly. There was never any doubt that the Colored Alliance was a distinct group, so as long as the white Alliance was not directly involved in politics, the parallel black organization was no more controversial than the Colored Methodist Episcopal Church or the segregated Negro Masons. A white Tipton County Alliance official could boast freely in 1888 that he had commissioned seventeen black organizers in Tipton County alone, and forty in the whole

33. Nashville *American,* August 16, 1888; Nashville *Weekly Toiler,* November 7, 14, December 5, 19, 1888, May 8, 1889.
34. Nashville *Weekly Toiler,* June 27, 1888, May 15, July 31, 1889, February 19, 1890; Nashville *American,* March 2, 1888, July 25, 26, 27, 28, August 18, 1889; Hicks, *Populist Revolt,* 112.

state, some of whom were working in Mississippi, Arkansas, and Alabama. The same year, the state Wheel had a special committee to organize black Wheels. This effort was impeded by a lack of evangelists, but the Negro Wheelers resisted the use of white organizers, to keep their own ritual secret. The black Alliancemen claimed one-fifth as many chapters as the whites did, but in 1889 only four counties sent delegates to a state Negro Alliance meeting: Shelby, Tipton, Lincoln, and Giles. Four white Alliance officials attended the Memphis meeting. One of them, J. H. McDowell, violated no southern taboos when he wrote that the stated purposes of the Colored Alliance were, among others, "to elevate the colored people of America, by teaching them to love their country and their homes . . . to labor more earnestly for the education of themselves and their children, especially in agricultural pursuits. . . . To become better farmers and laborers, and less wasteful in their methods of living. To be more obedient to the civil law, and withdraw their attention from political partisanship. . . ." [35] This was simply a prescription for docility. White Alliance leaders could afford a casual, paternal attitude toward the weak Negro Alliance.

A student of southern white Alliance attitudes on race has stated that "the outstanding characteristic of the Tennessee order was its close association with the Colored Wheel." This assertion, supported only by quotations from white Alliance sources, is highly dubious. Perhaps this student believed literally a claim by the *Weekly Toiler* that white Alliancemen in Tennessee had sympathy for poor black farmers unmatched in any other state. In the same issue the *Toiler* played up interracial cooperation in Alliance business agencies, which was part of a general effort to drum up customers, not a breakthrough for integration. In the absence of an organ for the black farmers, the official Alliance newspaper occasionally printed announcements from the state Colored Alliance president, and sometimes made friendly statements like this one: "We are glad to see the colored people organizing to help defeat the oppressions of combined capital and we trust our white brethren everywhere will

35. Nashville *American,* July 26, 1889; Nashville *Weekly Toiler,* June 28, October 17, 1888, February 27, March 27, June 19, 1889; Morgan, *History of the Wheel and Alliance,* 111.

lend them a helping hand, and give them every assistance possible."
But assistance did not include support for an attempted strike of
black cotton pickers, which the *Toiler* brushed aside as a foolish
idea.[36] Since neither the *Toiler* nor any other white Tennessee Alliance spokesman ever advocated racial equality or differentiated
Alliance racial views from the southern norm, and since no move
was made in Tennessee toward joining the segregated branches of
the Alliance, it must be assumed that the apparent goodwill toward
the Colored Alliance fit the pattern of condescending white paternalism prevailing among many southern politicians. Despite the occasional claims to the contrary by liberal scholars looking for antecedents, the racial attitudes of white Alliancemen in Tennessee did not
differ significantly from those of their non-Alliance neighbors.

It is hardly surprising that Alliancemen shared their white neighbors' attitudes on race. But it is remarkable how easily the Alliancemen forgot their effort to escape dominance by local elites. In an age
when "commanding presence" was still an explicit qualification for
appointive office, the Alliance sometimes tried to recruit those accustomed to success in politics, business, or the professions. It seemed
axiomatic that a prosperous organization would attract successful
men. As a breathless Alliance organizer explained, "We want Legislators, Governors, and Congressmen, and everything else." [37] In
some important cases, the Farmers' Alliance bowed to the old custom of social deference by embracing men of property and status.

It seems that the local politicians joined the Alliance en masse in
rural Cheatham County. A president of the county Alliance had run
for county register a dozen years before, and the Alliance doorkeeper
had run for sheriff. The president of the county Wheel was a man
who had been sheriff and a delegate to at least two Democratic state
conventions. The Wheel secretary had run twice for sheriff and had
also attended a state Democratic convention. A chairman and another member of the county court and other Democratic party func-

36. Gerald H. Gaither, "The Negro in the Ideology of Southern Populism, 1889–1896"
(M.A. thesis, University of Tennessee, 1967), 29; Nashville *Weekly Toiler,* October 10, 1888,
May 1, December 18, 1889, October 14, 1891.

37. J. Patterson to R. Olney, August 12, 1896, in Cleveland Papers; J. D. Ewell to R. L.
Taylor, June 11, 1888, in CGO, TSLA.

tionaries joined the Cheatham Alliance too. Two presidents of the Lauderdale County Alliance had been county delegates to state Democratic conventions, and another member was a former editor of the county's weekly newspaper.[38] Thus the Alliance admitted rural men who were as much politicians as farmers, and others who were not really farmers at all; despite its intentions, the Alliance was not completely free of entanglement with local elites.

Those who rose to leadership in the Alliance were not typical members, but men with political experience and ambition. In the summer of 1890 the Tennessee Alliance selected delegates to the national convention at Ocala, Florida. Of the five delegates, two or three were farmers. John Buchanan, outgoing Alliance president, owned a farm of 325 acres, the fourth largest in his civil district in Rutherford County. He had chaired an 1881 low-tax protest meeting, had run for county court clerk, had represented his district on the county Democratic committee, and had sat in the legislature—all before the coming of the Alliance. W. C. Lightfoot, probably also a farmer, had been a noted Lauderdale County low-taxer, with enough local influence to see his view on the state debt prevail at a public meeting over a resolution offered by the chairman of the county court.[39] A. L. Mims was a farmer and former schoolteacher of Davidson County. He ran for the legislature as a Democrat in 1884 and 1886, but lost both times. The other two Ocala delegates were not farmers, but, like the first three, had been in politics before joining the Alliance or Wheel. State Alliance Secretary E. B. "Eth"

38. Nashville *Weekly Toiler*, June 27, August 22, 1888, February 12, May 7, June 25, 1890, January 27, 1892; Ashland City *Cheatham County Plaindealer*, January 17, 1878; Ashland City *Cheatham County New Era*, October 13, 1881, April 27, 1882; Nashville *American*, June 21, 1882, June 12, 19, 1884, July 8, August 12, 1886, April 23, 1888; Nashville *Banner*, August 11, 1891; Ashland City *Reporter*, July 17, 1884; *History of Tennessee, from the Earliest Time to the Present: Together with an Historical and a Biographical Sketch of Montgomery, Robertson, Humphreys, Stewart, Dickson, Cheatham, and Houston Counties, Beside a Valuable Fund of Notes, Original Observations, Reminiscences, etc. etc.* (Nashville, 1886), 957.

39. Nashville *American*, July 27, 1889, August 16, 1890; Rutherford County tax book, 1889, film, TSLA; Murfreesboro *Free Press*, May 6, 1881, July 7, 1882, July 2, 1886; *House Journal*, 1887, p. 4; Memphis *Public Ledger*, September 3, 1880; Memphis *Avalanche*, December 11, 1877; *History of Tennessee, from the Earliest Time to the Present: Together with an Historical and a Biographical Sketch of Lauderdale, Tipton, Haywood, and Crockett Counties, Beside a Valuable Fund of Notes, Original Observations, Reminiscences, etc. etc.* (Nashville, 1887), 801.

Wade was a friend of Buchanan, a brother-in-law of a nephew of President James K. Polk, and owner of one of Murfreesboro's finest houses. Wade was active in community affairs and in the Democratic party, having been chairman of his county Democratic committee before the Alliance came, and having served as chief clerk of the state House of Representatives for several terms. The remaining Ocala delegate, John H. McDowell, had been a cotton farmer for seven years in Arkansas, but then returned to his native Tennessee to acquire first a Union City weekly newspaper and then the *Weekly Toiler.* He was listed as a "manufacturer" after his election in 1884 to the second of his three terms in the legislature. Now, in 1890, McDowell was the new president of the state Alliance.[40] Each of these five men was able to advance his political career after joining the Alliance.

A few other examples will serve to show how inarticulate, inexperienced Alliance members relied on relatively wealthy, sophisticated men to lead them. An assistant lecturer of the Lauderdale County Alliance held a law degree from Cumberland University in Lebanon, Wilson County, an incubator of Tennessee politicians. He had been chairman of the county court for five years, but quit his law practice for farming. A Shelby County delegate to a state Alliance convention had attended the medical school of the University of Nashville and belonged to the Episcopal Church. An unsuccessful candidate for state Alliance president in 1890 had received two degrees from East Tennessee University at Knoxville plus a Vanderbilt law degree. He had been a partner in the most prominent law firm in Clarksville, but left it to farm some land he gained through marriage. Another unsuccessful candidate for state Alliance chief, the president of the Giles County branch, had once been a physician, had served two terms on the board of the University of Tennessee, and had been chairman of the committee on education of the national Grange. A member of the state executive committee of the Alliance was the son of a merchant who was a director of the First National Bank of Memphis. A Jefferson County delegate to a state

40. Nashville *American,* September 4, 1884, January 8, 1885, April 11, September 26, 1886, April 22, 1887, August 16, 1890, April 12, 1894; Speer, *Sketches,* 26–27, 579; Morgan, *History of the Wheel and Alliance,* 268–70.

Alliance meeting had been a Whig legislator in 1855, director of a major railroad for four years, and director of a Knoxville bank. A graduate of Randolph-Macon College in Virginia became lecturer of the Fayette County Alliance. First vice-president of the Tennessee Wheel in 1887–1888 was a man who had been clerk of the Hardin County court for fourteen years.[41] These were not typical Alliancemen, but that they were Alliance leaders reveals much about the movement. There is no known case in which a man without property became an officer in the Farmers' Alliance in Tennessee.

The men of the Farmers' Alliance were ambivalent about how to regulate their relations with nonfarmers: theoretically, they drew a firm line against membership by town people, yet they admitted wealthy, educated farmers whose status was close to that of town elites and who would therefore enhance the social standing of the Alliance. In practice, farmers were not sure whether they should beat the towns or join them. The latter alternative was more attractive about 1889 when the Alliance was at its zenith, and established elites were impressed enough, and still complacent enough, to tolerate the movement. Another ambiguity in Alliance attitudes was the uncertainty about where the enemy was—in the local towns or in the East. To the extent that the farmers' enemy seemed to be in Wall Street and the Republican party, the Alliance could win the praise of the Bourbon Nashville *American* and admit some like-minded local Bourbon politicians to membership. But whenever the Alliance found its enemy closer at hand, it would provoke fierce opposition and frighten away many of the farmer-politicians upon whom it depended for leadership.

41. Nashville *Banner,* March 15, 1890, August 11, 1891; *History of Tennessee: Lauderdale, Tipton, Haywood, and Crockett Counties,* 801; Nashville *American,* August 13, 1890, February 11, 1892; Nashville *Weekly Toiler,* August 1, 1888, December 11, 1889, August 27, 1890; Memphis *Appeal-Avalanche,* March 15, 1892; *Dow's City Directory of Memphis, 1891* (Memphis, 1890), 57; Speer, *Sketches,* 5.

6

The Alliance in Politics

Ostensibly, the Alliance was nonpolitical. A man presented for initiation into membership was assured by his suballiance president that the oath would not "conflict with your political or religious views." Indeed, the "obligation" sworn by new members involved not political activism, but loyalty to the order and to brother members. The Tennessee Alliance, though strongest in Democratic areas, avoided identification with either political party before 1890. But as a prohibitionist editor asked in 1888, "Why have not the farmers, as Wheelers or otherwise, as much right to dictate the policy of this government as the saloon element?" Or the commercial element, the farmers might add, or the local bar association. A few astute politicians began to see the Alliance as political dynamite. "Don't make the wheelers mad watch that point," a Dickson County man warned Governor Taylor. One mad Wheeler was J. H. McDowell, who called Taylor a "scheming politician," and "advise[d] the brotherhood against him." In parts of West Tennessee, Wheelers worked locally against Taylor's renomination.[1] The restless Alliancemen were seeping into politics at the grass roots, and the cheerful governor neither understood nor controlled their discontents.

Meanwhile, the growing self-consciousness of farmers throughout the South and West was producing not only efforts for organizational unity but also an impulse toward articulation of national political

---

1. *Ritual for Subordinate Lodges Working under the Jurisdiction of the Farmers' and Laborers' Union of America* (Nashville, n.d.), 4, 5, 7; Murfreesboro *Rutherford Democrat,* June 6, 1888; I. M. Bowers to R. L. Taylor, July 11, 1888, Zachary T. Gattin to R. L. Taylor, April 19, 1888, in CGO, TSLA; Nashville *Weekly Toiler,* quoted in Knoxville *Tribune,* April 19, 1888; Nashville *American,* April 28, 1888.

goals. The Alliance platforms announced at St. Louis in 1889 and at Ocala in 1890 would mostly concern matters requiring federal legislation: banking and currency, tariffs and taxation, public control of transportation and communication, and direct election of the Senate. Tennessee Alliancemen, however, were not much concerned with these issues, even in an election for United States senator. John D. C. Atkins, commissioner of Indian affairs under President Cleveland, was running against Senator Harris with the support of A. S. Colyar, whose son held a clerkship under Atkins. "If all the signs do not fail I think we will warm Senator Harris' jacket with Gen Atkins," wrote old Redeemer W. H. Jackson. The *Weekly Toiler* warmly endorsed Atkins, whose strong showing in Gibson County Colyar attributed to Wheel strength there.[2] Alliancemen were neither consistent nor united in statewide political races in 1888, except perhaps in tending to oppose incumbents.

Most Alliance political energy in 1888 was spent in winning a few Republican and many Democratic nominations for the legislature. There was bitterness in Lauderdale County, where the farmers' opponents had reportedly promised to nominate a "certain farmer," but double-crossed the Wheel, joined its enemies, and effected the "undemocratic nomination of [T. Bun] Carson." Angry farmers then held a mass meeting and nominated an independent candidate who would represent farmer interests, regardless of party. The irregular candidate, with Republican help, came very close to defeating Carson, who lost one Democrat in six. Carson learned his lesson; two years later he was a county Alliance officer.[3] Perhaps the Alliance learned something too. In most other counties the Alliancemen did not need to bolt because they were seizing Democratic nominations.

Local political organization was aided by publicity in the *Weekly Toiler,* but it drew its energy from local interest and participation. The long-dormant farmers found leaders blossoming among them. Quite often a minor politician offered his experience, eager to ride

2. George B. Tindall (ed.), *A Populist Reader: Selections from the Works of American Populist Leaders* (New York, 1966), 75–77, 88–89; Nashville *American,* September 4, October 12, 1888; Knoxville *Journal,* August 20, 1886; W. H. Jackson to D. S. Lamont, September 21, 1888, in Cleveland Papers; Nashville *Weekly Toiler,* July 4, 18, August 1, 1888.
3. Nashville *Weekly Toiler,* October 31, November 14, 1888, February 5, 1890.

the most dynamic political movement in Tennessee since the low-tax Democratic party of 1880. As a result, the *Toiler* could count 41 Alliancemen and Wheelers among the 132 legislators elected in November, 1888. They included Senator J. C. Apple and Representatives T. B. Harwell and J. C. Moore, presidents of the Smith, Giles, and Tipton County Alliances; and Representatives C. C. Adams and John P. Buchanan, past and present state officers of the Wheel and Alliance. Brother J. M. Crews was temporary chairman of the Shelby County Democratic convention, then went on to the Senate. Either the bandwagon was hard to resist, or the *Toiler* missed a few in its November count, because after the session opened in January it found 52 Alliancemen in both houses, mostly Democrats from West and Middle Tennessee.[4]

When this vanguard of the agrarian revolt reached Capitol Hill in Nashville, they worked quietly within the old parties. While the Senate Democratic caucus was nominating Benjamin J. Lea for Speaker, most Alliance senators supported the winner, a veteran politician and lawyer who somehow got into the Alliance. The larger House of Representatives had more Democratic aspirants for Speaker than the Senate did. In addition to the former session's Speaker, W. L. Clapp of Memphis, they were Allianceman J. W. Lewis of Henry County; Bourbon anti-Taylor leader J. B. Fort, who had defeated an Allianceman for his seat; former United States Assistant District Attorney W. B. Stephens of Monroe County; and T. O. Morris, a spokesman for Nashville businessmen. Lewis did not get solid Alliance support—in fact, state Alliance president Buchanan nominated Clapp in the caucus. Democrats voted together on the House floor for caucus nominee Clapp.[5]

The House caucus votes on Speaker and United States senator reveal that Alliance legislators were interested in overturning established leaders. Former Confederate congressman John D. C. Atkins,

4. *Ibid.*, July 18, November 21, 1888, January 23, December 11, 1889, January 8, 1890; Morgan, *History of the Wheel and Alliance,* 110; Nashville *American,* March 2, 1888; Memphis *Avalanche,* April 10, 1888.

5. Nashville *American,* November 5, 1888, January 8, 1889; Nashville *Weekly Toiler,* September 19, October 31, 1888, February 6, 1889; Nashville *Banner,* May 9, 1888, March 15, August 9, 1890; A. D. Bright to J. D. Porter, February 4, 1875, in CGO, TSLA; *Senate Journal,* 1889, pp. 8, 9; *House Journal,* 1889, pp. 9–10.

a kinsman of Redeemer Governor Porter, was the champion of the anti-Bourbon Cleveland men. Atkins also had the support of the *Weekly Toiler* until J. H. McDowell bought out the other co-owner and disengaged the paper from the race.[6] Alliancemen were divided

Table 18

VOTING BY KNOWN ALLIANCEMEN AND OTHER DEMOCRATS
ON FIRST BALLOTS FOR NOMINATIONS FOR SPEAKER AND
FOR U.S. SENATOR, 1889 HOUSE DEMOCRATIC CAUCUS [7]

	Known Allianceman (21 voting on both)			
	Harris	Atkins	Savage	Totals
Lewis	1	10	0	11
Clapp	4	1	0	5
Fort	2	1	0	3
Stephens	0	1	0	1
Morris	1	0	0	1
Totals	8	13	0	

	Other Democrats (31 voting on both)			
	Harris	Atkins	Savage	Totals
Lewis	4	2	1	7
Clapp	7	1	1	9
Fort	7	1	1	9
Stephens	1	0	3	4
Morris	2	0	0	2
Totals	21	4	6	

in the House Democratic caucus on the Senate nomination as well as on the speakership. Nearly half the Alliancemen voted for both Lewis and Atkins, but the traditional influence of geography showed itself more clearly than Alliance discipline. Lewis and Atkins were both from Henry County, and of the ten Alliancemen voting for them, nine lived in counties within fifty miles of Henry and all in counties within seventy-five. Fiery old low-taxer and railroad regulator John Savage drew no Alliance votes. In supporting old Redeemer

6. Nashville *American,* August 19, 1888; Nashville *Banner,* June 23, 1888; Speer, *Sketches,* 35; Nashville *Weekly Toiler,* July 4, 18, September 5, 26, 1888.
7. Nashville *American,* January 8, 12, 1889.

Table 19
LEADERSHIP POSITIONS IN 1889 HOUSE OF
REPRESENTATIVES, BY ALLIANCE MEMBERSHIP [8]

	Alliancemen		Non-Alliancemen	
	Certain	Probable	Probable	Certain
Total in category	34	7	28	30
Speaker & key committee chairmanships	1	0	2	4
All other chairmanships	5	1	3	10

Atkins and railroad attorney Lewis, Alliance legislators demonstrated no strategy beyond simply rotating incumbents out.

Despite their numbers, Alliancemen failed to dominate the leadership of the legislature itself, or to control the elections of state officers. In the House, Alliancemen received a disproportionately low share of key positions, and although nearly all Democrats chaired committees in the smaller Senate, Alliancemen were more likely to be left out in appointments than others.[9] It seems that the legislators whom rank-and-file Alliancemen trusted and elected were not those best prepared for the machinations of Nashville's Capitol Hill. J. H. McDowell had failed to persuade the legislature to elect him comptroller, and the *Toiler* reflected his disappointment:

> There was [sic] from Speaker to Sergeant-at-arms, including State officers, sixteen wheel and Alliance candidates and about twice that number who were not wheelers, out of fifteen or sixteen offices filled by the General Assembly. Judge B. J. Le[a], Speaker of the Senate and Eth Wade, clerk of the Lower House, were the only ones elected, and very few knew they were members when they voted for them. During the contest for several offices the expression was frequently used: "We must beat the dam wheelers," and they did, with these two exceptions.[10]

Alliance legislators did not vote as a bloc in the routine business of the House of Representatives, as a cluster-bloc analysis shows.[11]

8. *House Journal,* 1889, pp. 92–95.
9. *Senate Journal,* 1889, pp. 60–62; Nashville *Banner,* September 12, 1890.
10. Nashville *Weekly Toiler,* January 30, 1889.
11. The Rice-Beyle cluster-bloc method defines the relationship of each pair of members by expressing the number of times they agreed on roll calls as a percentage of the number of times they both voted. A voting bloc is found by designating a minimum level of agreement and a fraction of the rest of the group with which each member must agree at this minimum level. Lee F. Anderson, Meredith W. Watts, Jr., and Allen R. Wilcox, *Legislative Roll-call Analysis* (Evanston, 1966), 59–76.

The use of this method on roll calls of the 1889–1890 House reveals that the only clusters were a central core group of Democrats and a smaller one of Republicans. The differences in party regularity among Democrats were slight, the Alliancemen being a little more regular on routine matters than were the others.

Table 20
KNOWN ALLIANCEMEN AND OTHER MEMBERS,
HOUSE OF REPRESENTATIVES, 1889 REGULAR AND 1890
EXTRA SESSIONS, BY MEMBERSHIP IN RICE-BEYLE CLUSTERS;
ALL ROLL CALLS WITH OVER THREE IN THE MINORITY ARE USED [12]

	Alliancemen		Non-Alliancemen	
	Certain	Probable	Probable	Certain
D	10	1	2	6
d	20	6	9	17
r	0	0	5	3
R	4	0	12	4

Key to symbols: D—Democratic core group, of which each member agrees with
                  each of at least ¾ of the others at least 80% of the time
                  d—all other Democrats
                  R—Republican core group (same criteria as D)
                  r—all other Republicans

Alliance Democrats followed their party on the most important legislation to emerge from the 1889 General Assembly. In the regular session and in a special 1890 session, new laws were enacted requiring a secret ballot and voter registration in the largest towns, and enforcing throughout the state the 1870 constitution's poll-tax requirement for voting. These laws were widely regarded as racially discriminatory in intent, and subsequent elections show a decrease in Republican votes that correlates significantly with black population. In West Tennessee the new laws broke the back of the Republican party for decades. The behavior of Alliance legislators during the consideration and passage of these laws is of particular interest because of the assertions by recent liberal historians that disfranchisement of southern blacks was perpetrated only after the Populist revolt revealed that black voters held a potential balance of power.[13]

12. *House Journal,* 1889, *passim.*
13. For an examination of these laws, the Alliance role in their passage, and their effects, see Appendix D.

Regulation of elections had long been of concern to Tennessee Democrats, but in 1885 Republican legislators blocked a quorum and prevented action. In 1889 the Democrats in the legislature attained unprecedented levels in both numbers and unity, and a national trend of election reform encouraged them to use their power. The resulting disfranchisement laws were not Alliance measures, but Alliance Democrats certainly concurred cheerfully in their passage, voting for them more heavily than other Democrats. Alliance Democrats were thinking of their party's advantage in 1889, and some of them, by ironic justice, found themselves later opposing as Populists the same laws they had favored as Democrats, and for the same reason.[14]

"We have noticed, session after session," remarked a Nashville observer in 1885, "that however large a proportion of the legislature may be agriculturists, they succeed in having very few laws passed that are of any substantial benefit to their class." This assessment remained true in 1889, despite the Alliance. Besides aiding the passage of the new election laws, which might have passed anyway, it secured with ease a law exempting its business agents from taxation. An Allianceman's bill to prevent cotton buyers from "docking each bale two pounds" was tabled, but the *Weekly Toiler* found solace in praising a new law reducing the number of wires in a legal fence from five to three. "Many of our farmers," explained the *Toiler,* "were without any legislative experience, and therefore could not do as much as they would have done with more experience. . . . Our greatest difficulty this session has been the want of proper unity of action among our members in the passage of bills, but they have done well, all things considered." [15] Lack of unity and experience, yes, but the problem was deeper than that. The Alliancemen did not know what to work for. They did not try to implement an Alliance program because they had none and because their performance was less important to most of their constituents than was the mere fact of their election.

Far from being discouraged by the 1889 legislature, the Alliance

14. *Ibid.*
15. Nashville *American,* January 11, 1885; Nashville *Weekly Toiler,* February 20, March 6 (quote), April 17, 1889; *House Journal,* 1889, p. 464.

pressed ahead with a campaign to capture the Democratic nomination for governor in 1890. The race for governor started in the usual chaotic way determined by the lack of clear issues or organized factions; various would-be candidates let their names be tossed around in the press, hoping for a response in the segments of the party most sympathetic to their general attitudes. By late 1889 one editor had narrowed the field down to House Speaker W. L. Clapp, Bourbon lawyer Josiah Patterson of Memphis, and Congressman Benton McMillin of Clay County. But Duncan Cooper's new Nashville *Herald* devoted its entire front page on New Year's Day to promoting thirty-eight-year-old Jere Baxter, a former president of the Memphis and Charleston Railroad with close ties to the Nashville business and financial community. Baxter said nothing about any economic interests of a farmer class, but he sought their favor by joining the Alliance. The *Toiler* was supporting state Alliance president Buchanan, and announced that Tennessee farmers deserved the governorship since they cast 70 percent of the Democratic votes. Others doubted that the farmers were "in a position to dictate the Democratic nominee for Governor." But the Nashville *Banner* remarked, "All the candidates (or nearly all) for governor in Tennessee are anxious to be known as farmers, or at least as the friends of farmers. The mere fact that a man allows a few borrowed hayseeds to cling to his locks does not stamp him as an agriculturist. The people understand these things." [16] Indeed they did.

An old-fashioned candidate who gave little recognition to the Alliance was Colonel Patterson. A native of Alabama and a Confederate veteran, he had moved to Memphis in 1872 and taken up a law practice. His outstanding speech as chairman of the 1882 Democratic state convention was probably the "telling speech in favor of Bate" by "a lawyer of Memphis" which John H. Savage remembered thirty years later as ensuring General Bate's nomination. In the 1883 legislature Patterson was a strong advocate of railroad regulation and a fifty-cent debt settlement. Three years later he still favored a railroad commission, and took a free-trade position on the tariff. In

16. Nashville *American,* February 12, September 5, 1889, February 8, September 22, 1890; Nashville *Herald,* January 1, 1890; Speer, *Sketches,* 570–72; Nashville *Weekly Toiler,* December 18, 1889, January 15, 1890; Nashville *Banner,* January 17, 1890.

1890 the colonel scorned the idea of the New South as implying that the South had a sin to repent. He was an enemy of New South men like Congressman James Phelan of Memphis, A. S. Colyar of Nashville, and Governor Taylor, whom Patterson could not bring himself to endorse while campaigning for Cleveland in 1888. Patterson told a Chattanooga crowd that the Union veterans among them had not fought to "Negroize" the South, and urged them to come over to the white man's party. One of his friends explained that he was a real "upper-case" Democrat, a lower-case Democrat being "the person who, or the thing which, is always going to revolutionize the state on economic questions, and never does it." [17] The Bourbon colonel was not about to revolutionize anything.

The Shelby County Democratic primary provided for an early contest between Patterson and a fellow Memphian, W. L. Clapp. After losing the city boxes by a ten-to-one margin, Clapp withdrew bitterly from the race, charging corruption and unfair influence for Patterson by the city government. Twenty-four Buchanan delegates elected in the rural districts were stifled by a unit rule adopted by the more numerous Patterson men.[18] In their attempt to regain the governorship after four years of Bob Taylor, the Bourbons had a solid urban base in Memphis.

Another city candidate, Jere Baxter, had his own big Davidson County delegation, plus the support of Democrats in towns across the state who hoped for a bustling, profitable New South. The friendly Chattanooga *Times,* longing for a "business Governor," called Baxter "a man of force, positive character, and direct methods . . . politician enough to keep his administration 'in line' . . . [who] would be, in the Governor's chair, something more and better than a politician." Two spokesmen for the Taylor administration asserted that Baxter could transform his business acumen into statecraft. From Memphis to Bristol, Taylor men were reported working for Baxter, and the governor was said to favor him privately. The ener-

17. [Savage,] *Life,* 191; Speer, *Sketches* 266–68; Knoxville *Chronicle,* January 20, 1883; Nashville *American,* August 12, 1886; March 4, June 19, 1890; Nashville *Union,* September 12, 1886; Nashville *Banner,* March 1, 5, April 10, 1890; Chattanooga *Times,* April 27, 1890. The revolution in question was the growth of an industrial New South.

18. Nashville *American,* May 25, 28, 1890; Memphis *Appeal,* May 23, 28, 1890; Nashville *Herald,* May 24, 1890.

getic Baxter collected $300,000 from Boston capitalists for his large farm during the campaign, a transaction sure to win the admiration of other businessmen and the suspicion of farmers, both of whom were interested not so much in what Baxter said as in who he was.[19]

Farmers' Alliance president Buchanan had a different sort of identity problem: some refused to take his candidacy seriously. A country editor first misspelled his name and then chortled, "The idea of J. P. having any of the symptoms of a statesman borders somewhat on the ludicrous." Buchanan was called "highly hilarious," an "alleged candidate for Governor." More soberly, a Republican editor commented that it was "strange how little is known about farmer Buchanan." And about the Alliance, he might have added, for he and his colleagues in journalism failed to realize that Buchanan's very obscurity caused his fellow farmers to trust him. By the middle of May, twenty-eight county Alliances and hundreds of suballiances had officially backed him for governor, which gave him a ready-made campaign organization no other candidate could hope to match. The farmers could pack county conventions and sway their neighborhoods where district conventions were used. In the seventh district of Coffee County only nineteen Alliancemen attended, but Democrats voted for Buchanan thirty-eight to three. "The farmers of Tennessee seem to be getting in their work pretty well," commented the Manchester *Times,* "judging from the number of counties which are instructed for Buchanan." [20]

Politicians and editors stopped joking about Buchanan as his delegate total moved steadily higher. On the morning of the Obion County Democratic convention, Alliancemen held a caucus led by state lecturer R. W. Tucker and by J. H. McDowell's son. In the afternoon the farmers marched into the convention, routed the com-

19. Nashville *American,* July 16, 1890; Chattanooga *Times,* February 14, 1890; Pulaski *Citizen,* May 22, 1890; Johnson City *Comet,* June 5, 1890; Bristol *Courier,* quoted in Knoxville *Journal,* April 26, 1890; Memphis *Scimitar,* quoted in Knoxville *Journal,* May 19, 1890; Chattanooga *Times,* quoted in Nashville *Herald,* July 16, 1890; Nashville *Weekly Toiler,* May 21, 1890.

20. Obion *Democrat,* quoted in Nashville *American,* January 20, 1890; Knoxville *Journal,* May 9, 23, 1890; Chattanooga *Times,* April 21, 1890; Nashville *Weekly Toiler,* May 14, 1890; Manchester *Times,* May 30, July 11, 1890.

bined opposition, and instructed the county's big thirty-vote bloc for Buchanan. The tumultuous Knox County convention was divided among front-runner Patterson, a strong Buchanan contingent, and a Baxter group with about a quarter of the votes. Baxter and Buchanan men joined forces to elect an Allianceman chairman and to divide the county delegation about evenly between them. The Alliance stepped on some toes in Hardeman County, where seventy-nine Patterson men of the eleventh civil district published a protest that they had not been notified of the district convention and so had been disfranchised. Reports kept coming from Democratic counties of Buchanan victories in conventions often described as the largest or most exciting in years. During the few days before the state convention, all sides agreed that Buchanan was the leading candidate, but city editors hoped that the farmers would be outwitted in Nashville, since they were "not politicians, and . . . what they accomplish[ed would have to] be done by main strength." The most convincing sign of Buchanan's strength was the announcement of gubernatorial candidate John M. Taylor, who was running a poor fourth, that he endorsed the Alliance platform verbatim.[21]

District-level primaries in some counties revealed where Alliance votes were concentrated. Giles County primaries gave the county seat and two adjacent districts to J. M. Taylor, two rich valley districts in the northern end of the county to Patterson, and four contiguous rugged, hilly districts to Baxter. Buchanan not only swept a broad U-shaped belt around the edges of the county, but reportedly carried his districts solidly, while the others were divided. The pattern in Giles suggests that Buchanan men were located not so much according to soil and land characteristics as by distance from Pulaski, the geographical, commercial, and political center of the county. In adjoining Maury County, Baxter's delegates were mostly confined to the town of Columbia. J. M. Taylor carried one rich farming district and Patterson won a few more. Buchanan, who

---

21. Nashville *American*, June 3, 19, 22, 24, 29, July 1, 8, 9, 16, August 13, 1890; Bolivar *Bulletin*, June 6, 1890; Nashville *Weekly Toiler*, July 9, 1890; Knoxville *Journal*, July 9, 15 (quote), 1890; Memphis *Appeal*, July 8, 1890; Nashville *Banner*, July 9, 1890; Chattanooga *Times*, July 13, 1890.

carried more districts than anyone else, found the bulk of his support in the less well-to-do farming sections away from the towns and rich alluvial riverbeds.[22]

A third county, Bedford, embraced part of the Inner Central Basin, a segment of the more hilly Outer Basin, and part of the rugged Highland Rim Escarpment. Of Taylor's three Bedford districts, one was in the poor Escarpment area and two in the fertile Inner Basin, good for general crops. Baxter apparently carried no entire district, but Patterson won the county seat and most of the rest of the Inner Basin, along with one Escarpment district. Buchanan gained nearly half the county's delegation by rolling up majorities in some Escarpment districts and in most of the Outer Basin area, famous for its Tennessee walking horses and similar to Buchanan's own neighborhood just across the line in Rutherford County. Once again, the general pattern, to which there were always exceptions, was for Buchanan strength to lie in the hillier sections away from the central town and lowlands. In his home county Buchanan carried three of the six wards of Murfreesboro, demonstrating that town people would vote for him when they knew him as a neighbor.[23] Elsewhere, Buchanan supporters were distant, both geographically and psychologically, from the local centers of power.

Did Buchanan men, then, live on the most infertile and rugged farmland? Not necessarily. Comparison of Alliance voting strength and land values in four Middle Tennessee counties indicates a pattern different from that of Texas, where Roscoe C. Martin found that Populists lived on poor farmland.[24] In Tennessee the pattern of 1890 was not so simply based on economic differences.

As Buchanan's delegate tally soared, Patterson and Baxter newspapers turned from attacking each other to notice the obscure man who was beating them as the fabled tortoise overtook the hare. A

22. Nashville *American,* July 7, 1890; Milton Whitney, *Field Operations of the* [U.S.] *Bureau of Soils for 1907* (Washington, D.C., 1909), 773–91, map; U.S. Department of Agriculture, *Soil Survey: Maury County, Tennessee* (Washington, D.C., 1959).

23. Nashville *American,* July 8, 13, 16, 1890; U.S. Department of Agriculture, *Soil Survey: Bedford County, Tennessee* (Washington, D.C., 1947).

24. Roscoe C. Martin, *The People's Party in Texas: A Study in Third Party Politics* (Austin, 1970), 61, 64–65. Perhaps this difference partly reflects a distinction between supporting the Alliance within the Democratic party and breaking out of that party.

Table 21
AVERAGE ASSESSED VALUE OF FARMLAND PER ACRE FOR
DISTRICTS (EXCLUDING COUNTY SEAT DISTRICTS)
KNOWN TO HAVE BEEN CARRIED BY FOUR CHIEF CANDIDATES
IN 1890 DEMOCRATIC PRIMARIES [25]

County	Bedford	Giles	Maury	Robertson
Number of districts	19	21	25	18
Districts for Buchanan	7	9	5	9
Average value/acre	$12.75	$ 7.77	$11.66	$ 7.97
Districts for Patterson	3	2	3	2
Average value/acre	$ 7.95	$10.65	$21.00	$ 6.11
Districts for Taylor	3	2	1	1
Average value/acre	$ 8.90	$ 9.75	$20.60	$10.20
Districts for Baxter	0	4	3	5
Average value/acre	......	$ 9.37	$ 9.41	$ 6.78

small-town weekly muttered that Buchanan was "without force of character, without experience, [and had] had no success in life." But most comments were more curious than derogatory. Buchanan "is a rather plain looking gentleman," said the Memphis *Appeal.* "He is considered by all who know him to be an honest and earnest man, who always minded his own business and never interfered with that of anybody else." Editor E. W. Carmack of the Nashville *American* expressed himself with unwonted mildness: "Mr. Buchanan entered the race an unknown man. For four years he had been a member of the legislature, but a native modesty prevented his name and fame from becoming by-words in the land. His canvass has been principally among the Alliance men, his theme the sub-Treasury measure, his song the advancement of the farmers." The Memphis *Commercial,* which predicted that "relentless enemies" would come out of a campaign full of "acrimony and bitterness," displayed only generosity in discussing Buchanan, whom it called "a plain farmer, strong with the Alliance folk because he is in personal sympathy and touch with their life and needs, is one of them, fully identified with

25. Maury County and Bedford County tax books, 1892, Robertson County tax book, 1883, film, TSLA; Giles County tax book, 1892, courthouse, Pulaski; Nashville *American,* July 7, 8, 1890; Nashville *Weekly Toiler,* July 16, 1890. For another example of how widely localities differed, see Appendix B, Table 17.

them and the advocate of all their pet schemes and measures of legislation, national and State." [26] Buchanan was a quiet man who did not arouse strong feelings in either his friends or his foes.

The Democratic state convention in July had many new faces, but professional politicians managed things because they knew how. The platform committee included old hands as Baxter men W. H. Jackson and J. D. C. Atkins, and Patterson-supporter S. F. Wilson. Even in the Buchanan caucus, though a distinctly rustic atmosphere prevailed, the politicians were in charge. John H. McDowell presided, former Democratic state chairman T. M. McConnell gave a speech, and a man was chosen for convention temporary chairman who was a lawyer, college graduate, and son-in-law of a Virginia legislator. The Buchanan meeting decided to support third-term Congressman James D. Richardson of Murfreesboro for convention chairman. Another veteran delegate instructed for the farmer candidate was Colonel John H. Savage, who snapped, "Yes, sir, I am for Buchanan. . . . For twenty-five years we have had fraud, corruption, deception, and deceit among Democrats. Now let's have a change. Give the farmer a chance." [27] The farmer's chance, and Buchanan's, depended on nonfarmers like Richardson, McDowell, and McConnell.

The national Alliance demands did not occasion controversy in the 1890 Democratic state convention any more than they had in the 1889 legislature. In the spring the Nashville *Banner* had attempted to make an issue of the Alliance subtreasury plan, which proposed that the federal government receive nonperishable crops as security for loans to farmers, the purposes being to save farmers from having to sell in a glutted market and to make the money supply more flexible. The proposal was an "agricultural pawn-shop policy," scoffed the *Banner,* which attacked Buchanan for "constantly urging this sub-treasury plan in his speeches." "Bro. Buchanan is not hidebound on the sub-treasury bill," retorted the *Weekly Toiler.* "He says if our national legislators will give us something better he is willing to accept it; but . . . one thing is certain, we are not going to

    26. Pulaski *Citizen,* July 10, 1890; Memphis *Appeal,* July 14, 1890; Nashville *American,* July 10, 1890; Memphis *Commercial,* July 3, 1890.
    27. Nashville *American,* July 15, 17, 1890; Nashville *Weekly Toiler,* July 23, 1890; Memphis *Appeal,* July 16, 1890; Speer, *Sketches,* 90–91.

surrender our convictions to Mills, Carlisle or any other leader on this question of relief unless they will propose some better remedy." [28] That silenced the *Banner* for a while, and no one was much interested in getting the subtreasury either approved or condemned in the state Democratic platform.

As provided by tradition, the platform was vague and platitudinous, designed to evoke and reinforce the feelings which had held voters loyal in the past. The ritual denunciation of the other party had an Alliance flavor:

> We declare that the agricultural interests are the mainstay and support of our dual system of government, State and Federal, and we arraign and condemn the Republican party for its legislative discrimination against this class, which has greatly reduced the price of farm lands and products; for its corrupt grant of large subsidies to special corporations; for its revolutionary methods to perpetuate its power; for its reckless spending of public money for party purposes; for its corrupting and debauching of the American franchise. . . .
>
> We denounce the McKinley tariff bill . . . oppressing the farmers and laborers of the country.

A plank demanding free coinage of silver, to be used equally with gold, stirred not a murmur from sound-money men. Besides free silver, the only plank resembling a national Alliance demand was one condemning the granting of public lands to corporations rather than to homesteaders. This mild, traditional platform was gaveled through without dissent.[29]

Next on the agenda was the gubernatorial nomination. Chairman Richardson recognized his brother, John E. Richardson, a Princeton man, former president of the Murfreesboro Democratic Club and respected board member of the Murfreesboro Educational Society. Buchanan was ahead of the "professional politicians," John Richardson proclaimed, in championing the rights of farmers. Allegations that Buchanan would give farmers an unfair advantage were false, he said. Then unpardoned Confederate General W. H. Jackson, the

---

28. For a summary of the subtreasury plan, and arguments for and against it, see Saloutos, *Farmer Movements in the South,* 119-21. Nashville *Banner,* May 20, 1890; Nashville *Weekly Toiler,* quoted in Washington *National Economist,* June 21, 1890. Roger Q. Mills and John G. Carlisle were Democratic leaders in Congress.

29. Nashville *American,* July 16, 1890; Tindall (ed.), *Populist Reader,* 75-77.

old Redeemer, rose and nominated Jere Baxter, the young capitalist. John M. Taylor and Colonel Patterson were presented, the latter, oddly enough, by a former supporter of Andrew Johnson and A. S. Colyar. Packed into the Hall of Representatives in the state capitol, the delegates waited for the first roll call of the counties. They knew that the crucial question was whether Buchanan could hold his men in line.[30]

On the first ballot, J. M. Taylor's delegates were from his neighborhood, as shown on Map 6. Patterson controlled his own big Shelby and adjoining Fayette, and Baxter won his home county, Davidson. Otherwise, the two city candidates drew most of their solid support from Republican counties in East Tennessee, where Democratic conventions were usually managed by party patronage appointees or aspirants. So the Bob Taylor administration carried some for Baxter, and Senator Isham Harris' friends swung others to Patterson. Buchanan delegates came mostly from Democratic counties, including the area which had followed low-tax bolter S. F. Wilson in 1880. The Alliance candidate was weak in the few counties with the heaviest black population, but was stronger in counties with above-average proportions of blacks than he was in the rest (see Appendix B, Table 14). The reason for Buchanan's strength in wheat counties, particularly in contrast to tobacco counties, is not clear, for the price of wheat in Tennessee had just hit an eight-year high in 1889. The first-ballot vote in the 1890 convention cannot be explained as well by economic, agricultural, and demographic statistics as by the structure of party politics and by the Democratic habit of responding to political rhetoric directed against alien oppressors.[31]

A two-thirds majority was needed for nomination, but Buchanan got fewer than half the votes on the first ballot. His hope lay in the mutual antagonism of Patterson and Baxter, each of whom controlled fewer than a quarter of the delegate votes. On the second day the minority position of the Alliance was underscored when an

---

30. *Who's Who in Tennessee,* 396; Nashville *American,* November 24, 1888, July 16, 1890.
31. *Annual Report of the Commissioner of Agriculture* (Washington, D.C., 1863–94), 1880, p. 197, 1881–82, p. 608, 1883, pp. 267–68, 1884, pp. 438–39, 1885, pp. 364–65, 1886, p. 397, 1887, pp. 560–61, 1888, pp. 431–32, 1889, p. 230, 1890, p. 296. The commissioner became secretary in 1889. Nashville *American,* July 16, 1890.

Map 6

1890 DEMOCRATIC STATE CONVENTION, FIRST BALLOT FOR GOVERNOR

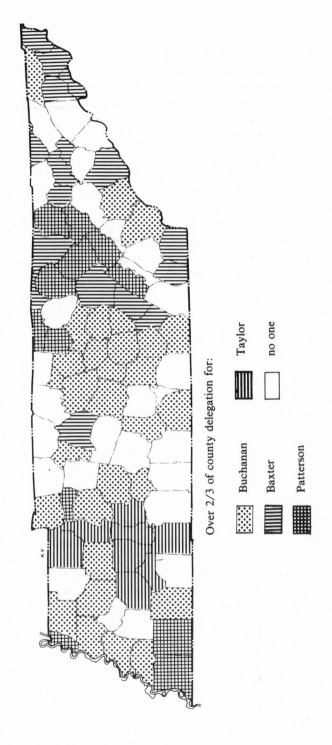

Over 2/3 of county delegation for:

Buchanan

Baxter

Patterson

Taylor

no one

Source: Nashville *American*, July 16, 1890.

anti-Buchanan man moved to end the unit rule, to allow counties with Alliance majorities to splinter: a McDowell motion to table this change was defeated, 736–869. Buchanan's gains from this change in rules nearly offset his losses, but then over several ballots he lost votes to Baxter. A White County delegate fell off a capitol balcony and killed himself, so Buchanan leaders used the recess to rally their men in a strategy meeting. Then they gained votes until J. M. Taylor gave up on the twenty-sixth ballot. When Hamilton County switched to Buchanan, resistance collapsed, and General Jackson moved that Buchanan's nomination be made unanimous. Compared to what was expected of them, the Alliancemen had "stood like a stone wall." The forty-three-year-old nominee, a not unhandsome man with a walrus moustache, went to the podium and pledged to fight for "the great principles enunciated by Jackson, Polk, and Johnson." [32] The politicians who had fought each other for control of the Democratic party for two decades sat and wondered what had happened.

John H. McDowell, the Alliance campaign manager, was understandably euphoric. "One of the grandest victories ever attained by farmers on this continent has passed into history," he gloated. "The shrewdest politicians in the State, trained for years in political wire pulling, have been outwitted and beaten by the 'hayseeds' in a fair, square, open fight." The reaction among other Democratic editors, however, ranged from fascination to apprehension. The Alliance, "like the fabled gourd, sprang into full growth in a night," marveled the Memphis *Commercial.* More typical was the Memphis *Avalanche,* dismayed at what it called "the first time in the history of the State that the representative of a class [had] been chosen to lead the great Democratic hosts to victory." This and other references to "certain class influences" witnessed to the inability of Tennessee's traditional governing class to see itself as it saw the Alliance. "What are known as the business interests are disappointed, to an extent, at the success of the alliance, because the alliance is believed to make unreasonable war on those interests," worried the Nashville *Herald.* But the harm he might do interested most Democratic editors far

32. Nashville *American,* July 16, 17, 18, 19, 1890; Chattanooga *Times,* July 19, 1890; Nashville *Banner,* July 19, 1890 (quote); Nashville *Herald,* July 19, 1890 (quote).

less than whether Buchanan was a "clean-cut Democrat." The Republican Knoxville *Journal* hoped that there were "hundreds and thousands of Democrats in Tennessee who would no more look to Mr. Buchanan as a leader, than would Wade Hampton look to Benjamin Tillman as a democratic leader in South Carolina." There was "a good deal of unpleasant talk about Mr. Buchanan's nomination among Democrats," one of them conceded. The muttering did not turn into organized mutiny, however, and most of the lawyers, editors, and businessmen who were accustomed to governing Tennessee accepted their defeat more or less gracefully.[33]

Because of their divisions, the Democrats were unable to conduct an integrated campaign. Buchanan seemed to be speaking more to Alliance meetings than to party rallies, and many Democratic leaders were reluctant to identify themselves with the head of the ticket, who was not a man to inspire a personal following. An inexperienced campaigner, he first spoke in Williamson County and then inadvertently addressed a Chattanooga crowd as "Boys of old Williamson." By using the motto "Sail on, O Ship of State," he sought to follow the *Weekly Toiler*'s advice, that "conservatism should characterize our every word and action."[34] An admirer of Jefferson, Buchanan held that "in all Governments there are two forces, the force of centralizing power and the force of the will of the people." The former was winning in America, he warned, under the promonopoly, high-tariff Republicans, who were generating increasing differentiation by wealth and a decadent trend like that of Imperial Rome. All this was welcomed by the British, who were trying to accomplish with gold what they had failed to do by force of arms—conquer the Americans. The contraction of the currency, said Buchanan, had been the most disastrous of the Republican policies, cutting into farm incomes. Yet the Force Bill was the "climax" of GOP sins, because

33. Nashville *Weekly Toiler,* July 23, 1890; Memphis *Commercial,* July 19, 1890; Memphis *Avalanche,* July 19, 1890; Nashville *Banner,* July 19, 21, 22, 1890; Nashville *Herald,* July 19, 1890; Knoxville *Journal,* July 20, 1890; Chattanooga *Times,* July 19, 1890; Memphis *Appeal,* July 19, 1890. Wade Hampton was a South Carolina patrician Redeemer, and Ben Tillman was a farmer leader who defeated the Hampton faction.

34. Tullahoma *Guardian,* quoted in Nashville *Banner,* August 7, 1890; Memphis *Appeal,* October 23, 1890; Knoxville *Journal,* September 24, 1890; Nashville *Weekly Toiler,* quoted in Nashville *American,* July 24, 1890.

"this land . . . has been, and ever will be, a white man's government," as sanctioned by "divine laws." The Democratic candidate favored more equitable taxation, support for schools, better roads, and the development of resources without abuses by capitalists. But he narrowed the basic issue to a question of whether democracy or plutocracy would rule. Finally, in response to criticism of his Alliance connection, Buchanan said he was only the second farmer ever nominated by Tennessee Democrats for governor. He almost invited martyrdom at the hands of the centralizing money power, which threatened at once to conquer and to corrupt.

> [If I am defeated] because I, knowing from experience the burdens and difficulties under which they [the people] are laboring, knowing that agriculture is the mainstay of the Government and the basis of the permanent prosperity of all classes, knowing that its very life's blood is being sucked up by vampires under the policy of the present Federal legislation—if, I say, I must fail because I, wedded to no special measures, always on the public rostrum have earnestly advocated the necessity of such relief as wise legislation may bring about, so that agriculture may have an equal chance in the race of life, then I shall be as proud of defeat as of victory.[35]

If Buchanan avoided party rallies, they shunned the Alliance. A Nashville crowd, for example, heard sixteen Democratic politicians including Bourbons and businessmen, but not one Alliance speaker. When a Prohibition party spokesman was almost mobbed in Murfreesboro for his attacks on the Alliance, Governor Taylor, who was next on the program, calmed the crowd by appealing to party tradition. Bob explained his support for Buchanan by assurances that the Alliance would soon fade away and was nothing to be afraid of. Buchanan's foes spread the word that Senator Harris could not support him, since Harris believed Alliance tenets "subversive of every principle of Democracy." These rumors persisted despite denials by the loyal party press.[36] The only reason the Tennessee Democratic party did not fall apart in 1890 was that the anti-Alliance

35. Memphis *Appeal,* September 3, 1890; Nashville *American,* September 3, 1890. The so-called "force bill" was Representative Henry Cabot Lodge's proposal for federal supervision of elections.

36. Nashville *American,* August 6, 20, October 3, 1890; Nashville *Banner,* October 10, 18, 1890; Tullahoma *Guardian,* quoted in Nashville *Banner,* September 30, 1890 (quote.)

politicians felt that the party rightfully belonged to them, that the nomination of Buchanan was a fluke, and that if anyone should get out of the party, it was the Alliance. The Democrats most reluctant to follow Buchanan were the merchants and professional men in the towns. "We know that in several portions of the State, and in Bedford county as well, there are some Democrats who will be slow to vote for Mr. Buchanan on Tuesday next, if they do so at all," noted the Shelbyville *Gazette*. "Some people are apprehensive that the lawyers and merchants will refuse to vote for Buchanan," remarked another small-town weekly, which then lamely concluded, "That is not true as to Pulaski. These gentlemen here are in honor bound to vote for him." [37]

The Nashville *American* felt compelled to deny a rumor that the bar of Murfreesboro, Buchanan's home town, would vote as a body against him; the *American* claimed that sixteen of the twenty-five lawyers were for him—a low proportion in a Democratic county. The Nashville *Herald* feared that since "the men in the rural districts, who have been in the habit of controlling and directing local politics . . . have been relegated to the rear," a counterattack was imperative. "Cities and larger towns should send lawyers and business men to the legislature," urged the *Herald*, "the best men they have, wherever they can. These men will be needed in the legislature, badly needed." In Shelby and Weakley, two strong Alliance counties, Democratic legislators who belonged to the order were accordingly replaced by non-Alliance men. In Rutherford County a meeting of anti-Alliance Democrats condemned the subtreasury and government ownership of railroads as well as the "force bill" and the tariff. Then they put up their own nominees for the legislature against the regular Buchanan Democrats. The insurgents' candidates, a lawyer and a farmer owning 275 acres, had been active for some years at the lower levels of the Democratic party, but stood no chance to win in Buchanan's home county.[38] Most town people across the state did not bolt like this, but were nonetheless unhappy.

---

37. Shelbyville *Gazette*, October 30, 1890; Pulaski *Citizen*, August 14, 1890.
38. Nashville *American*, May 30, June 10, 1886, October 25, 1890; Nashville *Herald*, September 10, 1890; Nashville *Banner*, October 13, 1890; Rutherford County tax book, 1889, film, TSLA; Murfreesboro *Free Press*, July 2, 1886.

A powerful voice of discontent with the political power of the Alliance was the Nashville *Banner,* which throughout the campaign verged on open opposition to Buchanan. Despite the candidate's disavowal of "special measures," the *Banner* insisted that he failed to confront the issue of the subtreasury. "Only a dolt can say that the Alliance political policy is not an issue in this canvass," the *Banner* declared. "If the standard-bearer of Democracy is unable, because of his pledge to a secret political organization, to meet all political issues and attack all undemocratic policies, then the party has come to a sad and perilous crisis in its history." In answer to the objection that the subtreasury was a national issue irrelevant to a state campaign, the *Banner* pointed out that Buchanan discussed the tariff, immigration, and the currency, all national issues.[39]

The fundamental quarrel of the *Banner* was not with the subtreasury itself, however, but with what it conceived to be the reason for Buchanan's silence about the plan. In Murfreesboro, Alliancemen were threatening a boycott of merchants opposed to their candidate. "This is the 'boycott' sort of 'Democracy' that freemen are asked to honor with office and power!" raged the editor, who urged Murfreesboro Democrats to go to the polls and defeat "every representative of dark-lantern proscriptive politics." The *Banner* likened Alliance boycotts of hostile newspapers to the methods of the Know-Nothing party of the 1850s. Having hit on this theme, the editor pursued it, denouncing Buchanan as the candidate of the "dark-lantern" Alliance, a "secret order" which the *Banner* called by the nickname "Sam." A generation earlier, in the heated campaign of 1855, Tennessee Democratic editors had called the Know-Nothings "Sam," suggested that they met "after night, way down in some dark cellar," and blasted them as a "secret oath-bound political organization." [40] *Banner* editor Gideon H. Baskette, perhaps the most intelligent journalist in Tennessee, was implying that the Alliance was similar to the Know-Nothing party not only in threatening the Democracy, but also in subverting the very principle of open, aboveboard political association in a free society. Baskette may have sensed

39. Nashville *Banner,* September 3, 27, 1890.

40. Nashville *Banner,* October, *passim,* November 3, 1890; Nashville *Union and American,* April 25, 26, May, 8, 23, June 3, 1855; Memphis *Appeal,* July 15, 25, 1855.

as well that the nativism of the Know-Nothings and the hostile suspicions of the Alliance were rooted closely together in the soil of folk traditions.

The Alliance tactic of turning against politicians who refused to endorse their demands provoked much of this sort of resentment. In the Memphis district the Alliance endorsed for Congress a lawyer and big landowner, but he was opposed in the Democratic nominating convention by a Memphis man. A stubborn rural-urban contest lasted through an incredible 5,053 ballots and ended only with the nomination of Josiah Patterson, defeated earlier for governor. In this race the substance of the Alliance demands was not discussed. The issue was whether the Alliance should run the party. In several other areas, non-Alliance Democrats resented the bloc-vote power of the farmers, but said little or nothing about the subtreasury plan itself. A critic of Buchanan complained that he was "the most prominent member of a secret order, which claim[ed] the right to propound questions to Democratic candidates and Democratic nominees, before giving its support, although claiming to be Democrats." [41] The Alliance demands, especially the subtreasury, were coming to be used by the Alliance as a test of sincerity and trustworthiness, and by their opponents as a symbol of illegitimate political tactics.

The Republicans tried to take advantage of discontent in the Democratic party, as they had in 1884 when many Democrats were disaffected by the Bourbons' railroad-regulation and low-tariff policies. Those most upset at the nomination of Buchanan were merchants and professional men who had supported Jere Baxter, so the Republicans nominated Lewis T. Baxter, who was said to be Jere's kinsman and who was a member of the same Nashville real estate firm. The *Weekly Toiler* commented that the Republicans had not chosen an Allianceman, but had gone the "opposite course," as truly they had. L. T. Baxter, son of a federal circuit judge, had been educated in the North and in Europe, had married well, and was

41. Memphis *Appeal,* July 4, August 6, 29, September 1, 2, October 1, 1890; Bolivar *Bulletin,* August 8, 1890; Charlotte *Dickson County Press,* quoted in Knoxville *Journal,* September 11, 1890, and in Nashville *Banner,* October 27, 1890; McMinnville *New Era,* quoted in Sparta *Expositor,* August 8, 1890; Nashville *American,* August 10, 1890; Nashville *Herald,* September 3, 1890.

the new president of the Nashville Commercial Club. The Democratic Nashville *Herald* called him "a well informed, active, progressive business man, a man of intelligence, and capable." The Republican nominee had grounds for his hope that businessmen would see
him as "the safest harbor in the storm." [42]

While trying to seduce town Democrats, the Republicans sought
to hold their usual constituency. Congressman L. C. Houk wrote a
letter to a Republican Alliance official which was published for the
purpose of hurting Buchanan. Houk argued that the GOP was the
best party for farmers, reminding them of the recent Sherman Silver
Purchase Act, and charged that the Alliance was only a subterfuge
to perpetuate Bourbon power. "I think I voice the sentiments of the
Republicans who belong to the Union [i.e. the Alliance], when I say
they will all with hardly an exception vote the straight Republican
ticket next November," said an Allianceman from Anderson
County. "Success to the F. & L. U. while it keeps aloof from politics,
and may God destroy it when it seeks to further the interests of the
democratic party." A black Republican editor of West Tennessee
would have no part of the Alliance. After praising a speech by
L. T. Baxter, the Jackson *Afro-American Sentinel* denounced Buchanan as a Bourbon by day and an Allianceman by night, depending on where he was, "and at all times the meanest specimen of
either." The *Sentinel* stressed Baxter's opposition to the new restrictive election laws, and charged that Buchanan was against the
Republican Lodge election bill because it threatened "[white] supremacy which is only another expression for Democratic rule." [43]
Under such leadership, most black and white Republicans stayed
with their party in 1890.

Lewis Baxter, trying to divide town Democrats from Buchanan,
called non-Alliance Democrats "Alliance negroes" because, he said,

    42. Nashville *Herald,* July 31, 1890; Nashville *American,* August 2, 3, 1890; L. T. Baxter
to J. B. Killebrew, July 6, 1889, in J. B. Killebrew Papers, TSLA; Nashville *Weekly Toiler,*
August 6, 1890; *Who's Who in Tennessee,* 402; Birmingham (Ala.) *News,* quoted in Nashville
Weekly Toiler, August 6, 1890; Nashville *Banner,* January 15, 1890; L. T. Baxter to L. C.
Houk, August 1, 1890, in Houk Papers, Lawson-McGhee Library, Knoxville.
    43. Houk to W. A. Simpson, in Knoxville *Journal,* August 8, 1890; W. J. Clark to Houk,
August 16, 1890, in Houk Papers; Jackson *Afro-American Sentinel,* October 11, 1890. For
the relation of race and the franchise, see Appendix D.

they had no part in the nomination process, but could only vote the party ticket—a comment that reveals much about how Baxter saw the blacks' role in his own party. The Tennessee Republican party in 1890 went on record for the Lodge bill, which provided for federal observation of voter registration and elections where requested by a citizens' petition. Baxter denounced the bill, however, partly because the new Tennessee laws forced him to rely less on black votes and partly because he wanted to attract non-Alliance Democrats. This strategy did not work. The Democratic press called on its party to stand together against the Lodge "force bill" to save the South from a return to "bayonet rule." A non-Alliance Democratic speaker compared the importance of the "force bill" to that of Fort Sumter, because it would put black heels on white necks. Not only did Baxter's stand convince few Democrats; it angered Republicans. William R. Moore, a wealthy Memphis businessman and white Republican leader, read of Baxter's stand on the Lodge bill and fumed, "I do not hesitate to say that he *ought to be* (as he will *certainly* be) *overwhelmingly defeated.*" [44] The "force-bill" issue served to strengthen Democratic party loyalty in 1890 and thus helped keep many non-Alliance Democrats for Buchanan.

Besides Baxter, another candidate hoping to draw middle-class town Democrats was the Reverend D. C. Kelley, nominee of the Prohibition party. A Methodist preacher, Kelley advocated a reformist Gospel far removed from fundamentalism. "This new age," he said in 1886 of a trend he saw in religion, "will be one of practical, earnest preaching, the center of which will be this life and its duties, one great factor of which will be to recognize goodness wherever it has been found, inside or outside the churches, as from God." Kelley offered a blend of religiosity and worldly optimism, expressed in the central progressive ideal of the state as an agent for moral reform. But many agreed with one farmer who feared that "a set of fanatics, and mostly Methodist[s, are] pushing their religion into the world."

44. Nashville *Herald,* September 28, November 1, 1890; Verton M. Queener, "The East Tennessee Republicans in State and Nation, 1870–1900," *Tennessee Historical Quarterly,* II (1943), 104–105; Vincent P. DeSantis, *Republicans Face the Southern Question: The New Departure Years, 1877–1897* (Baltimore, 1959), 198–99; Nashville *Banner,* September 29, 1890; Nashville *American,* July 27, 1890; L. O. W. Brandon to Houk, August 12, 1890, W. R. Moore to Houk, September 29, 1890, in Houk Papers, emphasis original.

This farmer had "no sympathy with any man or set of men who aid indirectly the Radical party," and said he "would have to [be] turned outside in, or inside out, remodeled, upset, capsized, swallowed by a whale & puked up, ground over, and then could not go with these [prohibitionist] folks." Rather than try to reach such voters, Kelley reportedly ridiculed Buchanan for his large family and rustic style of life. He won 27 percent of the vote in urban Davidson County, but elsewhere his support was held to a minimum by three factors: the gulf separating his middle-class attitudes from most voters' rural folkways, his suspension from his Methodist pulpit near the end of the campaign for improperly secular activity, and especially the strength of Democratic party loyalty [45] (see Appendix B, Table 15).

These efforts by Republicans, prohibitionists, and a handful of insurgent Democrats to defeat Buchanan failed. His victory in 1890 resulted from the continuity of voting habits, the organized support of the Alliance, and the discriminatory effect of the new election laws, in that order of importance (see Appendix B, Table 14). The Farmers' Alliance maintained its strong numerical position in the legislature, generally for the same reasons. Fourteen of thirty-three senators-elect and forty-one of ninety-nine new representatives, mostly Democrats, were members of the order.[46] The men of the Alliance won a startling triumph in 1890, but had done nothing, in the legislature or in the Democratic state convention, to indicate how they would use their power.

45. Jackson *West Tennessee Whig,* January 6, 1886; Cartmell Diary, October 4, 1890; Nashville *American,* August 20, 1890; *Tribune Almanac,* 1891, p. 312; Memphis *Appeal,* October 12, 16, 1890.
46. Miller, *Official and Political Manual,* 246–48.

7

The Alliance in
Power

After the Farmers' Alliance displayed such great vigor and unity in the 1890 campaign, its conduct of the state government was lackluster and aimless. Without even such a rudimentary, half-conceived program as the Bourbons had in 1883, the Alliance lost the initiative and soon found itself under attack from the politicians it had displaced. The Alliance had little, if any, record to defend, but its enemies struck on another level. They used symbols to imply that Alliancemen were not true Democrats, or even true southern white men. By the end of 1891 it was clear that the issue was not public policy but access to the power which anti-Alliance Democrats had lost but were poised to regain.

Governor Buchanan's first and easiest problem was the distribution of patronage. He conscientiously sat up till midnight receiving office seekers, then made solid and politically astute choices for his three top appointments. The new superintendent of prisons was Eth B. Wade of Murfreesboro, secretary of both the state Farmers' Alliance and the state Democratic committee, and an old acquaintance of the governor. Wade was no novice in politics, having served as clerk of the Tennessee House of Representatives for several terms and clerk of the Committee on Printing of the lower house of Congress. The second top job in the Buchanan administration, that of commissioner of agriculture, went to D. G. Godwin of Arlington, near Memphis. Godwin was a veteran of the legislature and an Allianceman. For state school superintendent the governor chose W. R. Garrett of Nashville, president of the National Education Association. Even the Nashville *Banner* conceded that the Garrett appointment was an excellent one. The Memphis *Appeal-Avalanche*

155

rated Garrett and Wade "entirely acceptable," and Godwin outstanding.[1] The Alliance regime was off to a smooth, conventional
beginning.

The most lucrative sinecure Buchanan could fill was that of coal-
oil inspector of Nashville, who could hire a deputy to do his work
for a fraction of his own income from inspection fees. This post was
eventually the center of much more controversy than appointments
which had some bearing on the conduct of the state government.
After the Alliance had won the gubernatorial nomination, the anti-
Alliance press granted to John H. McDowell the right to a generous
helping of spoils. Buchanan waited until a week after the legislature
adjourned, probably to maintain by the hope of patronage what little
influence there his office gave him, and then announced that his
foremost lieutenant, the state president of the Alliance and editor
of the *Weekly Toiler,* would be Nashville oil inspector. One Nashville
Democrat merely remarked that McDowell was "one of the best-
known men in the state." Another admitted that Buchanan owed
his office to McDowell, a political "genius," but predicted that his
heretical ideas would bring the governor under suspicion.[2] Indeed
McDowell's prominence proved to be a great source of trouble, as
well as strength, for the Buchanan administration.

The city press had not always been hostile to John McDowell. In
earlier years, when he represented Obion County in the legislature
and championed moral causes from prohibition to virginity to ban-
ning baseball on Sunday, he was criticized mainly for egotism. Of
his ambition there can be little doubt: he ran unsuccessfully for
Senate Speaker in 1885 and for state comptroller in 1889, and may
have wanted to be agriculture commissioner in 1891. But ambition
was a sin easily overlooked by men like A. S. Colyar, whose Nashville *Union* said of McDowell in 1886 that there had been "but few
more reliable and valuable public men" in Tennessee. His effective
leadership of temperance legislators in 1885 moved a group of Nash-

    1. Memphis *Appeal-Avalanche,* January 21, 27, 1891; Nashville *American,* July 29, 1889,
August 13, December 19, 1890, January 27, 1891; Nashville *Banner,* January 27, 1891.
    2. Pulaski *Citizen,* August 14, 1890; Nashville *Banner,* February 4, April 7, 1891; Nash-
ville *American,* April 7, 1891.

ville ladies to present him with a silver tea service.[3] The same personal qualities which had drawn forth such gratitude would bring McDowell under the most severe public attack any Tennessee politician had suffered since the days of Governor W. G. Brownlow.

Other Buchanan appointments did not fall to Alliancemen like Wade, Godwin, and McDowell. When a district attorney-generalship became vacant in West Tennessee, the governor named a two-term legislative veteran and former mayor of Trenton. Thomas M. McConnell was a Chattanooga politician who had fought Bob Taylor and had helped Buchanan get his nomination. Now he was handsomely repaid by appointment as chancellor. The governor was playing the old game, trying to satisfy friendly politicians without causing their jealous rivals to turn against him. When the Memphis chancellorship became vacant, Buchanan appointed a leading attorney, the father of defeated gubernatorial candidate W. L. Clapp. The younger Clapp was chosen for the three-man Shelby County Taxing District board, which was equivalent to a city council for Memphis. For oil inspector there Buchanan picked Andrew J. Harris, nephew of the Bourbon senator and a director of the Mercantile Bank of Memphis. The president of the Third Congressional District Alliance became Chattanooga oil inspector. He was the only Farmers' Alliance member among these men, but was also a former Hamilton County judge, and was recommended to Buchanan by the president of a mining company and by publisher A. S. Ochs.[4] Governor Buchanan clearly demonstrated a pragmatic patronage policy, designed to build an independent base for his administration but with more regard for party harmony than for Alliance membership or even agricultural interests. The men around Buchanan found in his

3. Nashville *American,* January 10, March 1, 21, 1885, January 7, 1887; Nashville *Weekly Toiler,* January 16, 1889; Knoxville *Journal,* November 22, 1890; Nashville *Union,* October 19, 1886.

4. C. E. Powell to R. L. Taylor, April 23, 1887, Robert Burrows to Taylor, March 9, 1888, E. Overton to Taylor, May 25, 1888, T. M. McConnell to Buchanan, July 3, 1891, W. G. M. Thomas to Buchanan, June 20, 1891, J. B. Ragon to Buchanan, June 20, 1891, M. H. Clift to Buchanan, January 31, 1891, A. S. Ochs to Buchanan, February 7, 1891, all in CGO, TSLA; Nashville *Banner,* September 14, 1891; Memphis *Appeal-Avalanche,* May 12, August 30, 1891, and quoted in Nashville *Banner,* March 24, 1891; *Who's Who in Tennessee,* 50, 316; Nashville *American,* October 14, 1886, July 15, 1890.

victory a chance to rise in the familiar game of politics, but no one thought to change the rules.

In view of Buchanan's lack of support among urban newspapers before his nomination, his press relations went quite smoothly for the first several weeks of his term. The Nashville *Banner,* which had hoped openly for his defeat in November, praised the governor's legislative message for supporting schools and a World's Fair exhibit. The Nashville *American* lauded his first veto, which blocked a bill granting money to a county for railroad construction. At the end of March a Memphis paper, quite content with Buchanan, stated: "So far as he has gone in his public acts, [his administration] is bound to be one of which the whole people will be proud. He has laboriously and intelligently addressed himself to his executive duties, won respect and made friends every day since his inauguration." [5] Another Memphis newspaper complained that "Gov. Buchanan [was] putting Alliance men in all the good offices," but praised the chief of them, J. H. McDowell, as a man with a "clean, straight democratic record." The only direct conflict with the press in these early weeks came when Buchanan physically expelled from his hotel room a Chattanooga *Times* reporter who Buchanan believed had misrepresented his campaign. [6]

The Alliance governor offered no proposals for social reform. He optimistically urged the legislature to do its duty: "In whatever will make our fields more productive, our manufactures more numerous, our business more prosperous, the investment of our capital more secure, the rewards of labor more remunerative and just; in whatever will lighten and equalize the burdens of taxation, make stronger the State Government, benefit and elevate the masses of the people, you will have my hearty sympathy and best efforts." [7] Buchanan did not really think the legislature should do "whatever" it could for the general welfare, for he believed that the "Jeffersonian non-interference theory of government is the wisest, leaving people to be happy

5. Nashville *Banner,* February 12, 1891; Nashville *American,* March 1, 1891; Memphis *Commercial,* quoted in Nashville *Banner,* March 31, 1891.
6. Memphis *Appeal-Avalanche,* January 11, April 29, 30, 1891; Nashville *American,* January 11, 1891.
7. White (ed.), *Messages,* VII, 372.

.

in their own way without undertaking to do for them what they can do better for themselves." Corporations, as well as government, Buchanan declared, should be prevented from expanding into the proper sphere of "individual effort and endeavor." The governor could report that Tennessee had "on the whole a good code of laws"; one of the few changes he asked was an increase in funds for the agricultural commissioner to hold farmers' workshops around the state. The only specific proposal Buchanan had for loosening what he called the "relentless grasp" of the "merciless tyrant" monopoly was a naïve suggestion that officers of corporations in Tennessee solemnly swear that they were not thinking about forming trusts to fix prices. He felt that his and the legislature's most important responsibility was to act unselfishly, conscientiously, and efficiently, "to guide 'the old ship of State' on toward her final and glorious destination." [8] Governor Buchanan left the location of that last harbor to the legislators' imagination.

Such was the conservatism the Farmers' Alliance leader urged upon the legislature. As a Democrat and an Allianceman, Buchanan should have gotten along well with the body, which contained more Democrats than any previous Tennessee General Assembly, and more Alliance members than the preceding one. The high number of Democrats resulted from the election of a few Alliance Democrats in counties with usual small Republican majorities, and probably from the effect of the new election laws in Knox County, as well as from the national Democratic tide of 1890. But the strong Democratic caucus nominated no Alliancemen for important offices. During the flu season the Nashville *Banner* punned that House Clerk C. W. Crockett had the Alliance "grip." Otherwise, Alliance office seekers met the fate of J. M. Crews, a veteran of the 1871 and 1889 legislatures, whose friends claimed that he had been denied renomination in 1890 as senator from Shelby County because he was an Allianceman. Crews then tried unsuccessfully for Congress and for the Memphis oil inspectorship before challenging the incumbent state comptroller in the Democratic caucus, where all his twenty votes except two were from Alliancemen or his home county. Many

8. *Ibid.*, 368, 369, 372, 382, 385, 387.

Alliancemen were among the sixty-seven voting for the incumbent.[9] Democratic Alliancemen in 1891, as in 1889, cooperated whole-heartedly with their party caucus, but did not try to control it. The formation of an Alliance subcaucus was prevented by the feeling of most Alliance legislators that they were Democrats first and Alliancemen second. The *Weekly Toiler* flayed Senator A. H. Woodlee of Grundy County for deserting a fellow Alliance senator in the caucus race for Speaker, and charged that Woodlee had traded his vote for a job for his brother-in-law. The Nashville dailies readily opened their columns to Senator Woodlee, who answered *Toiler* editor McDowell with a sarcastic personal attack. The senator loftily announced that he was a Democrat and would not take the dictation of the Alliance or of certain "selfish and designing men" who had thought since Buchanan's election that the Alliance should run the state, and who were "doing more to break up the Alliance and the Democratic party than all else combined."[10] Another Democratic legislator who put his party above his Alliance membership was James Wood Jones of Hardeman County. During the summer of 1890 the state treasurer wrote Jones and urged him to run for reelection:

> I expect a large number of Alliance men in the next House and will need some good, true, and capable friends to watch my interests. I don't mean that they would feel necessarily antagonistic to me, but some designing fellow who would use the order to further his personal interests might try to work up an opposition to me on the ground that he was an Alliance man and I am not. . . . I do not want to make the impression that I am expecting any special opposition from the Alliance for this of course would be inviting opposition and would be [to] get it.[11]

Allianceman Jones promised to help.[12] He and Woodlee would stay in the Alliance only as long as it did not undermine the Democratic party.

9. Miller, *Official and Political Manual,* 246–48; Nashville *Banner,* January 7, 9, 1891; Wheel #947, Shelby County, to J. P. Buchanan (n.d. [1890]), in CGO, TSLA; Knoxville *Journal,* July 28, 1890; Nashville *American,* January 24, 1891.

10. Nashville *Banner,* January 14, 15, 1891; Nashville *American,* January 15, 1891.

11. M. F. House to J. W. Jones, July 9, 1890, in Jones Family Papers, TLSA. The treasurer of Tennessee was elected by the legislature.

12. Nashville *American,* September 14, 1891; House to Jones, July 27, 1890, in Jones Family Papers.

Roll-call votes which divided Democrats in the 1891 legislature did not separate Alliancemen from other members. When it became necessary to elect a temporary Speaker, one Allianceman and four other Democrats tried for the position. The Alliance member received the votes of two Alliance Democrats, one Alliance Republican, and five others. On the second ballot the Allianceman and the two other minor candidates withdrew, leaving John A. Tipton, a Covington lawyer, and A. G. Hall of Nashville. The Democrats split roughly by region, and Hall won because nearly all Republicans voted for him. Alliance Democrats divided twenty-three to thirteen for Tipton.[13]

If Alliancemen showed only a moderate tendency to prefer a small-town lawyer to an urban one, they were more closely divided over a railroad-regulation bill introduced by Tipton and opposed by Hall. It was a Democrat from Eagle Creek in Overton County, listed as a "drummer" and a non-Allianceman, who explained his vote to prevent railroad discrimination by citing "the fact that under the fostering protection of our Federal Government we are to-day confronted by a monied aristocracy whose growth has been phenomenal and unparalleled in the history of governments." Alliance Democrats voted against the Tipton bill, seventeen to twenty-two, a division close to a random distribution.[14] According to the familiar pattern, Democrats were divided and the united Republicans killed the bill. A comparison of this roll-call vote to the Speaker's election reveals that Alliance Democrats, unlike other legislators, failed to conceive of a relationship between the two questions. Not only did the Alliance legislators fail to cohere; they divided in ways of which the logic, if any, remains obscure.

Railroad regulation took so much of the Senate's attention that a newspaper commented that "a majority of its debates are founded on that subject." Van Leer Polk of Maury County and Flournoy Rivers of Giles, neither one a friend of the Alliance, introduced similar bills to reestablish a railroad commission. Their most promi-

13. *House Journal,* 1891, pp. 295–96. Excluding courtesy votes by candidates, Democrats voted by region: for Tipton, West 19, Middle 15, and East 2; for Hall, West 4, Middle 22, and East 3.
14. Miller, *Official and Political Manual,* 247; *House Journal,* 1891, pp. 247, 248 (quote).

Table 22
VOTES ON TEMPORARY SPEAKER (SECOND BALLOT)
AND ON TIPTON BILL FOR RAILROAD REGULATION, 1891
HOUSE OF REPRESENTATIVES [15]

Alliance Democrats

| | | Temporary Speaker | |
		Tipton	Hall
Tipton bill	yes	8	7
	no	12	6

$$\phi = -.14 *$$

Republicans and non-Alliance Democrats

| | | Temporary Speaker | |
		Tipton	Hall
Tipton bill	yes	9	5
	no	3	20

$$\phi = +.53 *$$

* For explanation of ϕ (phi), see Appendix A.

nent public supporters, in contrast to the regulation movement of 1883, were not Bourbon types but businessmen, led by the head of the Nashville streetcar line. A legislative committee heard him and Duncan B. Cooper argue against railroader E. B. Stahlman, who testified that rate discrimination was good for the public. Discussion at a special meeting of the Nashville Commercial Club pointed to a clash between the trolley company and the Louisville and Nashville Railroad. After much debate, the club rejected the idea of regulation.[16] In the Senate, Rivers' bill was then defeated by a vote of nine to nineteen. Alliancemen in the Senate were more inclined to oppose railroad regulation than their fellow Alliancemen in the House, and more than non-Alliancemen in the Senate.

In 1896 a Democratic editor who favored railroad regulation had occasion to denounce E. B. Stahlman, and he alleged that the "Farmers Alliance Legislature" of 1891 had been a prime example of Stahlman's insidious lobbying activity. "The farmers had elected

15. *House Journal,* 1891, pp. 247, 296.
16. Nashville *American,* January 20, 29, February 10, 11, March 17, 1891, March 11, 1892; Nashville *Banner,* February 16, 1891.

Table 23
PARTY, ALLIANCE, AND OCCUPATIONAL BREAKDOWN OF VOTE
ON RIVERS RAILROAD COMMISSION BILL, AND ON BILL
TO PREVENT JUDGES WHO RODE ON FREE PASSES FROM
HEARING CASES INVOLVING RAILROADS; 1891 SENATE [17]

	Rivers Bill		Anti-free-pass Bill	
	Yes	No	Yes	No
Democrats	8	12	9	11
Republicans	1	7	3	4
Alliance	2	9	3	7
Non-Alliance	7	10	9	8
Farmers	3	8	5	5
Lawyers	6	6	6	5
Merchants and Professionals	0	5	1	5

John P. Buchanan governor, and overwhelmingly controlled the Legislature," recalled the editor.

> It was loudly heralded by the Legislature that every trust and corporation in the State would be torn up, root and branch. . . . [M]embers piled in bill after bill about regulating the railroads and curbing the power of corporations.
> There were forty-two bills against railroads alone, and but one of them passed. That one was to provide Jim Crow cars for negroes, and Stahlman had to go on the floor and request members to vote for that bill.[18]

This editor not only fallaciously equated Alliance numbers with control, but was mistaken in implying a direct link between the Alliance and the railroad bills. Of thirty-nine bills evidently concerning railroads in some way, two-thirds were introduced by non-Alliancemen. At the close of the 1891 session, senators rose to excoriate Stahlman and other lobbyists in acid terms like "contemptible crawling creature," but the one Allianceman who spoke out was the mildest of the group.[19] If the Tennessee Farmers' Alliance had any influence in the area of railroad regulation, it was on the side of the railroads.

17. *Senate Journal,* 1891, pp. 364, 367; Miller, *Official and Political Manual,* 246.
18. Nashville *Sun,* June 18, 1896.
19. *House Journal,* 1891, pp. 504–26; *Senate Journal,* 1891, pp. 501–13; Nashville *American,* March 31, 1891.

Another hot issue in the 1891 legislature was a bill singling out mills and factories in towns with populations of over fifty thousand for higher taxation, which was quickly labeled the "gouge" bill by its foes. Its chief advocate was a Democrat from Williamson County who was a farmer but whom the Alliance had opposed for election because he had refused to endorse their principles. His strongest opponent in committee was a Memphis lawyer. Alliance spokesmen took pains to dissociate their organization from the measure. "The Allen-Akin revenue bill has been dubbed the 'anti-enterprise bill' by the Banner," remarked the *Weekly Toiler.* "A very good name, as it would have driven cotton factories and flour mills out of the State instead of encouraging capital to build them." After the legislature adjourned, five Alliance senators published a statement disclaiming Alliance responsibility for the "gouge" bill, and pointing out that two of its sponsors were strongly against the organization.[20] The Alliance did not try to punish industry any more than railroads.

During its regular session the 1891 legislature enacted only two important laws. The first, mentioned in the 1896 editorial quoted above, required railroads to provide separate cars for the two races. The lopsided vote in the House (seventy-one to seven, with six Republicans and a Knoxville Democratic Union veteran in the minority) prevents contrast of Alliance and non-Alliance attitudes, as does the Senate vote (twenty-one to eight, an all-Republican minority) for a similar Jim Crow bill. When the new law went into effect during the summer of 1891, the Nashville *Banner,* out of solicitude for the railroads rather than for their segregated passengers, printed an angry, articulate letter from two black men. They said the colored section on Louisville and Nashville trains was divided by a partition from the white smoking area, so that they and their families had to run a gauntlet of smoke and tobacco juice (and insults, perhaps) when boarding a train. The two men said they only demanded equal treatment and declared, "The signs of the times unmistakably show that unless public sentiment will cry down such injustice, the future of the two races will be (let us put it mildly)

20. Nashville *American,* March 24, 1891; Nashville *Banner,* March 21, 25, April 4, 1891; Knoxville *Journal,* September 11, 1890; Miller, *Official and Political Manual,* 247.

anything but peaceful."[21] Alliancemen and other Democrats were equally deaf to this warning.

The other notable law passed during the 1891 regular session caused a minor crisis two years later, after the state supreme court upheld its constitutionality. Introduced by a Republican of Union County who was not an Allianceman, the bill required all corporations doing business in Tennessee to file their charters with the secretary of state. The measure went through the House with only one member, a Democratic Allianceman, voting against it, and then was passed in the Senate with twenty votes in favor and two Republicans and three Democratic Alliance members opposing it. By 1893 the enemies of the Alliance had taken control of the state government, but they stood firm against out-of-state corporations which feared they would be subject to Tennessee taxation if they let the state have their charters. Despite threats by insurance companies that they could hurt Tennessee's economy, Governor Peter Turney refused to call the legislature into extra session to repeal the law, and the companies thereupon began complying with the statute by filing their charters. Thus, ironically, the one controversial piece of legislation aimed at "monopoly" during the height of the power of the Farmers' Alliance was sponsored by a nonmember, was passed over some Alliance opposition, and was eventually enforced by the man who deposed the Alliance governor from office.[22]

The farmers' revolt of the 1890s is often described as a major factor in undermining the laissez-faire theory, and in promoting the idea that government should be an agency for the people's welfare. The farmers' own words can be used to support this interpretation: "We believe that the power of government—in other words, of the

21. *House Journal,* 1891, pp. 271, 330; *Senate Journal,* 1891, pp. 332, 412; *Nashville Banner,* June 12, 1891.

22. Memphis *Commercial,* June 13, 29, July 3, 6, 19, 1893. House Bill 350, "To Prohibit Trusts in Restraint of Trade," has been given as an example of Alliance legislation, in Robison, *Bob Taylor,* 153, and in S. J. Folmsbee, R. E. Corlew, and E. L. Mitchell, *Tennessee: A Short History* (Knoxville, 1969), 399–400. But this bill was passed in the House by a vote of eighty-two to three, and in the Senate by twenty-nine to one. It could hardly have been seen by corporations as a threat. Its sponsor, Representative Story of White County, had been a sky-blue in 1882 and had opposed Buchanan's nomination in 1890. *House Journal,* 1891, pp. 327–28, 330, 514; *Senate Journal,* 1891, pp. 412, 471; S. E. Cunningham to Eth Wade, April 28, 1891, in CGO, TSLA.

people—should be expanded (as in the case of the postal service) as rapidly and as far as the good sense of an intelligent people and the teachings of experience shall justify, to the end that oppression, injustice, and poverty shall eventually cease in the land." [23] It may well be that such rhetoric of national platforms did weaken laissez-faire ideas. But if welfare-state liberalism was sprouting in national Populist conventions, it was not necessarily rooted in the rank-and-file membership. In Tennessee, neither Governor Buchanan nor the Alliancemen in the legislature tried to expand the stunted power of the state government.

During the first months of Buchanan's term, criticism of him and of the Alliance legislature was minimal. Conflict, when it did come, arose not over public policy but from the charge that the Alliance was bound to divide or betray the Democratic party. Some Democrats feared that the Alliance could be used by third-party organizers as a base without itself becoming officially involved. The Ocala meeting of the southern Alliance, in December, 1890, stirred a premonitory fluttering in the Democratic press, especially when Eth Wade was reported as having put the Ocala platform over party loyalty (Wade denied the report).[24] The Alliance was attacked both for working within and for working against the Democratic party, a reflection of the increasing confusion of the Alliance itself.

A key symbol for both sides in the approaching clash was the Alliance subtreasury plan. The Democratic press assailed it on the muddy theoretical ground that it was "paternal and communistic" or "nearly in accord with the Republican idea of paternal government," that it tried to cure the evil of governmental favoritism to manufacturing with favoritism to agriculture. Alliance spokesmen answered that the general-welfare clause of the Constitution covered their plan, that it would meet the needs of the people and was the best thing in sight, and that it would be much cheaper than its enemies claimed. But all this was really beside the point. "[T]he newspapers are discussing the subtreasury scheme," the Memphis

23. "National People's Party Platform of 1892," in Tindall (ed.), *Populist Reader,* 92.

24. Memphis *Appeal-Avalanche,* December 5, 18, 1890; Nashville *American,* December 4, 6, 7, 17, 19, 20, 1890; Nashville *Banner,* December 3, 6, 15, 17, 1890; Jacksonville *Florida Times-Union,* December 6, 1890.

Commercial noted frankly, "and are almost without exception condemning it as inimical to the interests of the [Democratic] party and opposed to its success next year." The Alliance was organizing to elect candidates favorable to the subtreasury, but since the Tennessee Democratic party presumably could not endorse the plan, and since the new third party would do so, a bolt from the Democracy seemed imminent. On the other hand, the Nashville *Herald* ominously revealed strange rumors that the Alliance planned to take over the next Democratic state convention, put the subtreasury in the platform, and then excommunicate its enemies from the party. The *Weekly Toiler* reasoned dangerously that if a Democratic convention endorsed the subtreasury, no one could call it un-Democratic. All those not on the Alliance side were its enemies, the *Toiler* threatened; the "wishy-washy, milk and cider fellows . . . will have to be dumped on the trash pile of worthlessness." [25] At issue was not the wisdom of the subtreasury system, but the political implications of advocating it.

In the middle of May the old Democratic leadership fired an echoing fusillade at the subtreasury. Congressman-elect Josiah Patterson issued a sweeping statement arguing that it would cost too much, destroy a stable currency, fail to give help to those who needed it, contribute to wicked Republican centralization of power, and disrupt the Solid South. Patterson was joined in the following few weeks by three other leading Bourbons including United States Senator W. B. Bate, and by Bob Taylor and other prominent non-Bourbons. Not all antisubtreasury arguments were as rational as those of Colonel Patterson. State Senator Flournoy Rivers explained that the plan had originated when Pharoah and Joseph locked up the wheat and made the farmers work on the pyramids. A former state senator revealed that the ancient Romans had tried the subtreasury and had proven its impracticality for all time. If the subtreasury was constitutional, Congressman Benton McMillin wondered, why had Thomas Jefferson not thought of it? Senator Isham Harris, never the

---

25. Nashville *American,* May 5, 29, 1891; Nashville *Banner,* November 11, 1890; Memphis *Commercial,* May 6, 16, 1891; Memphis *Appeal-Avalanche,* May 6, 16, 1891; Nashville *Weekly Toiler,* May 13, June 3, 1891; Nashville *Herald,* May 3, 1891; Washington *National Economist,* April 11, 1891.

first to speak out in a controversy, waited until October and then announced that he was "unalterably opposed" to the subtreasury as "class legislation[,] which is the most vicious and unjust of any that a government could adopt." [26] Harris left the dirty work to local politicos and editors of small weekly newspapers, like the one which said, "If the thing [the subtreasury] went into practice . . . low-down white Republicans and negroes would be appointed to grade, value, and have charge of the farmer's grain deposited in the warehouse. . . . The average Republican official loves to humiliate the southern white people by appointing, in many instances, negroes and the sorriest specimens of white men in their party to many of the offices in the South." [27] Against such a propaganda barrage the Alliance leaders could muster only a handful of small newspapers and one first-rate orator, John H. McDowell.

The choice of the subtreasury as a symbol of Alliance heterodoxy was South-wide and not determined by conditions unique to Tennessee. In fact, the Tennessee Alliance leadership was very conservative on the issue: at Ocala the state delegation voted one to three against the plan, while the total vote was seventy-nine to ten in favor. The Tennesseeans explained that they would have voted for the original plan, which called for loans on "approved security," without mention of commodities. At the abortive organizational meeting of an antisubtreasury Alliance in St. Louis in the fall of 1891, the Tennesseeans present included six legislators and Superintendent of Prisons Eth Wade, who was deposed as state Alliance secretary for his apostasy. Another St. Louis delegate, prominent early in the Rutherford County Wheel, was one of the wealthiest citizens of Buchanan's home county.[28] Alliancemen who feared jeopardizing their careers in the Democratic party and losing their local social status bowed to the prescribed test of party orthodoxy. Thus the subtreasury issue hurt the Alliance by decimating its leadership.

26. Memphis *Appeal-Avalanche,* November 9, 1890, May 13, 30, June 21, October 4 (quote), 1891; Nashville *American,* June 12, 15, 22, August 1, 10, 1891; Nashville *Banner,* June 5, 1891; Nashville *Weekly Toiler,* October 21, 1891.

27. Sparta *Expositor,* November 6, 1891.

28. Woodward, *Origins of the New South,* 239; Washington *National Economist,* January 3, 1891; Nashville *American,* August 25, September 15, 1891; Nashville *Weekly Toiler,* January 30, 1889; Rutherford County tax books, 1889, 1890, film, TSLA.

An important part of the campaign to discredit the Farmers' Alliance in 1891 was a powerful assault on its president, J. H. McDowell. At the end of March came a hint of what was in store for him. "A South Pittsburg paper dares to declare that Brother McDowell was a Republican in Arkansas," the Nashville *Banner* noted tersely. A few days later New South Democrat J. W. Sparks published a letter saying that he disagreed with McDowell on the subtreasury, but felt bound to say that the charge that he had been a Republican in Arkansas was entirely false. Like Buchanan, Sparks was a Rutherford County man, and it is easy to imagine that the governor prompted Sparks's letter. But the rumor would not be stamped out—two newspapers brought it up again in June.[29]

Meanwhile, when McDowell received his sinecure as Nashville coal-oil inspector and was thereby freed to travel around, his foes began censuring his promotion of congressional-district Alliances, condemning his advocacy of the subtreasury, and ridiculing his ambition. The Alliance president was especially criticized after he went to Mississippi to debate United States Senator J. Z. George.[30] E. W. Carmack of the Nashville *American* turned his talent for acid sarcasm against McDowell's self-denied plan to be elected to the Senate. "We know that God Almighty never gave him that mass of storm-stricken and insurrectionary whiskers and made him look like a weather-beaten tintype of Senator Peffer for nothing. . . . United States Senator McDowell, noble knight of the horny hand and stone-bruised heel, we, the played-out Bourbon, moss-back, upper-case Democrats salute thee." [31] At the end of May the *American,* the state's leading partisan Democratic newspaper, came under the control of Duncan B. Cooper, and prepared to attack McDowell with all its might.

Near the end of June the *American* appeared on the streets of Nashville bearing an extraordinarily long story which claimed to expose McDowell's past. A reporter who had gone to Desha County,

29. Nashville *Banner,* March 31, 1891; Nashville *American,* April 12, 1891; Memphis *Public Ledger,* quoted in Nashville *Banner,* June 23, 1891.

30. Nashville *American,* April 8, 1891; Nashville *Banner,* April 8, 1891; Memphis *Appeal-Avalanche,* May 6, 1891.

31. Nashville *American,* April 9, 1891. William A. Peffer was a Populist U.S. senator from Kansas.

Arkansas, on the Mississippi River south of Memphis, wrote that McDowell had lived there for seven years during Reconstruction. In 1873 he deserted the Democratic party to run for justice of the peace with the support of the Radical Loyal League, and during his campaign McDowell actually sat down and ate dinner with Negroes. Once elected, continued the *American* article, he greatly increased the yield of his office in fees, then moved up to be deputy under a black Republican county clerk. McDowell's activities made him the most unpopular man in the county by 1876, so that when he ran for county clerk with Radical support, many whites voted for his victorious black opponent. Beaten, forsaken, and disliked by both races, McDowell returned to Tennessee in 1877. The *American* followed this article with several signed statements by Arkansas people witnessing to the truth of the report. Other newspapers responded very gravely and called on the Alliance leader for an answer.[32]

McDowell, who was in Mississippi debating "Private" John Allen, a prominent Democrat, fired off a letter to Memphis flatly denying the *American*'s charges. "It is a conspiracy," McDowell declared, "on the part of the Nashville *American* and its political backers to accomplish, by falsehood and slander, what they could not do by argument—that is, to ruin me politically because I have the courage to follow my convictions and advocate the demands of the farmers' alliance."[33] Editor Carmack contemptuously dismissed the conspiracy charge, began goading McDowell repeatedly to sue the *American* for libel, and quoted eleven other Tennessee newspapers which asked the Alliance leader to defend himself. The Nashville *Banner* revealed that during the 1880s antiprohibitionists had dug into McDowell's past but had filed away their findings. J. W. Sparks, McDowell's former defender, now let it be known that he was having second thoughts.[34] McDowell's public life was in mortal peril.

The Alliance leader canceled his speechmaking and hurried to Arkansas to prepare his defense. Born in Gibson County, Tennessee,

32. *Ibid.,* June 25, 1891; Nashville *Banner,* June 25, 1891; Memphis *Appeal-Avalanche,* June 25, 1891.
33. Memphis *Appeal-Avalanche,* June 26, 1891.
34. *Ibid.,* July 3, 1891; Nashville *American,* June 26, 28, 29, 1891; Nashville *Banner,* July 2, 1891.

around 1845, he had attended school between harvesting and sowing but dropped out to fight for the South. After the war he rented land for five or six years until he had saved anough to buy land in Desha County, where he raised mainly cotton for seven years. In Arkansas he joined the Grange and became an early member of the Wheel after moving to a farm in Obion County, Tennessee. His older brother was able to finish college and law school, establish a practice in Memphis, and win an appointment to the chancery bench from Redeemer Governor Porter. A state senator in 1889, W. W. McDowell was praised by the New South Chattanooga *Times* as "one of the ablest jurists in the state." He had connections with some of the old Whigs and sky-blues of Memphis.[35] John, however, did not put down such roots anywhere.

On July 13, about three weeks after the Nashville *American* aired its charges against him, McDowell published his defense in two other newspapers. In length, thoroughness, and documentation, his answer was at least as impressive as the *American* article, and McDowell lost no time in getting to what he considered the most serious of the accusations. "Any man or newspaper has the right to sift or bring to public view the official or public record of any public man," he admitted, "but to attempt upon the statement of one negro in Arkansas to degrade me and my family socially by charging that I socially affiliated with and eat with negroes was the most dishonorable and most ungentlemanly course I have known pursued by white men who claim to possess principles or sense of honor." In order to prove that it was no crime to have been a Republican, he cited the cases of prominent Democrats in Tennessee and elsewhere with party irregularities in their pasts. The whole purpose of the "conspiracy" of the *American,* Josiah Patterson, and others, McDowell explained, was to weaken the Alliance by ruining him. His own defense was followed by fifty-one statements by Arkansas people, many of them sworn or notarized. One after another, they maintained that McDowell had been known as a temperance man, that he had not been

35. Nashville *Banner,* October 11, 1884, March 6, 1890; *Who's Who in Tennessee,* 559; Morgan, *History of the Wheel and Alliance,* 268–70; Miller, *Official and Political Manual,* 186; Chattanooga *Times,* quoted in Nashville *Weekly Toiler,* June 25, 1890; W. W. McDowell to Porter, September 19, 1877, in CGO, TSLA.

a Republican or Loyal Leaguer (thus raising the question of why McDowell tried to excuse party irregularity), that several of the *American*'s supporting statements were distorted before publication and one of them was by a man guilty of miscegenation, that Mc-Dowell had always been a strong Democrat, that he had built a Baptist church himself, and so forth. Tennessee Ninth District Congressman Rice A. Pierce, the chairman of the Obion County court, and six other Obion County officials affirmed that McDowell had always been a Democrat and a true gentleman.[36]

Carmack promised a reply in good time, contenting himself for the present with muttering that McDowell's friends were "hoodlums and hog thieves." The *Weekly Toiler,* of course, congratulated McDowell on his "complete vindication." It was all a "conspiracy," explained the *Toiler,* of "scheming politicians," especially Josiah Patterson. Among Alliancemen, McDowell was acquitted by election in August to another term as their state president, and his refutation was widely accepted as satisfactory. But Carmack's smear was hard to forget: months later McDowell was still referred to in the press as the "Arkansas rascallion," "the odiferous coon leader," and "greasy Johnny." [37]

Shortly after McDowell's reply to the *American,* public attention was distracted by an upheaval at the Briceville coal mine, the first of a series of explosions from the mining district of the Cumberland Mountains. Some of the mines leased convicts from the state and maintained them at a cost of about forty cents per day per prisoner, which cut the general wage levels and angered free miners. In February, 1891, a Nashville newspaper called the lease system "human slavery," an apt description since 80 percent of the prisoners in the mines were black. The remarkably patient and self-disciplined free workers succeeded in embarrassing the weak state government and, by 1896, in ending the convict-lease system.[38]

36. Nashville *Banner,* July 13, 1891; Memphis *Appeal-Avalanche,* July 14, 1891.

37. Nashville *American,* July 14, 1891, February 13, 14, 1892; Nashville *Banner,* July 14, 1891; Knoxville *Journal,* July 15, 16, August 15, 1891; Memphis *Appeal-Avalanche,* July 14, 1891; Memphis *Scimitar,* Memphis *Commercial,* Memphis *Public Ledger,* Chattanooga *News,* Nashville *Weekly Toiler,* quoted in Nashville *Banner,* July 15, 1891; Nashville *Herald,* February 1, 1892.

38. Nashville *American,* September 9, 1891; *Journal of the Knights of Labor* (Philadelphia), August 20, 1891; "Report of the Warden, Superintendent, and Other Officers of the Tennessee Penitentiary," in *House Journal Appendix,* 1889, p. 119; Davis, "Arthur S. Colyar,"

In July, 1891, the trouble started when the Briceville mine managers brought in convicts to tear down strikers' homes and build a stockade for a large number of convicts to replace the free workers. Over three hundred armed miners promptly put the convicts and their guards on a train for Knoxville. Governor Buchanan called out five companies of the state militia and personally took the prisoners back to the mine, where he explained that he had to uphold the law, however unjust. His state labor commissioner met with the miners and helped keep them quiet, but the militia grew nervous as the workers received reinforcements. On July 20 several hundred armed miners, some from as far away as Kentucky, forced the militia to take the prisoners back to Knoxville again, then proceeded to a second mine and removed its convicts too. Five hundred more state troops rushed to East Tennessee, but a possible serious clash was averted when Buchanan agreed with the miners that if the convicts could return to the mines for sixty days, the militia would leave and the legislature would meet in extra session to consider ending the lease. This time Buchanan took the convicts back to the mines without troops, meeting no resistance. He was praised for firmness and courage, and demonstrated his sympathy with the miners by an unsuccessful attempt to take convict labor away from Briceville on a legal technicality.[39] A solution now depended on the legislature.

The state Farmers' Alliance convention, in August, 1891, proclaimed that the convicts should be worked on the roads, away from competition with free labor, and that the convict lease should not be renewed at its expiration. When the legislature met in September, however, the Alliance members helped outvote the prolabor Republicans. The toothless Cochran resolution was a cheap way of going on record for reform. On more substantive matters the Alliance Democrats voted to retain the existing lease and to strengthen law and order. Only three Democratic Alliancemen voted for their own organization's compromise position of respecting the lease contract

317; Nashville *Banner,* February 5, 1891 (quote). For a summary of the report of state officials on the strike, and of the Knoxville *Journal* account, see A. C. Hutson, Jr., "The Coal Miners' Insurrections of 1891 in Anderson County, Tennessee," *East Tennessee Historical Society's Publications,* VII (1935), 103–21.

39. Nashville *American,* July 16–24, August 14, 1891; Hutson, "Coal Miners' Insurrection," 106–107, 109, 114, 115; Memphis *Appeal-Avalanche,* July 26, 29, 1891; Nashville *Banner,* July 30, 1891; Knoxville *Journal,* July 25, August 14, 1891.

but taking the convicts out of the mines.[40] The important results of
the extra session were stronger militia laws, disillusionment among
the miners, and the breakdown of Buchanan's compromise.

Table 24
VOTES ON THREE ROLL CALLS,
1891 EXTRA SESSION, HOUSE OF REPRESENTATIVES,
CONCERNING MINE CRISIS, TABULATED BY PARTY AND
(FOR DEMOCRATS) ALLIANCE MEMBERSHIP [41]

1. Cochran resolution, expressing "the wish of the General Assembly that the State
never again lease its convicts at the expiration of the present lease contract."

	Yes	No
Democrats	31	36
Alliancemen	20	17
Others	11	19
Republicans	19	0

2. Davis bill, to abrogate the convict lease immediately.

	To Table	Not to Table
Democrats	58	8
Alliancemen	31	4
Others	27	4
Republicans	0	20

3. Senate bill 25, "to give the Governor more power over the military."

	Yes	No
Democrats	70	3
Alliancemen	40	1
Others	30	2
Republicans	0	16

The workers' negotiating committee soon resigned, and at the
beginning of November nearly six hundred convicts from the Anderson County mines were released rather than sent to Knoxville under
guard as before. The helplessly weak state government could only
offer a reward and ask the local sheriff to capture the escapees. By
January, 1892, the mine at Briceville, where the crisis had begun,

40. Memphis *Appeal-Avalanche,* August 13, 1891; *House Journal,* 1891 extra session, p.
109.

41. *House Journal,* 1891 extra session, pp. 61–62, 119, 95.

had decided not to use prisoners after all, but convicts were back at the other Anderson County mine, watched by three hundred new prison guards and ninety entrenched militiamen equipped with a Gatling gun and a howitzer. Such force disheartened the miners: as one of them reported a few months later, "many of our best men have left the state." [42]

Governor Buchanan was hurt by a crisis not of his own making. He was caught between businessmen who considered the strike "a crime without parallel" [43] and laws he felt duty-bound to enforce, on the one hand, and, on the other, the strong feeling of labor and reformers that the lease system was a disgraceful injustice. He was unable to satisfy those who blamed him for negotiating with law-breakers, but he won the resentment of the miners for sending in the militia. Although it is hard to imagine how he could have been more fair, the feebleness of Buchanan's official powers and the paucity of his political experience made him vulnerable to the enemies of the Alliance.

The Farmers' Alliance was weakened during the summer of 1891 by the arguments against the subtreasury, by the attack on McDowell, and, indirectly, by the coal strike. The enemies of the Alliance, moreover, began to organize against it to ensure its downfall, justifying and supporting their campaign by declaring more and more explicitly that the Alliance was politically illegitimate, disrespectable, and subversive of the Solid South.

In May the Nashville *Herald* began sounding a new note of urgency and open hostility which had not been heard in Tennessee since Buchanan's election. "McDowell and the Alliance," it said, "as a part and parcel of the Democracy, must go. The methods of the latter and its insolence are as offensive as is the prominence of McDowell." And later, "The Alliance, as a political factor, has been already too long tolerated. . . . It is now time for the drawing of lines and for hewing to such lines." Other Democratic newspapers

---

42. A. C. Hutson, Jr., "The Overthrow of the Convict Lease System in Tennessee," *East Tennessee Historical Society's Publications*, VIII (1936), 86–91; Nashville *American*, November 1, 2, 7, 1891, January 1, 2, 1892; Memphis *Appeal-Avalanche*, December 4, 1891; E. C. Prescott to J. C. Houk, October 10, 1892, in Houk Papers.

43. A. S. Colyar, quoted in Nashville *American*, November 3, 1891.

joined the *Herald,* denouncing the Alliance as a "secret, oath-bound, one-class political party" which had no right to dictate to the Democracy. Another tactic was to make the Alliance look disreputable. One newspaper pointedly mentioned that the South-wide Colored Alliance had over a million members, and another reported that the Alliance included thousands of leftover Republicans, Greenbackers, and other assorted cranks and malcontents. Looking to his own reelection, Senator Bate intoned, "The Solid South is still a political necessity, because our section is a minority and unable to protect itself, but is powerful so long as united and presenting an unbroken front, to give power to a national Democracy." How could a man defend his party "through long years of bloody warfare," asked the old general, and then desert it for the heretical subtreasury scheme? [44] The underlying premise was that Alliancemen could not be true Democrats.

Two examples from country newspapers will illustrate how party loyalty was invoked against the Alliance. Democratic leaders in White County planned a big fall barbecue complete with partisan oratory, but the Alliance scheduled a rally at the same time. Several days later the local newspaper published an anonymous letter purporting to be from a farmer but full of transparent rusticisms, like the prose of a novelist trying to write in dialect. The "farmer" related how Alliance leaders had made him promise not to go to the Democratic rally, so he went to the Alliance meeting instead, where McDowell spoke. But hostility toward the Democratic party, the party of his poor old father, made the "farmer" uneasy. A rally companion explained that the speaker was

> "tellin' his personal experiences of the better days of the country when he was in the Legislature and they wouldn't let Democrats vote and we wasn't bothered with Democrats." I felt mean anyway, a sneakin' down there and leavin' Nancy and Tom to go by theirselves to a Democratic meetin', and when I heard him a talkin' that away I thought o' my pore old father, now dead and gone, who fought through the war and wasn't afraid of anything, how the tears ran down his dear old face when he

44. Nashville *Herald,* May 6, 11, 1891; Nashville *Weekly Toiler,* May 13, 1891; Nashville *American,* August 13, 15, 24, December 2, 1891; Nashville *Banner,* August 11, 1891; Memphis *Appeal-Avalanche,* June 12, December 7, 1891.

came home from the election and told my mother how they let niggers vote and drove him and Silas' father from the polls. I can't tell you how mean I did feel.[45]

Despite the dialect form, which a real farmer might have taken as an insult, this fake letter was representative of the pressure used to weaken the Alliance. An editor in another small town was less melodramatic.

The Democratic members of the Alliance cannot delay action. . . . Immediate steps must be taken. They must either abjure the eternal principles of Democracy, which would be a sacrilegous act, or absolve themselves of all connection with the organization of dangerous heresies and condemnable ideas. To do the former would be execrable in the extreme. . . . To cast off the heresies of an undemocratic, proscriptive, restrictive, secret political society would be a worthy deed; and it is a deed that every Democrat must do who finds himself in the Alliance camp.[46]

Such propaganda was effective. A farmer who as late as August, 1891, noted with approval that "the *Alliance* . . . [was] moving around *briskly* to *right* matters" had decided nine months later that the "Democrats who are not alliance want a man, who is not mixed up with a secret political party, [which] demand[s] all sorts of absurd measures . . . led by disapppointed office seekers[;] since the war a large no[.] of men have been acting with the Democratic party, who never were Democrats. These men will go off into a 3rd party[;] . . . ready for any new ism, led on by designing and corrupt men, they would ruin the country." [47]

Indoctrination was supported with action. Impressed by the effectiveness of grass roots organization in the Buchanan campaign of 1890, some suggested a network of clubs to combat the farmers' lodges. The men who gathered in May to found the State Business Men's Association listened to A. S. Colyar first explain that there were no hostile classes in Tennessee, and then urge them to form clubs in every town to fight political candidates representing only one class. This plan was attractive, but a more practical and direct

45. Sparta *Expositor,* October 23, November 6, 1891.
46. Fayetteville *Sun,* September 16, 1891.
47. Cartmell Diary, August 15, 1891, May 6, 1892, emphasis original.

suggestion was to use the subtreasury as a test to exclude all but "straight Democrats" from county Democratic committees and conventions. Both of these methods were used during 1891. Democratic clubs and mass meetings passed resolutions against the subtreasury and secret oath-bound political orders, and in Lincoln County a meeting was called in an effort to depose the Alliance-controlled county Democratic committee.[48]

Thus the first year of power for the Tennessee Farmers' Alliance was a time of lost opportunities and rising opposition. Hobbled by inexperience and an ideology of limited government, the Alliance did not promote or even conceive a legislative or administrative program. Weighted down by the conservatism of white supremacy and property rights, it failed to seek allies among blacks or labor unions. But ineffective as it was in using power, the Alliance had shown in the campaign of 1890 that it could dominate the Democratic party. The losers of 1890 were not going to underestimate the Alliance again, nor did they intend to divide and weaken their forces a second time. No one knew how far the Alliance might try to press its claims, especially after the Cincinnati conference of May, 1891, heralded the founding of a third party.[49] It was after Cincinnati that Bourbons and New-South men alike began to prepare for an impressive and very effective mobilization to destroy the Alliance.

48. Nashville *Banner*, May 5, August 12, 19, 1891; Nashville *American*, August 22, October 29, 1891; Memphis *Appeal-Avalanche*, October 28, November 1, 1891; Manchester *Times*, quoted in Fayetteville *Sun*, September 16, 1891, and in Memphis *Commercial*, May 11, 1891; Sparta *Expositor*, July 10, November 20, 1891.
49. Hicks, *Populist Revolt*, 214–15.

8

The Conservative Counterattack

The opposition to the Farmers' Alliance which gathered during 1891 grew naturally into a movement to prevent Governor Buchanan's renomination in 1892. This movement may be divided into three phases. During the first period, when Peter Turney's candidacy was developing, Buchanan still had wide support, including non-Alliance politicians. The second phase saw anti-Alliance Democrats transform a convention for choosing national convention delegates into a rule-making body for the state party, and thereby exclude Alliance-men from county primaries. The Tennessee People's party then quickly organized. In the last phase of the campaign, Democratic nominee Turney received help from most Democratic leaders as Buchanan's independent candidacy failed to become a strong challenge from outside the party. The successful conservative counterattack thus deposed the Alliance by a coup, and then crushed the People's party which formed largely in protest against that coup.

As early as September, 1891, editor Walter Cain of the Nashville *Herald* was sending up trial balloons for possible alternatives to Buchanan. He drew some response with the name of state Supreme Court Chief Justice Peter Turney. Then in February, 1892, Cain succeeded E. W. Carmack as editor of the larger Nashville *American,* which began an insistent drumfire of criticism of Buchanan. Both the *Herald* and the *American* declared themselves opposed to Buchanan's renomination but received little immediate support. One anti-Alliance country editor supposed that politicians were afraid to defy the farmers, who had earned a formidable national reputation. Judge Turney formally announced his candidacy on February 25 and was hailed by several country weeklies, one of which called him a

179

God-given savior. The important urban dailies remained cool, except the *American* and two or three others. Adolph Ochs' Chattanooga *Times* withheld judgment, declaring itself "as a whole, . . . satisfied" with Buchanan as governor. But many more small-town editors began endorsing Turney.[1]

The only Democrat in the field against Buchanan, Peter Turney was a large, hearty, but dignified man with a taste for liquor. A group of friends, complimenting his "all-round substantialness," once gave him a suit with a forty-nine-inch waist and a forty-six-inch chest. An ardent secessionist in 1861, he was so impatient at Tennessee's delay in joining the Confederacy that he led a movement to attach his native Franklin County to rebel Alabama. When Tennessee seceded he was already raising troops for the South.[2] He became a supreme court judge in 1870, but a judicial career did not cool his ardor. In 1888 he addressed a meeting of Tennessee Confederate veterans, reasoning that to protect the raison d'etre of the organization, "we cannot and must not in anywise in the least sympathize with that spirit of seeming apology we sometimes meet. We retract nothing, and believe the cause in which our comrades fell was just. . . . Our cause was worth all we sacrificed to it. Though lost, it deserves vindication. Its defence by our arms at least checked centralization." Later he said that if he were to die he would wish one word inscribed on his tombstone: *secession.*[3] Turney was not a man of outstanding ability, but his Confederate record and long removal from intraparty battles made him acceptable to diverse anti-Alliance elements.

While the Turney boom was getting underway, John McDowell kept up his activity, organizing Buchanan clubs and promoting his

1. Nashville *Herald,* September 1–6, October 9, 1891, February 15, 26, 1892; Nashville *American,* February 15, 19, 21, 23, 25, 1892; Nashville *Banner,* February 15, 23, 26, 27, 29, 1892; Pulaski *Citizen,* February 25, 1892; Shelbyville *Gazette,* March 3, 1892; Memphis *Appeal-Avalanche,* February 26, 27, 1892; Memphis *Public Ledger,* February 25, 1892; Memphis *Commercial,* February 25, 1892; Chattanooga *Times,* February 26, March 8, 1892.
2. Speer, *Sketches,* 472–74; Nashville *Banner,* July 31, 1886; Nashville *Herald,* April 2, 1892; Robison, *Bob Taylor,* 179.
3. [Peter Turney?] "They Wore the Grey—The Southern Cause Vindicated: An Address by Hon. Peter Turney, Chief Justice of the Supreme Court of Tennessee, before the Tennessee Association of Confederate Veterans, at Nashville, August 8th, 1888," *Southern Historical Society Papers,* XVI (1888), 319, 338; Knoxville *Journal,* November 5, 1891.

own senatorial candidacy. He convened and controlled a Tennessee Labor Congress, an effort to win over the state's few organized workers. A Nashville union leader spoke of the continuing struggle between capital and labor, but Governor Buchanan threw a chill over farmer-worker cooperation by telling the meeting he regretted that Tennessee unions were not always reasonable and conservative, and warning sternly of the dangers of anarchy and public reaction to lawlessness. The demands issued by the Labor Congress should have been sufficiently cautious even for Buchanan: an end to the convict lease, a ban on child labor under age fourteen, a juvenile reform school, and safety laws for factory workers. Although there were actual labor leaders at the conference, it was really conducted for them by the Alliance. Buchanan was endorsed a few days later by the Trades Council of Memphis, where the Alliance supported a strike against the hostile Memphis *Commercial.*[4] But McDowell's efforts to woo labor yielded no other evidence of success. The Knights of Labor would hardly rally to the governor who had sent troops to the mines.

The Turney campaign was aided by the absence of any other anti-Alliance candidate. The Chattanooga *Times* "reluctantly" veered around to oppose Buchanan when it became clear that he would not renounce the subtreasury, and by late March all seventeen Democratic dailies in Tennessee opposed the governor's renomination. The Turney men took a leaf from their well-organized enemies' book and called an unusual statewide meeting. Bourbons and railroad lawyers, editors and merchants, past officeholders and aspiring young hopefuls were there, and friends, appointees, or allies of every Democratic governor from 1860 to 1890, with the possible exception of Marks. Former governor James D. Porter chaired the meeting, which included many old sky-blues as well as low-taxer S. F. Wilson. The 150 anti-Alliance Democrats testified by their diversity to the menace they saw in the Alliance. Men who had fought each other bitterly in the past now joined to fight a common threat, a "movement," in the words of the Nashville *Herald,* "that ha[d] effectually

4. Knoxville *Journal,* January 1, 1892; Nashville *American,* March 2, 1892; Memphis *Appeal-Avalanche,* February 21, March 1, 3, 14, 1892; Nashville *Weekly Toiler,* March 30, 1892; Nashville *Herald,* March 6, 1892.

quenched all open, honest, and intelligent political aspiration in the state as if the human mind had been suddenly subjected to some enervating blight." [5] The quenching of political ambition was nothing new, as blacks, Republicans, and small farmers had often discovered. But now the Alliance was presenting the state's traditional governing class with its first serious challenge since the 1860s. The result was a degree of unity among leading former Confederates resembling the Redemption of 1869–1870.

During the first phase of the Turney-Buchanan campaign, the governor had considerable support outside the Alliance. Two of the leaders denounced by Turney men for arranging a "snap" county convention were W. L. Clapp and A. J. Harris, both Buchanan appointees in Memphis. While E. W. Carmack charged that the Shelby County primaries were rigged "in the interest of [Alliance] demagogues and ringsters," Buchanan got only an uninstructed delegation to the state convention, split between his and Turney's men. However, the standoff in urban Shelby was an improvement over the governor's 1890 showing there.[6]

In Rutherford County the Alliance-dominated county Democratic committee summoned a mass meeting which resulted in what was rightly called the "first open split in Tennessee Democracy" of 1892. Farmers poured into the county seat, and the meeting's chairman, who was Buchanan's own preacher, ran things in the governor's favor. Turney men pushed for a primary to elect state convention delegates, claiming that Buchanan's neighbors were afraid to stand up against him in an open meeting, or that businessmen feared an Alliance boycott. When the mass meeting chose a Buchanan delegation, the Turney men retreated to the courthouse and voted to hold a primary to elect a rival delegation, though at this time the governor clearly controlled the Democratic rank and file of his own county.[7] The regular or Buchanan delegation from Rutherford in-

    5. Chattanooga *Times,* March 12, 13, 17, 22, April 2, 1892; Nashville *American,* March 11, 23, 1892; Nashville *Herald,* February 27, 1892.

    6. Nashville *American,* March 9, 10, 17, 1892; Nashville *Banner,* March 10, 1892; Nashville *Herald,* March 10, 1892; Memphis *Appeal-Avalanche,* March 17, 1892; Memphis *Commercial,* March 10, 16 (quote), 1892.

    7. Memphis *Appeal-Avalanche,* April 3, 1892; Nashville *American,* April 3, 1892; Nashville *Banner,* April 4, 1892.

Table 25
COMPARISON OF PROPERTY HOLDINGS OF BUCHANAN DELEGATES
AND TURNEY COUNTY COMMITTEE, RUTHERFORD COUNTY
OUTSIDE THIRTEENTH DISTRICT (MURFREESBORO), 1892 [8]

	Buchanan Delegates	Turney Committee
Size of group	72 men	24 men
Property unknown	12 men	5 men
Property known	60 men	19 men
Average landholding per man	209 acres	229 acres
Average total assessed property per man	$2,972	$3,522

cluded some of the county's leading lawyers and professional politicians. But the Turney faction was not without its share of social status, either. Table 25 gives property-holding comparisons between the Buchanan state convention delegates and the Turney faction's county committee, for Rutherford County outside the Murfreesboro district. The unknowns in Table 25 could be men who owned no taxable property and paid no poll tax, and so were not listed in the tax book, but the proportion of unknowns is about the same for both groups. The governor probably held more of the local elite in his home county than elsewhere. But in this one county the leadership of the Buchanan and Turney factions within the Democratic party were not separated by significant differences in wealth.

Outside Shelby and Rutherford counties Buchanan had more friends who were not farmers or Alliancemen. They included a former legislator for Maury County who was a wealthy promoter of coal and iron properties, leading Knoxville politicians, an old Redeemer and sky-blue from Paris trying to make a comeback, and others with their own reasons for betting on Buchanan over Turney.[9]

The governor had one foot on the Democratic dock and the other in the Alliance rowboat. Committed to both, he was embarrassed

8. Nashville *American,* April 3, 24, 1892; Rutherford County tax book, 1889, film, TSLA.
9. W. J. Whitthorne to J. B. Killebrew, January 4, 1890, in Killebrew Papers; R. P. Cole to A. S. Marks, January 24, 1879, in CGO, TSLA; F. M. Thompson to S. A. Champion, February 27, 1883, in Champion Papers; Nashville *Banner,* March 15, 1890; Nashville *American,* April 2, September 4, 1892; Nashville *Weekly Toiler,* May 18, 1892.

by the increasing distance between them, but he could not control the trend of national farmer groups toward the People's party. The Alliance meeting at Indianapolis the previous November, despite disavowals by Tennessee Alliance leaders, had been reported in the press as a sign that the Alliance would back a third party. The National Industrial Conference, held at St. Louis in February, 1892, had been quite sympathetic to the Populists, and Turney had cleverly announced his candidacy on the very day the press was full of news about St. Louis linking the Alliance and Populism.[10] Buchanan sought to dissociate himself from Populism by issuing a public statement:

> If you wish a declaration of principles from me, look at the Democratic platform of 1890, upon which I was nominated, by which I pledged myself to stand . . . am still standing, and expect to stand until the Democracy . . . shall formulate another. . . .
> I am opposed to a third party or people's party . . .
> There is need of an unbroken front in the ranks of the Democratic party against Republicanism and third partyism, and I regret to say that the radical elements in the party are endeavoring to array faction against faction. The great conservative masses will, however, I believe, hold in check these elements in accord with the spirit of the call issued by the National Democratic Committee.[11]

But Buchanan could not turn the clock back to 1890. When McDowell announced that he would not support Turney under any conditions, the Memphis *Commercial* quickly put him "already in the third party." A front-page letter in the *Weekly Toiler* alleged that the statewide Turney conference had threatened to "wipe the Alliance gang off the face of the earth," and warned that "hundreds of men in my county and myself among them, will leave the Democratic party and forever" if the abuse continued.[12] Among town people and politicians, such bellicose words hurt Buchanan by as-

10. Nashville *American,* November 20, 1891; Memphis *Appeal-Avalanche,* November 20, 24, 1891; Nashville *Weekly Toiler,* December 2, 1891; Hicks, *Populist Revolt,* 227–28; Clarksville *Tobacco Leaf-Chronicle,* March 8, 1892.

11. Chattanooga *Times,* March 28, 1892.

12. Nashville *American,* April 29, 1892; Nashville *Herald,* April 29, 1892; Memphis *Commercial,* April 29, 1892; Nashville *Weekly Toiler,* March 30, 1892.

sociation, because he refused to repudiate McDowell or renounce the subtreasury.

In the first phase of the campaign, or until about the first of May, Buchanan and Turney were running fairly evenly in delegate strength, if the governor was not ahead. The haphazard methods of selecting state convention delegates, varying from county to county and unregulated by law, allowed misunderstanding and trickery which greatly increased the bitterness on both sides and convinced many Buchanan men that Turney was winning delegates by illegitimate means.[13] This hostility developed into an open split during the second part of the campaign and contributed much to the growth of a new party.

The People's party of Tennessee was founded not by leaders of the Farmers' Alliance, but by former adherents of the Union Labor party, which had polled forty-eight votes in Tennessee in the previous presidential election. Union Laborite leaders, who were acquainted with J. H. McDowell, became involved with the national Populist organizers in 1891 and then issued a call in May, 1892, for a Tennessee Populist convention.[14] They were putting up a skeleton structure in case the Alliance needed to move into it later.

One Alliance leader jumped the gun. In mid-May the editor of the official *Weekly Toiler,* also secretary of the state Alliance, resigned from his district Democratic committee, and his newspaper ran up the Populist colors. This sudden move had not been coordinated with McDowell, who said he was still a Democrat though he would never support Turney. Another top state Alliance official announced that he would support any Democratic nominee and predicted that it would be Turney since Buchanan had just lost the delegations of two strong Alliance counties. Buchanan was now in a very difficult position; many of his men were following the *Toiler* out of the Democratic party, while others were going over to Turney

13. Nashville *Banner,* April 5, 6, 7, 18, May 5, 1892; Memphis *Scimitar,* quoted in Knoxville *Journal,* April 20, 1892; Nashville *Herald,* April 6, 1892; Memphis *Appeal-Avalanche,* April 17, 1892.

14. Nashville *American,* November 18, 1888, February 19, 1890; Nashville *Weekly Toiler,* December 19, 1889; Cincinnati (Ohio) *Enquirer,* May 20, 1891; Memphis *Appeal-Avalanche,* May 21, 1891; Nashville *Herald,* May 16, 1892.

to avoid association with Populism. Either way, Buchanan was losing supporters for his renomination. He stubbornly tried to maintain
his impossible position by reaffirming his loyalty to the Democracy,
yet emphasizing that he favored free silver, a lower tariff, more
currency, and, in vague terms, the subtreasury.[15] At this most critical
point in his campaign, Buchanan could do little to shape its direc-
tion.

Another development in May that transformed the gubernatorial
race was the state Democratic convention for selecting delegates to
the national convention. Anti-Alliance men had arranged for this
to be handled in a separate meeting because they expected, correctly,
that the Alliance would tell farmers to put all their effort into the
gubernatorial convention. At the May convention the sky-blues and
other Turney men were in firm command. They chose a railroad
attorney for the national party committee, failed to urge Bourbon
Senator Bate's reelection (ostensibly because the convention would
not stop cheering Cleveland), and chose national convention delegates who were solid for Cleveland.[16] This convention also went
beyond its official function and adopted a platform intended to force
Alliancemen to abandon either the subtreasury or the Democratic
party, a strategy feared for weeks by Turney moderates as a "fire-
brand." After May the Tennessee Democratic party was officially
on record as opposed to "every species of class legislation," especially
the subtreasury, which was "illusory, impracticable, and unconstitutional." This declaration, in effect, changed the rules in the middle
of the game. Pro-Turney county Democratic committees, which had
been trying to disfranchise Alliancemen in the primaries, now excluded them easily by requiring an anti-subtreasury oath. Buchanan's considerable remaining strength inside the Democratic
party was increasingly neutralized. McDowell charged that the May
convention had been "controlled by the money powers of Wall
Street," and called on all Alliancemen to cease activity within the

15. Nashville *Weekly Toiler,* October 28, 1891; Nashville *Banner,* May 10, 11, 1892;
Memphis *Appeal-Avalanche,* May 16, 18, 1892; Nashville *American,* May 18, 1892; Nashville
Herald, May 12, 1892; Chattanooga *Press,* May 13, 1892.
16. Nashville *American,* August 28, 1885, March 18, May 26, 27, 1892; Nashville *Weekly
Toiler,* quoted in Clarksville *Tobacco Leaf-Chronicle,* March 26, 1892; Nashville *Banner,* May
26, 27, 1892; Chattanooga *Times,* June 21, 1892.

Democratic party. By June 1 Peter Turney was assured of the Democratic nomination for governor.[17]

At the end of May, McDowell summoned about a hundred Alliance leaders to Nashville for a secret strategy meeting. Continuing to work for Buchanan inside the Democratic party no longer made sense, but enough leading Alliancemen opposed the third party to prevent the Alliance from simply moving as a body over to Populism. The conference avoided direct mention of the People's party but praised the Populist *Weekly Toiler* and asked farmers not to support anyone not endorsing their demands—which was tantamount to an invitation to bolt. As though on signal, Populist organizations quickly sprang up in many counties, led by Alliancemen who were nearly always former Democrats. The speed with which the Alliancemen organized and put local Populist or joint Populist-Republican tickets in the field indicates that they required no persuasion to desert the Democracy. A Populist newspaper predicted that the third-party men could not be enticed back into the Democratic party, since they were "not out through anger and ill treatment; they [were] out from principle, and they [would] stay." [18] This was a dubious distinction, however; underlying the Populists' principles was the feeling that they had been ill-treated, and the unfair coup of the May convention caused many Alliancemen to stand by their principles more resolutely.

If any Allianceman had reason to act from resentment, it was Governor Buchanan, who was being called "the most ignorant man who ever attained the honor of a Governor's chair in these United States." But the cautious, earnest man hesitated to join the new party

17. Memphis *Appeal-Avalanche,* March 26, 1892; Nashville *American,* May 23, 27, 1892; Nashville *Herald,* February 1, 1892; Nashville *Banner,* May 21, 1892. Because Buchanan's pre-June strength did not show up at the August convention, it has been overlooked. Even during May, Buchanan was carrying Democratic mass meetings in Warren, Cheatham, and Campbell counties, and losing the 850-man Sumner County mass meeting by only seventeen votes. As late as September the state Democratic chairman confided that "at least a third" of his county committees were "unorganized owing to the [farmers'] revolt." Nashville *Herald,* May 8, 1892; Nashville *American,* May 20, 22, 1892; Memphis *Commercial,* May 23, 1892; Nashville *Banner,* May 13, 25, 1892; W. H. Carroll to W. F. Harrity, September 5, [1892], in Cleveland Papers (quote).

18. Nashville *American,* May 31, June 2, 9, August 5, 1892; Nashville Banner, May 31, June 1, 7, 30, 1892; Memphis *Appeal-Avalanche,* June 2, 1892; Nashville *Herald,* June 8, 1892; Carthage *Record,* quoted in Nashville *Banner,* June 16, 1892.

for two special reasons: first, his recent condemnation of Populism had been well publicized; and second, he knew that many of his most valuable political friends, as well as thousands of non-Alliance voters, would never follow him if he bolted. To avoid embarrassing the governor, McDowell waited as long as he could before publicly joining the third party, but had to make the expected announcement in late June so he could attend the state Populist convention.[19] Buchanan remained silent.

McDowell and his friends dominated the first state convention of the People's party of Tennessee, composed of about 250 men representing forty-five of the state's ninety-six counties. He was chairman of the platform committee, and he convinced the assembly to delay in nominating a candidate for governor, in the hope that Buchanan would be available later. While McDowell was outside the room, J. R. Beasley, the Greenback nominee of 1882, put through a strong low-tax resolution on the old state-debt question. McDowell rushed back inside and talked the delegates into reconsidering and rejecting the motion as raising a distracting side issue. Clearly, Tennessee Populism was not a resurrected Greenback party. The convention ratified a platform denouncing both major parties and demanding free coinage of silver, inflation to fifty dollars per capita, direct election of the United States Senate, and an end to the convict lease. The subtreasury was prudently omitted. In reorganization, Alliancemen replaced the old Union Laborites on the state Populist committee, so that party and Alliance would be thenceforth virtually indistinguishable. The new party had a constituency and a platform but lacked a candidate for governor.[20]

Competition in the Democratic primaries continued in some areas where the Alliance was strong, and in Nashville, where Buchanan carried three wards including the city's two wealthiest. But in most counties a hush descended—a Nashville newspaper called it "ominous"—and Turney men found that they could simply walk in

19. Chattanooga *Times,* June 22, 1892. The *Times* had reversed itself since February 25. Nashville *Weekly Toiler,* quoted in Nashville *Banner,* June 15, 1892; Nashville *Banner,* June 22, 1892.
20. Nashville *American,* June 29, 1892; Nashville *Banner,* June 29, 1892; Memphis *Appeal-Avalanche,* June 29, 1892. For text of platform, see Appendix C.

and collect delegates. A month after the Populist convention, Buchanan finally withdrew from the race for the Democratic nomination, defending his own consistency and the farmers' right to organize on occupational lines. He blamed the "vituperative" campaign against him, dominated by "sky-blue bolters," for the bitter division in the party, for the "haughty" and "vindictive" May convention, and for barring thousands of Democrats from their party by the unprecedented loyalty oaths. Later, sky-blues like J. D. Porter and W. H. Jackson indeed dominated the August Democratic convention, though not to the exclusion of Senator Bate and some of Bob Taylor's friends. The remarkably calm and dignified body quickly nominated Turney. About two hundred Buchanan delegates met to discuss an independent race and split into two camps over the question. Thus the second phase of the campaign, which had begun with Buchanan and Turney on fairly even terms within the Democratic party, closed with some Buchanan men at the Democratic nominating convention putting up token resistance and others urging him to run as a Populist.[21]

The third phase of the campaign began inauspiciously for Buchanan. A new miners' revolt broke out, this time in Grundy County, whence over six hundred convicts from two mines were sent under guard to Nashville. In Anderson County, too, the convicts were soon surrendered again to the miners. Governor Buchanan sent five hundred militiamen to Anderson County, where their commander began making mass arrests. But the press blamed the governor for the outbreak. A. S. Colyar, speaking to two thousand persons in Nashville, cried, "The greatest humiliation to me is that we have reached the point where the people are willing to put a fool in the office of Governor. (Great applause)." Buchanan reacted defensively to the uprising and the criticism, and once again was made to appear the victim, rather than the master, of circumstances.[22]

21. Nashville *American,* July 6, 19, 20, 31, August 7, 10, 1892; report of Davidson County tax assessor in Nashville *American,* July 28, 1892; Nashville *Banner,* July 19, August 2, 4, 9, 10, 1892; Nashville *Herald,* June 17, 1892; Knoxville *Journal,* July 16, 1892; Clarksville *Tobacco Leaf-Chronicle,* July 4, 6, 1892.

22. Nashville *American,* August 14, 16, 17, 18, 20, 21, 1892; Nashville *Banner,* August 16, 19, 20, 22, 1892; Memphis *Commercial,* September 6, 1892. For the 1892 mine crisis, see Hutson, "Overthrow of the Convict Lease System."

While Buchanan was coping with the strike, Alliancemen were going to Nashville for their annual meeting, and the governor timed his announcement of an independent candidacy to coincide with their arrival. His personal platform was much more specific and less bombastic than those written by committees. Several of his planks were progressive and forward-looking, especially those asking for direct election of the United States Senate, free trade, limitation of trading in agricultural futures to stop manipulation, a graduated income tax, an end to the convict-lease system, legal provision for arbitration of strikes, child-labor legislation, and generous support for the public schools. But he also called for an end to the national banking system and rejection of the Lodge "force bill." The Alliance influence shows in his demands for free silver at sixteen to one, inflation of the currency, and a ban on alien land ownership. The Alliance delegates read this platform, heard J. H. McDowell urge that party loyalty be subordinated to Alliance principles, and elected Populists to most leadership positions. Many Alliancemen stayed around for the reconvened Populist state convention, which met to endorse Buchanan's independent candidacy. He was not leading the Populists, but following them. "Governor Buchanan . . . is a weak man, who commands but little confidence and respect," reported Judge Howell Jackson to Grover Cleveland. "The Peoples party is led and controlled by an unscrupulous demagogue (named J H McDowell)," [23] who may have wished that he did not need Buchanan.

The main speaker at the reconvened Populist convention was a black preacher, who was reportedly well received. He talked about race relations, not the Populist program. Speaking as a black man to whites, not as one Populist to others, he pled gently for understanding and trust between the races, arguing that race was used in politics to divert attention from real issues. This speech is the only evidence of direct cooperation between Populists and blacks in Tennessee, except for the inclusion of one Negro in the twenty-five-man Hickman County delegation to the party's 1892 state conven-

23. Nashville *American,* August 16, 1892; Nashville *Banner,* August 17, 18, 19, 1892; Howell E. Jackson to Grover Cleveland, September 17, 1892, in Cleveland Papers.

tion. Many blacks voted for Tennessee Populist candidates, but they did so by casting fusion ballots given to them by their Republican leaders, usually whites. The Democratic press, which certainly would have made much of significant racial integration at a Populist convention, did not mention the subject. Although Buchanan accused the Democrats of using the Lodge "force bill" as a false issue, he agreed with them in opposing the measure. On at least one occasion the Populists appealed directly to racism, sharply criticizing Cleveland for signing a bill integrating New York City schools. Tennessee Populists did not differ significantly in racial attitudes from Tennessee Democrats.[24]

A group of Buchanan supporters met secretly after the Populist convention and selected an independent campaign committee for the governor in order to attract disgruntled Democrats not willing to identify fully with a new party. The seven-man committee included a former mayor of Memphis and two low-tax men of the late 1870s. J. H. Burnham, their chairman, published a long statement in which he described the Alliance as a natural outgrowth of the Democratic party. Invoking Andrew Johnson's warning against a "moneyed aristocracy," he recited the old Democratic doctrines of opposition to high tariffs and national banks, advocacy of a bimetallic currency, and enmity to class and sectional legislation. "All this," he said, "was strong and inflammatory language—prophesies uttered through Democratic tongues of fire. It was the red-hot coals of revolution, and, by greeneyed bondocracy, is now called rampant anarchism. But were these teachings true? is the all-important question. We answer yes, verily; true and righteous altogether." Thus the Farmers' Alliance was the most effective propagator of true Democracy.[25]

Why, then, if they were the best Democrats of all, did the Alliancemen leave the old party? They had tried not to, Burnham explained. From "that strange and undefinable unrest of heart akin to suspicion, in those hours of longing born of impatience, that natural and intuitive reaching out for help, the Farmers' Alliance asked that 'one of

24. Nashville *Banner,* June 30, August 19, 1892; Nashville *Weekly Toiler,* November 2, 1892.
25. Nashville *Banner,* August 30, 1892; Nashville *American,* February 2, 1890; J. W. Newman to J. D. Porter, August 23, 1878, in CGO, TSLA.

their own sort' be called to the head of the state." But then "all the old recognized leaders of the party" had turned against Governor Buchanan. Their excuse was the subtreasury, though they tolerated doctrinal differences among themselves. Their real motive was to make Buchanan a "scape-goat" for his friends among the "humbler class," who were " 'the most defenseless victims' of all Democracy's children." After paraphrasing the Declaration of Independence of 1776 and cataloging the arrogance, insensitivity, and injustice of the party leaders' policies, Burnham urged the election of Buchanan, "that justice may be done and injustice be rebuked. And, let weal or woe come, we stand prepared for either, supported by an approving conscience; for we believe that ours is a fight for the right, for the 'defenseless' against the strong, for the 'dependent and helpless' against the encroachments of the powerful. And this is why we bolt, and why the party lash hath lost its sting." This Burnham manifesto is the most candid and revealing exposition of Tennessee Populism by a participant. Significantly, its rhetoric is conservative in appealing to tradition, and is focused not on broad questions of social justice, but on the political events of the previous several weeks.[26]

In his campaign speech Buchanan mentioned some of the proposals of his personal platform, but the Populists depended more on the attitudes expressed by the Burnham manifesto than on programs for governmental action. An "Old Fayette Democrat" wrote to a Memphis paper pledging a vote for Buchanan despite his weak record, in order to assert the farmers' right to organize and take their rightful place beside businessmen and mechanics in politics, and also to retaliate for the insult of exclusion from the party by a clique of lawyers and corporation men. J. H. McDowell was reported as saying simply that the Populists quit because they were proscribed and vilified.[27] A Democratic Coffee County newspaper painted a gloomy picture, also stressing the emotions of the Populists:

> Men who have always voted the straight ticket are leaving the [Democratic] party by hundreds, and there seems but little chance of getting them back the present year. There is a spirit of unrest among the people

26. Nashville *Banner,* September 12, 1892.
27. Knoxville *Journal,* October 6, 1892; Memphis *Appeal-Avalanche,* August 22, 24, 1892.

never before seen, and neither speeches nor literature have any effect. The split in the party is wide and deep; the people are mad, and determined to rebuke the leaders of the party. In the towns the sentiment is strong for the ticket, but as soon as you reach the country districts it is just the other way. The bitter things said by public speakers and newspapers before the convention brought about this unhappy state of affairs. Farmers feel as if they had been badly treated and are ready to take anything which promises to bring them relief.[28]

Buchanan's specific campaign proposals can mostly be seen as corollaries of the basic feeling of having been "badly treated." From this feeling the early Alliance had drawn its strength, and on it the third party rested.

The Republicans used specific issues too, but they were more traditional than Buchanan's platform. GOP nominee G. W. Winstead attacked the Democrats for the convict lease, heavy taxes on merchants, and the new election laws. The Knoxville *Republican* appeared with a five-column headline over a picture of convicts in the mines and hungry children of free miners, with a caption blaming the scene on the Democrats. The Republican party could assume that its adherents were already fortified by former Unionism and intrastate sectionalism, but took every opportunity to strengthen those group identities. The Knoxville *Journal* kept up a running attack on Turney for insisting that his secessionist stand had been right, and called him an anarchist when he stated that the campaign was "a question of going to the ballot-box now or to the cartridge-box later." [29] The Republican strategy was to hold their voters in line and hope for another minority victory like that of 1880.

The Democrats argued that the Populists were "essentially a party of paternalism, which, ignoring the Democratic theories of government, demands that the Federal power shall take hold of and regulate things." The assumption was that there was no middle ground for Populism between Hamiltonian and Jeffersonian ideals. Such misdirected forays into political philosophy were rare, however. The Democratic campaign, like the Republican, sought to strengthen the group identities the party always used. To prove that Buchanan did

28. Manchester *Times,* quoted in Nashville *Banner,* September 16, 1892.
29. Nashville *Banner,* August 24, 1892; Knoxville *Republican,* November 4, 1892; Knoxville *Journal,* September, *passim,* September 26 (quote), 1892.

not deserve honor and power, Democratic newspapers tried to make him appear uneducated, a "blundering politician," moved by "whims, grievances, and vanity," "a good enough sort of fellow to run a farm, or to read almanacs." The governor's response to the mine crisis was termed a "disgrace" which "daily [added] to the humiliation that must be felt by every proud citizen of the old Commonwealth." [30]

The Populists were scorned as "a free coinage and general get-something-for-nothing aggregation"; by contrast, a Democratic rally was "a great enthusiastic success . . . a gathering of intelligence. And decency. And respectability. And patriotic devotion," with "a gratifying absence of anarchistic presences and sentiments." Turney was put forward not as a man with a plan, but as a dignified, reliable old war hero. "One thing that will operate in favor of Democracy in the coming election, as opposed to the People's party, is the shrewdly conceived idea advanced that the latter organization is made up of a poor and uneducated class," remarked an astute observer. "However aristocratic rule may be abhorred by the good citizens of this commonwealth, none of them care to be classed with the rag, tag, and bob tail, and that sort of pride, though it may be very foolish, will keep a great many in line with the Democracy." Thus Democratic leaders acted on the assumption that most voters preferred securing their social status under the existing system to challenging the community consensus. Although the Populists in West Tennessee were reportedly "numerous, wild & wooly, and . . . making a vigorous campaign," a Hardeman County Democrat said his county was "in an uncertain condition—with very many voters not satisfied with affairs & yet not ready to go to a third party." [31]

An appeal aimed at these borderline voters was the white-supremacy argument, that the Democratic party had fought the "battles against sectional intolerance, the Federal bayonets of reconstruction and negro domination. The Democratic party made the

---

30. Nashville *Banner,* July 7, 1892 (quote); Memphis *Appeal-Avalanche,* July 6, August 26, 1892; Nashville *Weekly Toiler,* October 19, 1892; Chattanooga *Times,* August 18, 1892; Memphis *Commercial,* November 2, 1892; Memphis *Public Ledger,* October 31, 1892.
31. Chattanooga *Times,* July 5, 1892; Nashville *American,* September 25, 1892; Nashville *Banner,* October 18, 1892; "Walker" to J. C. Houk, September 27, 1892, in Houk Papers; A. T. McNeal to J. W. Jones, August 29, 1892, in Jones Family Papers.

white man master of the South[.]" Democratic orators and editors wrung every drop of rhetoric from the Lodge election bill, strongly implying that it would reestablish the legendary horrors of Reconstruction. When J. H. McDowell asked for federal election supervisors the old Arkansas charges were dragged out again, and E. W. Carmack attacked him on the stump with a vicious racist diatribe worthy of Ben Tillman or Theodore Bilbo. Carmack's paper charged that the Colored Alliance was training black people to strike and boycott like the Briceville miners. Judge Turney said that the Republicans, who would benefit from Populist votes, wanted to end the social barrier between the races, and to repeal the antimiscegenation laws (the Republican Knoxville *Journal* exploded that he was "either a fool or a knave" to utter such "insane drivel"). "Democrats, do your duty," urged a country weekly. "Stand up and contend for the principle of white supremacy and all will be well." "Democracy in the South means white supremacy, peace and prosperity," explained another small-town paper; "Republican success means to us negro supremacy, strife and a reign of terror." [32] The unusual shrillness and frequency of such warnings in 1892 reflected the crisis of a major challenge to Democratic party grass-roots loyalty, and the reaction of Democratic leaders in making the white-supremacist basis of their party explicit.

The way to make the Populists the targets of racist rhetoric was to show that the two minority parties were cooperating, which in fact they were. By late September the Republicans agreed to "clear the field" in Congressional Districts Four through Ten (Middle and West Tennessee), giving Populists a chance at three of these seats, in exchange for their keeping third-party gubernatorial and presidential tickets in the campaign to draw off Democratic votes. In local and legislative races, explained GOP leader John C. Houk, "In counties that went Democratic in 1888 we are giving the 3rd party the right of way. In counties that went Republican in 1888 we are

32. Nashville *American,* July 23, September 10, 1892; Ripley *News,* July 8, 1892; Memphis *Commercial,* April 13, 1892; Memphis *Appeal-Avalanche,* June 29, October 6, 1892; Memphis *Public Ledger,* October 11, 1892; Nashville *Banner,* October 14, 1892; Knoxville *Journal,* October 7, 1892; Bolivar *Bulletin,* November 4, 1892; Clarksville *Tobacco Leaf-Chronicle,* May 26, 1892.

side-tracking, by mutual understanding, the 3rd party candidate."
In addition, McDowell was counting on Republican support to win
Bate's seat in the Senate. The Democratic press treated evidence of
this cooperation as proof of a hideously evil conspiracy.[33] Its real
significance was not that it was illegal or immoral, but that it showed
that the chief end of the Populists was to defeat Democrats, to whom
they rightly attributed their ideology. In short, Populists were less
interested in programs than in revenge.

Several days before the election, the Democratic press came up
with a scandal. Spread across its pages was an exchange of letters
between two state Republican leaders mentioning an agreement to
pay McDowell fifteen thousand dollars in funds of the national
Republican committee in return for keeping Buchanan in the race
to help Winstead. "A Damnable Deal," "the Most Infamous Conspiracy in the History of Tennessee Politics," "a diabolical conspiracy," screamed the Democratic dailies, as McDowell and Buchanan were classed with Benedict Arnold and John Brown. The two
Republicans involved did not deny writing the letters, and Republican papers growled darkly about treason in the party and Democratic bribe money. The bitter factional split in the GOP ranks
probably tempted an anti-Winstead man to sabotage his own ticket.[34]
The disclosure was a disaster for the Republicans as well as for the
Populists. "Please write me at once," begged a Republican postmaster of Congressman Houk, "if [*i.e.* whether] there is any truth in the
report about McDowell selling to our Party. We had them beat bad
here but if this proves to be true it will drive the Third Party back
to the democrats. . . . Write at once." McDowell and Populist chairman L. K. Taylor denied selling out to the Republicans. The *Weekly
Toiler* argued that even if the charges were true, nothing would be
wrong with a major party paying for Populist speakers to propound

33. J. C. Houk to Anthony Higgins, September 23, 1892, Houk to J. H. McDowell,
September 23, 1892, in Houk Papers; Nashville *American,* October 23, 1892; Memphis *Appeal-
Avalanche,* October 14, 1892; Memphis *Commercial,* October 17, 1892.

34. Nashville *American,* October 23, 24, 1892; Memphis *Appeal-Avalanche,* October 23,
1892; Memphis *Commercial,* October 23, 1892; Chattanooga *Times,* October 23, 1892; Chat-
tanooga *Press,* October 24, 1892; Knoxville *Journal,* October 25, 1892; S. H. Haynes to J. C.
Houk, September 27, 1892, in Houk Papers. For a discussion of Republican factionalism, see
J. A. Sharp, "The Farmers' Alliance and the People's Party in Tennessee," *East Tennessee
Historical Society's Publications,* X (1938), 109–12.

Populist doctrine.[35] The image of McDowell as a disreputable plotter was sharpened, and the People's party suffered. Thus ended the last, and, for Buchanan, the worst, phase of the campaign.

Analysis of the election returns of 1892 may reveal deeper causes of Populist discontent than their recent treatment by the Democrats. A familiar explanation of Populism is that farmers revolted because of economic distress caused partly by the falling prices of staple crops. Although it is true that Tennessee cotton prices had been skidding downward for two years, and reached a ten-year low in the spring of 1892, this trend is not related to the 1892 election: the simple product-moment correlation between per capita cotton production and Buchanan's percentage of Democrats and Populists, in ninety-four Tennessee counties, is only +.08.[36] Another standard view of Populism in the South traces it back to the burdens of debts and the tenant-farming system. But outside East Tennessee, where Populism was weakest, these factors seem unrelated to the movement in Tennessee (see Appendix B, Table 16, Part A).

If falling prices and debt cannot explain Populism, perhaps other quantitative indicators can point toward an understanding of the revolt. In West Tennessee, only two generations from the raw frontier, new farmland was still being brought under cultivation during the 1880s, and Populism correlates with increased cultivated acreage. In older Middle Tennessee, Populism tended to occur where the rate of increase in the number of farms dropped from the 1880s to the 1890s. In the one case, new men could have felt less tied to their localities and readier to rebel than more settled residents. In the other case, frustrated upward social mobility could have helped generate dissatisfaction. Both situations show how alienation from local communities could parallel and reinforce the alienation from the state-level elites exacerbated by the conservative counterattack of 1892. Confederate, low-tax, and Bourbon rhetoric had prepared Populists to blame outside oppressors for their troubles, but by 1892

35. J. B. Riggs to J. C. Houk, October 25, 1892, in Houk Papers; Nashville *Weekly Toiler,* October 26, November 2, 1892.

36. Cotton prices from Nashville *American,* 1883–1893, *passim; Tribune Almanac,* 1894, 345–46; 1890 Census, *Population,* 39–40; U.S. Census Office, *Report on the Statistics of Agriculture in the United States at the Eleventh Census: 1890* (Washington, 1895), 396.

some voters were ready to turn against the very leaders of those past movements (see Appendix B, Table 16, Part A).

Some voters were ready, but not all. Of the approximately 50,000 Alliance members remaining in 1892, between 15 and 25 percent were probably Republicans, teen-agers, and women, so that Buchanan's total of 31,500 votes was a good Alliance turnout. But he failed to add to his Alliance base. For every Democrat driven by alienation and discontent to leave his party for Buchanan, four stayed behind to defend respectability and white supremacy. Buchanan received 1 vote in 8, and Turney beat Winstead by a 26,000-vote margin [37] (see Map 7). Now largely purged of Alliancemen at the county leadership level, the Democratic party retained control of both houses of the legislature. Populists tried for twenty-one state Senate seats, taking one, and entered sixty-four of the ninety-nine House races, winning only five. Congressman Rice Pierce, who like Buchanan ran for reelection as an independent Democrat, was defeated, leaving in the congressional delegation only one erstwhile Alliance sympathizer, Democrat James D. "Slippery Jim" Richardson. [38] A three-way race for the Senate among Democrats Bob Taylor, John H. Savage, and successful incumbent W. B. Bate did not split the party since all of them opposed the Populists. The campaign of 1892 showed that although the Farmers' Alliance could conquer when its enemies were divided and complacent, the Alliance stood no chance against the united and aroused lawyers, businessmen, and other county magnates who normally controlled the Democratic party.

37. J. A. Sharp, "The Entrance of the Farmers' Alliance into Tennessee Politics," *East Tennessee Historical Society's Publications,* IX (1937), 78; Nashville *Herald,* November 23, 1891; Knoxville *Journal,* April 14, 1892; Nashville *American,* August 18, 1892; *House Journal,* 1893, p. 21.

38. Nashville *American,* August 25, September 23, November 6, 13, 1892; Memphis *Commercial,* October 7, 1892. One Populist legislator was elected as an Independent Democrat. W. H. Jackson wrote that Richardson was "oily & tricky & known as 'Slippery Jim' in Tenn[essee]." W. H. Jackson to Grover Cleveland, May 3, 1893, in Cleveland Papers.

Map 7
SUPPORT FOR BUCHANAN IN 1892 ELECTION

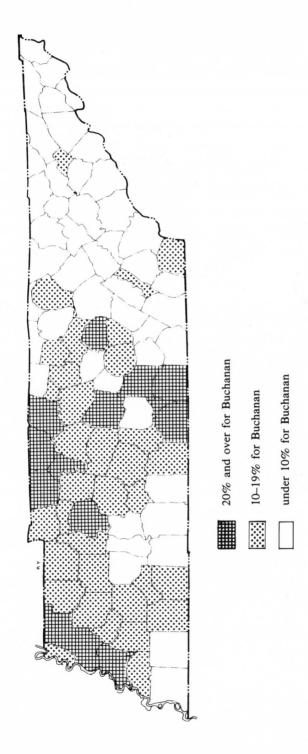

20% and over for Buchanan

10–19% for Buchanan

under 10% for Buchanan

Source: *Tribune Almanac,* 1894, pp. 345–46.

9

The Failure of
the People's
Party

Perhaps one reason for the variety of historical interpretations of
Populism is the diversity of the states in which it occurred. The
People's party could hardly be more uniform nationally than the
established major parties, which were merely quadrennial federa-
tions of state organizations. John D. Hicks's classic *Populist Revolt,*
which overlooked the southern states, saw the movement as based
on economic grievances and as a forward-looking precursor of twentieth-century liberalism. In correcting Hicks's neglect of the South,
C. Vann Woodward contended that southern Populists sought cooperation with blacks and labor and were, if anything, more radical
than their midwestern counterparts. Richard Hofstadter and other
subsequent writers, however, have suggested that the Populists were
irrational and retrogressive, motivated in part by nostalgia and fear
of conspiracies.[1] After the defeat of 1892 Tennessee Populism continued to fit the pattern of Hofstadter somewhat better than that of
Woodward. Having left behind the irresolute and faint-hearted in
its exodus from the Democrats, the People's party survived in the
wilderness as a small and shrinking minority. Although their rhetoric divulged their Bourbon ancestry, Tennessee Populists continued
to cooperate with Republicans, who also placed tactics before ideology. Populist legislators accomplished nothing, handicapped by
small numbers and lack of definite goals. The silver Democratic tide

1. Hicks, *Populist Revolt;* Woodward, *Origins of the New South;* Richard Hofstadter, *The
Age of Reform: From Bryan to F.D.R.* (New York, 1955). Some of the revisionists are listed,
and rebutted, by Woodward in "The Populist Heritage and the Intellectual" in his *Burden
of Southern History* (Baton Rouge, 1960), 141–66; for a more recent bibliography of the
controversy see Sheldon Hackney (ed.), *Populism: The Critical Issues* (Boston, 1971), 166–67.

of 1896 virtually obliterated a party already weakened by bitter internal divisions. Judge Turney was ill for some time after his victory in the 1892 election and so was inaugurated at his home in Winchester. He was pliable enough to appoint as his private secretary, at an associate's urging, an old sky-blue banker Turney had not even considered ten minutes before signing the appointment. Sickness did not prevent the old judge from remaining on the supreme court until the very moment he became governor, so that he could appoint to his own seat the son of an intimate friend of his father. Governor Turney survived his illness, causing disappointment in the Senate, which expected its Speaker to become governor, and embarrassment in the House, which had over-hastily resolved to attend the funeral.[2] Turney never gained a significant personal following.

Table 26
BILLS INTRODUCED BY POPULISTS,
1893 LEGISLATURE [3]

	House	Senate
Number of seats	99	33
Total bills introduced	695	528
Average bills/member	7.0	16.0
Number of Populists	5	1
Bills introduced by Populists	31	16
Average bills/Populist	6.2	16
Number of Populist bills related to Populist platforms	3	0

Like Turney, the People's party barely survived the campaign. Six Populists were elected to the legislature: one senator and two representatives from districts including Montgomery County, and one representative each from Rutherford, Lauderdale, and Weakley

2. Nashville *American,* July 12, 1882, January 17, 19, March 9, 1893; Sparta *Expositor,* March 24, 1893; Memphis *Appeal-Avalanche,* December 11, 1892; Knoxville *Journal,* December 30, 1892.

3. *House Journal,* 1893, pp. 881–903; *Senate Journal,* 1893, pp. 820–835. The three bills related at all to Populist platforms were labeled "to amend the election law," "to repeal uniform [*i.e.* secret] ballot law," and "to request the secretary of state to account for stationery."

Table 27
POPULIST VOTING ON KEY ROLL CALLS,
1893 LEGISLATURE [4]

Question	Vote of House		Vote of Populists	
	Yes	No	Yes	No
1. HB 6, no children under age 12 in factories	52	44	4	1
2. table HB 162, repeal Bureau of Labor Statistics	47	29	4	0
3. SB 201, RR terminal bill, opposed by Bourbons as too generous with railroads	68	30	4	1
4. SB 19, move penitentiary & buy farm & coal land	55	39	0	5
5. SB 321, bonds for new prison	52	42	0	5
6. HB 14, reform fee system in local government	72	24	5	0
7. SB 259, permit women to be notaries public	40	46	3	1
8. HB 181, funds for World's Fair exhibit	36	58	0	5
9. table HRes 29, to decrease House staff	45	46	0	5
10. HB 114, salaries for Supreme Court (opponents say amount too high)	40	50	0	5

counties. All of them received the majority of their votes from Republicans, most of whom were black except in the Carroll-Weakley district. To analyze these six Populist legislators we will seek to find whether they tried to enact their platforms, who their friends were in the legislature, and whether they were cohesive or individualistic in voting behavior. Populists in the 1893 legislature did not try seriously to implement their 1892 platform. The most remarkable thing about the behavior of the six legislators is that of the forty-seven bills they introduced in both houses, only three had possible connection with any Alliance or Populist program or platform. Fur-

4. *House Journal,* 1893, pp. 129, 153, 238, 266, 304, 313, 426, 473, 546–47, 812.

thermore, Populist voting on measures introduced by other members was not always predictable from third-party rhetoric. Both voting behavior and rhetoric were unclear refractions of a general suspicion of powerful men and institutions.

The Rice-Beyle cluster-bloc method of analysis of legislative voting reveals that the five Populists in the House did not form a highly cohesive voting unit. One of them tended to vote with Democrats, another with Republicans, and the other three with other Populists. With the exception of Gooch, of Buchanan's own county, the Populists formed a small, loose voting bloc closely tied to the larger Republican bloc. In the routine matters occupying most of the time of the House, most Populists continued the friendly relations with the Republicans established in the campaign of 1892.[5]

Table 28
POPULIST VOTING, 1893 HOUSE OF
REPRESENTATIVES: PARTIES OF MEMBERS AGREEING
MOST OFTEN WITH EACH POPULIST MEMBER (ROLL CALLS
WITH FEWER THAN 3 IN MINORITY NOT USED)[6]

	Dem.	Rep.	Pop.
Blackford	0	1	2
Gooch	2	0	1
Gwynn	0	3	0
Ledbetter	0	1	2
Pierson	0	1	2
totals	2	6	7

A more subtle method for analyzing legislative voting is the Guttman scale.[7] The roll calls of the 1893 session of the House of Representatives were narrowed down for Guttman scaling in the following manner: under a hypothesis of an urban-rural attitudinal range, five Democratic members were selected who agreed highly with an urban viewpoint, and five with Bourbon attitudes. All roll calls in which at least three of one group opposed at least three of the other and in which at least twenty legislators voted in the minority were used

5. See Chapter VI, n. 11, above.
6. *House Journal,* 1893, *passim.*
7. Anderson, Watts, and Wilcox, *Legislative Roll-call Analysis,* 89–122. The Guttman scale indicates which roll calls reveal degrees of intensity of one fundamental attitude, and it ranks legislators by intensity.

for Guttman scaling. The twenty-nine roll calls thus selected were
cut to the seventeen forming the clearest pattern. The ten members
used as standards, of course, ranked at opposite ends of the scale—
city men at the top, rural at the bottom. Table 29 shows the party

Table 29

PARTY DISTRIBUTION IN GUTTMAN SCALE BASED ON
CITY-COUNTRY CRITERIA, 1893 HOUSE OF REPRESENTATIVES

	Democrats	Republicans	Populists
Top 33 (city)	27	6	0
Middle 34	14	19	1
Bottom 33 (country)	27	2	4

distribution of the one hundred members (a contested seat changed
hands during the session). On these seventeen selected roll calls, the
Democrats tended to polarize. Most Populists voted with the
country Democrats (roughly, Bourbons), giving the Republicans the
balance of power.

The graduated voting differences reflected in the city-country
Guttman scale would be more significant if related to the constituencies of members. This relationship may be discovered, in part, by
a rank-order correlation of the members' Guttman scale positions
with the race-urban indices of their home counties.[8] With the Guttman scale inverted to put the Bourbons at the top, this rank-order
correlation is +.53 for the whole House, and +.82 for the five Populists—clear indication that on certain roll calls the House divided
not by party, but along lines roughly reflecting their constituencies.
Of these seventeen roll calls, only five decided questions other than
the mechanics of political power.[9] Although the Populists routinely

8. Herbert Arkin and Raymond R. Colton, *Statistical Methods* (Rev. ed.; New York,
1956), 85–87; a rank-order correlation of +1.0 would indicate that two rank orders were
identical. The race-urban index is the percentage of blacks in the population minus the
percentage of population in towns over 2,000, in 1890. 1890 Census, *Population*, 317–28,
428–29.
9. These are the roll calls used in the city-country scale, in reverse order of the number
of errors (*i.e.* in order of how well they fit the Guttman scale pattern): 1. Concerning Malone
bill, which would reform fee system making many state and county offices lucrative and
inefficient. 2. Passage of Malone bill (city position: opposed). 3. Adopt rules of previous
session, instead of rules proposed by Rules Committee controlled by the Speaker, a city man
(city position: opposed). 4. Concerning Malone bill. 5. Expunge from *House Journal* the

Table 30
BILLS INTRODUCED BY POPULISTS,
1895 LEGISLATURE [10]

	House	Senate
Number of seats	99	33
Total bills introduced	707	502
Average bills/member	7.15	15.2
Number of Populists	7	3
Bills introduced by Populists	29	12
Average bills/Populist	4.14	4.0
Number of Populist bills related to Populist platforms	1	1

voted with the Republicans, on issues related to the access to power the Populists did not mind lining up with rural Democrats in such a way as to suggest that rural constituencies' attitudes could override partisanship. In other words, on some nonpartisan roll calls the Populists revealed their kinship to Bourbonism.

The Populist contingent in the legislature increased to ten in 1895, but all were elected from districts where Democratic control was normally precarious. The Republican leadership delivered their followers to Populist candidates in these counties, and a few third-party voters provided the margin of victory. The Republican upsurge of 1894 apparently explains the increased number of Populist legislators over 1893, since the statewide Populist vote for governor decreased.

The legislature of 1895 was so preoccupied with a contested gubernatorial election that it considered little else of importance. Populist

---

charges against Speaker Davis, a city man; these charges forced him out of the speakership (city position: in favor). 6. Amendment to revenue bill. 7. Concerning Malone bill. 8. Amendment, concerning railroads, to revenue bill. 9. Adjourn. 10. Concerning recess. 11. Amendment to revenue bill. 12. Amend bill to facilitate construction of railroad terminal in Nashville. 13. Recess. 14. Passage of railroad terminal bill, #12 (city position: in favor). 15. Decrease staff of House (city position: opposed). 16. Concerning impeachment of Shelby County criminal court judge. 17. Amendment to resolution setting time for election of state officers by legislature.

10. *House Journal,* 1895, pp. 606–27; *Senate Journal,* 1895, pp. 702–18. The two bills related at all to Populist programs were labeled "to protect shippers of grain" and "to define trusts, etc."

members introduced fewer bills than others, and the few they sponsored had little or nothing to do with Populist programs.

Few roll-call votes concerned important issues besides the gubernatorial contest, but Table 31 shows Populist voting in the lower

Table 31
POPULIST VOTING ON KEY ROLL CALLS,
1895 HOUSE OF REPRESENTATIVES [11]

Question	Vote of House		Vote of Populists	
	Yes	No	Yes	No
1. Cut down printing of reports of state officials	50	37	7	0
2. Register births & deaths	35	55	0	7
3. Appropriation for Tennessee Centennial	29	65	0	7
4. Chicamauga Park war monument	51	26	1	4
5. Support investigation of penitentiary (Democrats were embarrassed by chance of scandal)	34	52	6	1
6. Abolish capital punishment	16	60	1	5
7. Accept Democratic report on gubernatorial contest	52	44	0	7
8. Support free silver	47	33	5	0
9. Make unbelievers competent witnesses	59	35	5	2
10. "To protect workingmen in their labels"	51	17	1	1
11. Regulate primary elections	25	55	4	3

house on some roll calls best indicating their attitudes. In 1895, as in 1893, Populist legislators placed a higher value on cheap and limited government than on modernization and economic progress. On occasion they failed to support progressive reform measures. Their most steadfast position was opposition to the Democratic party. Populist legislators, like Governor Buchanan, clearly did not seek public office in order to carry out constructive, coherent programs.

11. *House Journal,* 1895, pp. 67, 171–72, 193, 330, 351–52, 355, 364, 449, 517, 562–63, 569.

Outside the legislature, Populist leaders seemed equally aimless, turning against each other after their defeat of 1892. During the winter following the election, when *Weekly Toiler* editor L. K. Taylor became national Alliance secretary, J. H. McDowell offered a "strong and active" Populist, J. G. Carrigan, a block of shares which McDowell said controlled the newspaper. However, he held back some stock because of debts against the *Toiler,* which Carrigan discovered when McDowell fired him as editor. In April, Carrigan mailed McDowell a postcard for which the former was arrested for sending obscene matter through the mail. This incident brought to light an old feud between McDowell and Taylor. Shortly before an 1893 state Populist committee meeting, Taylor published a statement detailing his grudge against McDowell—a glimpse into Tennessee Populism revealing mutual jealousy, suspicion, and mistrust. Taylor's denunciation, at least equaling the Democratic abuse of McDowell, called him "a moral coward, a spiteful villain, a treacherous wretch, a venomous reptile, and a voluminous liar. He has not even the vacuum where a conscience should be. The slime from his trail on earth will remain a stench in the nostrils of decency, and the fumes from his polluted heart will corrode the smokestacks of hell." The state party committee unanimously stripped Taylor of his state and national Populist committee memberships. The next month the man who had brought the *Toiler* into the party in May, 1892, was admitted to the Nashville bar.[12]

Despite his falling-out with McDowell, L. K. Taylor attended the 1894 state Populist convention, which reflected the leaders' quarrel. The three hundred delegates, representing forty-four counties, were pronounced mostly "staunch farmers, men of high standing and influence in their communities" by a Nashville newspaper. Staunch farmer John P. Buchanan was at the convention, although he may not yet have considered himself a Populist, since he still maintained a separate Independent Democratic party in Rutherford County. For the nomination for governor, McDowell backed T. J. Ogilvie, former head of the Bedford County Farmers' Alliance, an unsuccess-

12. Memphis *Commercial,* June 17, 18, August 6, 16, 1893; Nashville *Banner,* August 15, September 25, 1893.

ful candidate for a Democratic legislative nomination in 1888, and a losing Populist candidate for Congress in 1892. L. K. Taylor and several other leaders supported A. L. Mims, a farmer and former schoolteacher, a two-time loser in Davidson County legislative elections, and state president of the Farmers' Alliance. Once a foe of a strong railroad commission, Mims had voted for Cleveland in 1892 and had urged the Alliance to give the Democrats a chance, since "Conservative but determined forces at the helm [were] both the safest and the best." His criterion for judging the Democrats was whether they wanted "the citizen, not the dollar, [to] rule in this country." In 1893, however, Mims spoke out for free silver, a graduated property tax, and governmental housing projects for the poor, which were not conservative proposals in the 1890s. At the 1894 Populist convention, his name drew such cheers from the delegates that McDowell and Ogilvie conceded defeat and supported Mims's nomination.[13] McDowell's loss indicates a decline in his prestige and also perhaps that rank-and-file Populists thought it fitting to nominate their state Alliance president, as they had done in 1890 as Democrats.

Both Ogilvie and Mims, and most other Populist leaders in 1894, were Alliancemen. An exception was A. E. Garrett, Populist nominee for the state supreme court. A native of Overton County, he was an attorney, a Union veteran, a member of the 1865 legislature, and a Democrat in the Congress of 1871–1873. Garrett was a sky-blue bolter in 1882 and a Prohibition party man ten years later. This most untypical Populist was the convention's sole nominee for the five-member court, so that he could run with four Republicans on a fusion ticket, where he would fit comfortably.[14]

The Populist state platform of 1894 contained three affirmative proposals: free silver and inflation, a graduated income tax, and direct election of the Senate. The major impulse expressed in the

13. Nashville *Banner,* April 12, 14, 1894; Memphis *Commercial,* August 16, 1893, April 15, 1894; Knoxville *Journal,* July 12, 1890; Nashville *Weekly Toiler,* November 14, 1888; Nashville *American,* September 4, 1884, September 26, 1886, August 14, 1892, April 4, 1894; Memphis *Appeal-Avalanche,* April 12, 1894; Washington *National Economist,* March 11, 1893 (quotes).
    14. *Biographical Directory of the American Congress,* 1002; Nashville *Banner,* June 3, 1892; Nashville *American,* April 12, 1894.

platform was to "hurl from power" the "plutocratic East" for the sake of the "liberties and prosperity of the American people." [15] The three positive demands were designed to strike down the mighty and/or the East. This platform represents the mood of the Tennessee Populists better than do the national platforms of their party.

Despite some rumbles of discontent in the Democratic party against Governor Turney, no one stepped forward to challenge his renomination. Pressed on the silver issue, he took refuge behind the currency plank of the 1892 national Democratic platform, which cheerfully demanded both free coinage of gold and silver and a firm, stable currency consisting of dollars of equal value. That was the kind of evasion used by Bob Taylor on the Blair bill and by John Buchanan on the subtreasury, but unlike his predecessors, Turney was not attacked for straddling, because Democrats feared further division in their party. E. W. Carmack asserted without explanation that "under a Populist governor the State was drifting steadily upon the breakers" and that Turney had rescued Tennessee and its reputation. At the state Democratic convention the governor's name was put forward by Carmack, a friend of Senator Harris, and seconded by a former sky-blue. Turney was escorted to the dais by a trio representing party harmony: General W. H. Jackson, the prominent Redeemer and friend of President Cleveland; T. M. McConnell, a former supporter of Buchanan; and Carmack the Bourbon. Turney was renominated unanimously.[16]

The unusual harmony of the Democrats was tribute to the threat seen in Populism. True, it had become traditional before 1888 to renominate an incumbent governor, but the last previous smooth renomination had occurred amidst a Donnybrook over the 1884 tariff plank. After the farmers' takeover of the 1890 convention, Democratic politicians arranged for harmonious rubber-stamp sessions. Table 32 demonstrates this effect of Populism. In 1896, for the first time in twenty-six years, a non-incumbent Democrat was

15. Nashville *American,* April 12, 1894. For platform text, see Appendix C.
16. Nashville *Banner,* January 23, February 23, August 16, 1894; Pulaski *Citizen,* April 11, 1889, and quoted in Memphis *Commercial,* February 18, 1894; McKee (ed.), *National Conventions and Platforms,* 265; Memphis *Commercial,* March 13, July 29, 31, 1894; Nashville *American,* June 22, 1882, July 15, 1890; W. H. Jackson to D. S. Lamont, October 23, 1887, in Cleveland Papers.

Table 32

DECLINE OF DEMOCRATIC NOMINATION CONTESTS
AS SHOWN BY FIRST BALLOT FOR GOVERNOR, DEMOCRATIC
STATE CONVENTIONS, 1870–1896 [17]

Year	Number of Candidates, First Ballot	Percentage of Votes for Top Two Candidates
1870	1	—
1872	1 *	—
1874	11	35
1876	1 *	—
1878	7	50
1880	(convention split in two before nomination)	
1882	6 **	66
1884	1 *	—
1886	4	74
1888	5	67
1890	4	70
1892	1 ***	—
1894	1 *	—
1896	1	—

* Incumbent.
** Regular Democrats after sky-blue walkout.
*** One actual candidate; insignificant scattering for others.

nominated with absolutely no opposition at the convention. This trend toward composing differences in private followed and paralleled the increasing use of the Democratic nominating caucus in the legislature (see Table 7 above).

The Republicans were divided, as before. Congressman John C. Houk's faction called itself "native born whites" and their opponents "carpetbaggers." The Houk side was hurt by the rumor that it had used the McDowell payoff scandal of 1892 to strike at the bonds between the "carpetbaggers" and the national party committee. A

17. Nashville *Union and American,* September 14, 1870, August 20, 1874; Memphis *Avalanche,* May 20, 1872; White (ed.), *Messages,* VI, 448, VII, 95; Nashville *American,* August 17, 1878, August 12, 1886, May 11, 1888, July 16, 1890, August 10, 1892; Nashville *Banner,* August 16, 1894, May 8, 1896.

sign of "carpetbagger" ascendency was the seating at the state convention of a racially mixed Davidson County delegation over a con-
testing lily-white group. The convention nominated "carpetbagger"
Henry Clay Evans, an iron manufacturer and Pennsylvania native,
for governor. A Union veteran, he had settled in Chattanooga, served
two terms as mayor, organized a public-school system, and gone to
Congress for one term. After his defeat for reelection to Congress,
he received a post in the Harrison administration.[18]

Evans was attacked for his northern birth by the Democrats, and
by Governor Turney for being a big businessman who had issued
scrip wages to his workers. "Force Bill Evans," taunted the Democrats, although he had actually opposed the Lodge election bill.
Turney charged absurdly that the Republican plank against the
state's Democratic election laws would permit seventeen hundred
convicts to vote. A Republican retorted that Turney had "deliberately exposed his moss-grown back, by dragging out from its musty
hiding place, and waving it aloft, the old confederate bloody shirt,
that was made to do duty a quarter of a century ago[.]" The Democratic Chattanooga *Times,* though cool to his Bourbon rhetoric,
praised Turney as a clean, reforming governor, which said more
about the *Times* than about Turney.[19]

Although the Republicans were the main threat to Turney's reelection, the People's party was not forgotten. "We are going to make
a desperate effort to snow the Pops under everlastingly," a Turney
lieutenant assured him. But the Populists, who needed unity the
most, could not attain it. Shortly after their convention another
internal squabble broke out: former governor Buchanan, a member
of the board of the *Farmers' Voice,* was sued in Nashville chancery
court by the editor, an ally of McDowell, for trying to exert an undue
influence over the paper's editorials. Buchanan answered that the
paper was wrong in trying to help the People's party—evidence that

18. Nashville *American,* October 26, 1892; Nashville *Banner,* August 22, 1894; J. Eugene
Lewis, "The Tennessee Gubernatorial Campaign and Election of 1894," *Tennessee Historical
Quarterly,* XIII (1954), 107; Queener, "East Tennessee Republicans as a Minority Party," 63;
Biographical Directory of the American Congress, 950.
19. Nashville *Banner,* September 26, 29, October 23, 1894; Knoxville *Journal,* October
2, 17, 1894; Chattanooga *Times,* May 30, 1890.

he still clung to his Independent Democratic organization.[20] The Populists had nearly as little confidence in each other as they had in major-party leaders.

The third party's best hope, as in 1892, was cooperation with the larger Republican party. For the August elections the two parties printed joint tickets for county offices and for the state supreme court. The Democratic judicial slate won, reversing a few local Winstead-Buchanan majorities of 1892. In scattered counties the Populists sharply changed old patterns of Democratic domination: in Rutherford the weakest Democrat got only one vote more than the strongest Republican; the fusion ticket carried Cheatham County with Populist Garrett leading; and the Democrats barely won Lauderdale.[21] But the third party was still insignificant except where it held the balance between the major parties.

For November the Republicans and Populists cooperated as in 1892. Each party ran its own nominee for governor, but they joined forces against the Democrats in legislative races. Once again, such arrangements were condemned by the Democrats as illegitimate, as a "conspiracy against the peace and welfare of the State." "The Populists as usual have been sold out to the Republicans," thought a Democratic voter. "They are *nothing,* the most contemptible party that has ever come into notice, more like a set of lunatics than anything else." [22] The third party lost three legislative seats controlled by Montgomery County, where Republican-Populist fusion broke down in legislative races, though Evans carried the county. But the Populists increased their House delegation from five to seven and elected three senators, relying on Buchanan's Independent Democrats in Rutherford County and on Republicans everywhere.[23]

Tennesseeans woke up the day after the election to find that the lackadaisical Democrats might have lost the governorship to a resur-

20. M. N. Whitaker, secretary of campaign committee of Franklin County Central Democratic Club, to Peter Turney, September 11, 1894, in CGO, TSLA; Memphis *Commercial,* May 31, June 1, 1894; Nashville *Banner,* June 1, 1894.

21. Memphis *Commercial Appeal,* July 28, 1894; Nashville *Banner,* August 8, 1894; Nashville *American,* August 12, 1894.

22. Nashville *Banner,* October 27, 1894; Memphis *Commercial Appeal,* November 3, 1894; Cartmell Diary, November 3, 1894.

23. Nashville *Banner,* October 27, 1894; Clarksville *Tobacco Leaf-Chronicle,* November 7, 1894; Memphis *Commercial Appeal,* January 29, 1895.

gent Republican party. The Knoxville *Journal* spread a huge eagle across the top of its front page, with the words, "Farewell Secession, Goodbye Old Pete, Hail Glorious Era of Light." The strongly Democratic Memphis *Commercial Appeal* proclaimed on its front page that Turney had won, though it noted on page two that many politicians thought otherwise. Days lengthened into weeks, and still the result was unclear, because state officials were following an unprecedented policy of keeping the official returns secret as they arrived in the mail. Meanwhile, a Democrat from Madison County who had been accused of printing fake ballots in 1884 to defeat the railroad commission began proclaiming Turney's victory and rounding up legislators to keep Evans out of office. Finally on December 13 the secretary of state released the official returns, showing Evans the winner with 105,104 votes to Turney's 104,356 and Mims' 23,088.[24] But the Democratic press opened a barrage of charges that East Tennessee returns were flawed because officials there had permitted voting without poll-tax receipts, an accusation not denied by the Republican Knoxville *Journal.* As Democratic partisans gained confidence, others became disturbed at the prospect that Turney would be kept in office beyond the expiration of his term, forcing Evans to appeal to a Democratic legislature to expel Turney from office.[25]

The legislature hastily enacted an election-contest law, which had been lacking, and appointed investigative committees to tour the counties where the returns were disputed. A Democratic justice of the peace supported by A. S. Colyar inaugurated Evans privately. But Turney retained physical possession of the office while the legislature resolutely exposed violations of the poll-tax law in Republican counties and, with equal determination, overlooked cases of outright fraud and false returns in Democratic counties. The operating premises of the Democrats were laid down by the state party committee: "It is the right and duty of the Democratic party to represent the State, and it has done so by large majorities and with ease"; therefore

24. Knoxville *Journal,* November 7, 1894; Memphis *Commercial Appeal,* November 7, 18, 1894; Nashville *Banner,* November 20, 30, December 13, 1894; Nashville *World,* October 31, 1884; *Senate Journal,* 1895, p. 177.
25. Nashville *Banner,* December 20, 24, 27, 1894; Memphis *Commercial Appeal,* December 30, 1894, January 2, 1895; Knoxville *Journal,* December 24, 1894.

a Republican victory was an impermissible aberration. Furthermore, declared racist E. W. Carmack, "the average Haywood county or Fayette county Republican voter" was the likely missing link between apes and men in the Darwinian chain of evolution.[26] Democratic legislators enforced the poll-tax law to invalidate otherwise legal Republican votes, but considered frauds by Democratic officials an appropriate way of neutralizing black voting power. There can be little doubt that according to the votes cast in 1894, H. Clay Evans was elected governor. Over the continuing and vehement protests of Republican, Populist, and a few Democratic legislators, however, Turney was "counted in" and inaugurated for a second term in May, 1895.[27]

Evans benefitted from a large Republican turnout, which exceeded that of 1892. This extraordinary feat of increasing the party's vote from a presidential to a nonpresidential election was accomplished mostly by tapping Republican reservoirs, rather than by gathering up disaffected former Populists. Another factor in the outcome was the Populist hold on some former Democrats. Mims's 10 percent was a drop from Buchanan's 15 percent of 1892, but it was enough to be decisive in the result. Ironically, an effect of this balance-of-power position was to emphasize the futility of a third-party politics that only delivered power to an unsympathetic major party. As a Democratic editor pointed out right after the election, "no prominent Populite politician [would] be allowed to expectorate upon the polished oaken floor of Governor Evans." [28] Most Populists did not calculate the effects of their votes, but the 1894 election drove home the lesson that Tennessee was a two-party state without the Populists, which could only accelerate the attrition in their ranks.

Mims voters of 1894, though fewer, were much the same as the

26. Nashville *Banner,* February 6, March 6, 1895. For the election contest, see Lewis, "Tennessee Gubernatorial Campaign and Election of 1894," 224–43; *Contest for Governor in Tennessee: Complete Proceedings of the Joint Convention and Investigating Committee, the Evidence in Full and Arguments of Counsel* (Nashville, 1895). Memphis *Commercial Appeal,* January 5, February 23, May 9, 1895.

27. Democratic newspapers outside Tennessee that condemned the count-in included the New York *World,* the Louisville *Courier-Journal,* the Atlanta *Constitution,* the Atlanta *Journal,* and the New Orleans *Times-Democrat.* Nashville *Banner,* January 17, 1895.

28. White (ed.), *Messages,* VII, 468–71, 555–57; *Senate Journal,* 1895, p. 177; Memphis *Commercial Appeal,* November 13, 1894.

Table 33
POPULIST VOTE BY PROPERTY-OWNERSHIP GROUP,
CIVIL DISTRICT 11, LAUDERDALE COUNTY,
1894 ELECTION [29]

Property Group	Voting Populists in Group	Potential Voters in Group	% Populists in Group
No taxes assessed or paid	48 ⎫	189	46
Poll tax only paid	40 ⎭		
Landowners	18	116 *	16
1–50 acres	5	29	17
51–100 acres	5	35	14
101–200 acres	6	36	17
201–500 acres	2	11	18
500 acres and over	0	5	0
Total	106	305 *	34

* Figure of 305 is 1890 population of district times ratio of voting-age male population to entire population for Lauderdale County in 1890. The total of 116 landowners includes a few women, making the numbers of landowning voters slightly more, and the number of nonlandowning voters slightly less, than they should be.

Buchanan voters of 1892 (see Appendix B, Tables 1, 16, and 18). In the eleventh district of Lauderdale County, which had a much higher proportion of blacks than the average Tennessee district, nearly half the nonlandowning potential voters, but only one-sixth of the property owners, voted for Mims in 1894.

The data from this one district offers evidence that Tennessee Populists were lower on the scales of wealth and status than their Democratic neighbors. Prominent landowning farmers willing to support the Alliance within the Democratic party balked at becoming Populists, as the Democratic strategists of 1892 had expected.

In 1895 the clamor for free silver posed a critical threat to the

29. Lauderdale County tax book, 1893, courthouse, Ripley; 1890 Census, *Population*, 317–28. A legislative committee took sworn testimony in hearings on the 1894 election which included a list of all Populist voters in this district; the list is in *Contest for Governor in Tennessee*, I, 958.

People's party, because the prosilver stand of the Tennessee Democrats made the third party seem pointless. The 1896 state Democratic convention chose Bob Taylor again, with no dissent, since a nephew of Senator Harris had dropped out of the race earlier. On the currency question there was no harmony, however; each side shouted down speakers from the other, but the sound-money Memphis delegates felt insulted as well as beaten in the voting. Bob Taylor jumped on the resulting free-silver plank "with all the agility of a practiced performer," grumbled the gold-bug Nashville *Banner.* Indeed, silver feeling ran so high in the convention that a sound-money delegate felt compelled to write President Cleveland to reassure him, "The rank and file of our people are honest and patriotic, but they have allowed sectional prejudice to influence them in party councils." [30] This "sectional prejudice" was so close to the attitude undergirding Populism that silver Democrats would find many third-party men receptive to their overtures.

Populist leaders struggled to keep their followers from trooping off after the Democrats' bright silver banner. The latter were encouraging Populists to return to their old party, perhaps in recognition that the proscriptive policy of 1892 had given the third party a major boost. Any persons, irrespective of past party affiliation, were invited to vote in the Democratic primaries on pledging to support the nominee. The Democrats, said a Populist newspaper, "argue with the Populists that they have accepted and are advocating the Populist demand for . . . [free silver at sixteen to one] . . . , and therefore the Populists should come back to the old party and help to win the fight for silver. Excuse us, gentlemen. If you were to adopt the entire Populist platform we could not trust you as long as you labelled it Democracy. You made a mistake. . . . The old parties are doomed." [31]

"We already belong to the oldest and strongest silver league in the Union, and can see no necessity for joining another," declared A. L. Mims, who went on to express confidence that silver Democrats would "lay aside prejudice and fall into line with the only

30. Nashville *Banner,* May 8, 1896; Memphis *Commercial Appeal,* April 1, May 8, 1896; M. Savage to Grover Cleveland, June 19, 1896, in Cleveland Papers.
31. Nashville *Banner,* April 1, May 24, 1896.

organized party through which the unlimited coinage of silver [would] ever be obtained." For the time being, Populist leaders placed party loyalty over principle—a reversal of their original position. But the pressure for cooperation with silver Democrats would increase. By January, 1896, Populists and Democrats in Haywood County were agreeing to vote in one county primary to nominate a single ticket for a local election.[32]

Many Tennessee Populists were angry at the third-party nomination of Democrat William Jennings Bryan for president, though Tom Watson was his Populist running-mate. John H. McDowell, speaking to the 1896 state convention, denied that the People's party would ever endorse Democratic vice-presidential nominee Arthur Sewall, and claimed that word was expected from the Democrats at any time about Sewall's withdrawal in favor of Watson. McDowell insisted that the Bryan nomination was compatible with middle-road, or antifusion, Populism. Not all his hearers were convinced. J. R. Beasley, the former Greenback leader, and J. W. James, who had been on the Populist national committee in 1891 when McDowell was still a Democrat, moved to condemn the Populist nomination of Bryan, objecting also to the Democratic plank for redemption of paper money in coin. The convention voted to support McDowell and Bryan.[33]

After their defeat the anti-Bryan men abstained from voting in approval of the state platform, which expressed limited, pragmatic goals, many of them negative. It echoed countless Democratic platforms in calling for economical government and low taxes, but it opposed that party in six planks demanding repeal of the election laws of 1889–1890 and denouncing the settlement of the contested 1894 gubernatorial election. The platform acknowledged the nativist American Protective Association in opposing any governmental appropriation for "sectarian purposes," and in calling for restriction of immigration to protect American workers. A. L. Mims, renominated for governor, stressed state issues in his campaign, rather than the national Populist demands.[34] Since the Democrats were preempt-

32. *Ibid.,* June 18, 1895; Nashville *Sun,* January 31, 1896.
33. Nashville *Banner,* July 28, 29, 1896; Memphis *Appeal-Avalanche,* May 21, 1891.
34. Nashville *Banner,* July 29, September 16, 1896.

ing the silver issue, and since the Republicans would reap the benefit of indignation at the 1895 "count-in," the Populists were struggling to maintain a justification for their existence. To do so they argued that no one else could be trusted.

Others besides the Populists were having problems with the silver stampede in the Democratic party: the gold Democrats. Encouraged more or less openly by several leading newspapers, some of the same men who had bolted their party in 1882 over the state-debt question began organizing again.[35] Perhaps because the issue this time was national, the gold Democrats in Tennessee were even less successful than the sky-blues had been. Once again some of the "best men" in the state and some of those normally most strongly partisan split from their party but failed to carry a mass of supporters with them.

One sky-blue who left his party again in 1896 was Congressman Joseph E. Washington of the Nashville district. In the strange and shifting course of politics, he was supported warmly in 1890 by the *Weekly Toiler,* but in 1896 he thought the Democratic silver plank represented capitulation to Populism. The same man who had warned in 1890 that Republican victory meant black heels on white necks now refused to support the party of white supremacy. A silverite won the Democratic congressional primary by default in 1896 when silver forces agreed to let only one of their number enter, which caused Washington suddenly to see the compelling power of his principles and withdraw. Nashville *Banner* owner E. B. Stahlman, who joined the Republican party outright earlier in 1896, persuaded the black Republican nominee for Congress in the Nashville district to withdraw so that GOP support would go to J. C. McReynolds, the champion of the organized gold Democrats of Nashville.[36]

The situation in the Tenth Congressional District was somewhat similar. Josiah Patterson of Memphis, who had won the seat in 1890 after losing the gubernatorial nomination to Buchanan, came into

---

35. *Ibid.,* October 15, 1896; Chattanooga *Times,* June 9, 1896; Nashville *Sun,* May 4, June 13, 1896; Clarksville *Tobacco Leaf-Chronicle,* November 4, 1896.

36. Nashville *American,* September 11, 1886; Nashville *Weekly Toiler,* August 13, 1890; L. O. W. Brandon to L. C. Houk, August 12, 1890, in Houk Papers; Nashville *Banner,* June 4, July 21, 27, August 5, 1896; Knoxville *Tribune,* October 10, 1896; Nashville *Sun,* October 21, 1896.

increasing conflict with silver Senator Isham Harris over the currency question, as well as over patronage. "The time has passed for attempting to conciliate men who are active in their opposition to the administration," Patterson wrote President Cleveland in 1895, in a clear reference to Harris. The congressman toured the South from Alabama to Texas to Kentucky, speaking for sound money. Patterson was out battling the silver dragon, editorialized E. W. Carmack in the Memphis *Commercial Appeal*: "His pathway shines with the white-bleached bones of gorgons, griffins, hydras, sea-serpents, paralblo-pipedons and other outlandish varmints." After Carmack quit his post as editor in the spring of 1896, he seemed the logical silver candidate to oppose Patterson. A drawback was that the Populists still resented his attacks on them. Carmack ran anyway, however, with the district's silver Democrats behind him. Patterson was hurt by the declaration of the state Democratic committee that Carmack was the official standard-bearer in the Tenth. The decisive blow came when William Jennings Bryan himself, whom Patterson considered "the worst of his type," gave Carmack his blessing before a vast crowd in Memphis. The race was the district's most evenly matched in years, however, because gold-bug Patterson had many Democratic friends in Memphis, plus the support of the Republican organization and of acrobatic Populist leader J. H. McDowell.[37]

The only statewide effort of the gold Democrats was to support the National Democratic ticket of John M. Palmer and Simon B. Buckner, which openly aimed at splitting the Democratic vote to elect McKinley. The Nashville *Banner* came out for Palmer-Buckner, as did the Chattanooga *Times,* now run by George W. Ochs since his brother Adolph's recent move to the New York *Times.* Only 1,951 voters cast Palmer-Buckner ballots in Tennessee, however, fewer than 1 percent of the votes cast, and not enough to take the state from Bryan.[38] More gold Democrats voted for McKinley

37. Nashville *Banner,* March 9, 1894, May 4, 1896; J. Patterson to Grover Cleveland, May 5, August 1, 1895, July 11, August 12, 1896, in Cleveland Papers; Memphis *Commercial Appeal,* April 19, 1895, October 6, 1896; Nashville *Sun,* April 29, September 5, October 19, 1896. Unlike J. E. Washington, Patterson had not been a sky-blue, but a Bourbon.
38. Woodward, *Origins of the New South,* 287; Chattanooga *Times,* August 9, 14, 1896; Nashville *Banner,* October 15, 1896; *Tribune Almanac,* 1897, p. 260.

than for Palmer. The small Palmer vote was concentrated in urban and/or growing counties, and in black counties—areas where the white people were most confident and prosperous (see Appendix B, Table 19).

The sound-money Nashville *Banner* hoped non-McKinley votes would also be divided, and cooperated with Populist leaders to hurt silver Democrats. Late in 1895 the *Banner* published charges that Democratic leaders had approached McDowell and urged him to work with them for the sake of silver. True or not, the report gave him a chance to reaffirm his loyalty to the People's party and also drove another wedge between the silver parties. The *Banner* took a curious interest in the integrity of the Populists, urging them to remain independent and not to forget their grudges against the Democrats.[39]

With no help from gold Democrats, who rubbed salt in their wounds, the problem of fusion became an insoluble one for the Populists after their national convention nominated Bryan and Watson. McDowell wrote national Populist chairman Marion Butler, "The uncertainity on Watson & Sewall is tearing our party to pieces. Advise me what to do at your earliest moment." McDowell overestimated the proportion of Populists who would refuse to vote for Sewall, as did a pro-Bryan Democratic editor who was worried about losing the state if two Bryan tickets were put forward. Sitting on a conference committee with the Democrats to negotiate a joint slate of electors, McDowell was in a strange position because he was getting Republican support in his race against a silver Democrat in the Ninth Congressional District. The negotiations stalled, breaking up in late September, and McDowell's *People's Friend* insisted that Sewall had to step down. A silver Democratic editor charged that the Populists cared nothing for silver, wanting only to keep their own party alive.[40] As far as J. H. McDowell was concerned, this accusation was correct.

Not all Populists were willing to follow McDowell. In October

39. Nashville *Banner,* October 14, 16, 1895, July 28, 29, 1896.
40. J. H. McDowell to Marion Butler, June 6, 1896, in Marion Butler Papers, Southern Historical Collection, University of North Carolina Library, Chapel Hill; Nashville *Sun,* September 9, 24, 27, 1896; Memphis *Commercial Appeal,* September 5, 1896.

two of the twelve Bryan-Watson electors resigned, urging support for Bryan and Sewall. The Davidson County Populist convention endorsed this mutiny, and condemned state Populist chairman Buchanan for supporting fusion with gold-bug Republicans in some legislative races. A faction of the third party decided to call on all Populists to vote for the Democratic Bryan electors.[41] The revolt spread, as local Populist leaders asked their neighbors to scratch the Bryan-Watson electors from their party ballots. The Democratic press delighted in printing notices like this one:

> To the Populists of Wilson County.
> In view of the fact that our state committee and the democratic committee have failed to agree upon a plan of fusion . . . [and since the] populist party has always prided itself upon its non-partisan principles . . . I earnestly call upon the members of the populist party in the county of Wilson to lay aside their feelings in the matter and vote for Bryan and Sewall, for in them is our only hope to attain the legislation that we believe is so vitally necessary for the prosperity of the country. H. C. PALMER.[42]

With its organization falling apart, the state Populist committee wrote the Democratic chairman late in October to ask for a reopening of negotiations. He saw clearly that fusion now would only help stop the disintegration of the People's party, so he turned them down. Just when Tom Watson's campaign tour took him through Nashville, the state Populist committee issued a statement ostensibly trying to keep the door open for fusion, but offering no new concessions, and urging all Populists to stand by their party organization, because if that collapsed, all was lost. But the Democratic press was emblazoned with names of Populists who were abandoning Watson, including another nominee for elector, J. H. Burnham. "The People's party was not made to be prostituted to the greed of Republicanism," he said. "Our party is a mighty protest against wrong and oppression, was begotten and born in the furnace of persecution. Therefore let us protest, not submit to such unhallowed bossism." Since it was no longer clear to them that both major parties were controlled by

---

41. Nashville *Sun,* October 11, 1896; Nashville *Banner,* October 12, 1896; Knoxville *Tribune,* October 13, 1896.
42. Lebanon *Democrat,* October 22, 1896.

Wall Street, many Populists refused to give aid and comfort in a national election to the one which apparently was. The Bryan-Watson ticket received scarcely a third of the mere twelve thousand votes given to Mims.[43]

Tennessee Populism never recovered from the debacle of 1896. Demoralized by a shrinking membership, the party was confused and fragmented by the dilemma of whether to fight the state-level enemy (the Democrats) or the national foe (the Republicans and Wall Street). By 1900 the People's party of Tennessee was a mere shadow: its candidate for governor in that year received fewer votes than Buchanan had polled in a single county in 1892. John H. McDowell turned to greener pastures, rising to the rank of "general" in the United Confederate Veterans and to the office of "chieftan" of the McDowell Clan of America. In 1912 he turned up in Theodore Roosevelt's Bull Moose party, after joining Buchanan and Mims in supporting their old, bitter enemy, E. W. Carmack, in his prohibitionist campaign of 1908. Populist voters probably returned to the Democratic party, or succumbed to apathy. But the suspicious hostility toward outsiders expressed in the Populists' anguished and futile struggle to "hurl from power" the high and the mighty, and to resist the "encroachments of the powerful," [44] would remain to find various expression in later generations.

Paradoxically, the very similarity of these Populist attitudes to Bourbonism is a clue to the relative weakness of the People's party in Tennessee. Despite Bob Taylor's personal popularity, the Bourbons had dominated the Democratic party in the state during the 1880s. The keystone of Bourbonism was support for the existing social order of the South, especially white supremacy. Such conservatism was combined easily with resistance to aggressive Yankee power as embodied in railroads, bankers, moral reformers, and

---

43. Nashville *Sun,* October 20, 22, 23, 1896; Nashville *Banner,* October 23, 1896; Knoxville *Tribune,* November 2, 1896; *Tribune Almanac,* 1897, p. 260. The silver Democratic tide swept Bob Taylor to a third term and defeated McDowell, McReynolds, and Patterson for Congress.

44. *Tribune Almanac,* 1901, p. 379; John Hugh McDowell, *History of the McDowells, Erwins, Irwins and Connections* (Memphis, 1918), [10], 93; Isaac, *Prohibition and Politics,* 16, 142; "State Populist Platform of 1894," in Nashville *American,* April 12, 1894; J. H. Burnham statement, in Nashville *Banner,* September 12, 1892.

Republican protectionists and race-mixers. Tennessee Populism borrowed its basic attitudes, as well as its voters, from Bourbonism. State Populist platforms agreed with defiance of outside oppressors, differing from Bourbon attitudes only on state questions: the election laws, the convict lease, and perhaps child-labor measures. But this difference was critical. Populists threatened the *status quo* by seeking access to political power. Tennessee's ruling elites therefore united to crush Populism as they had driven the Alliance from the Democratic party, and with Bryan's help, discontent was again channeled against outsiders alone. The state's strong Republican party was a convenient and familiar symbol for convincing voters that political disruption would bring social upheaval and Negro rule. Under these conditions, Populism's failure is not so remarkable as its occurrence.

10

Conclusion

It has been generally assumed among historians that Tennessee Democrats in the last quarter of the nineteenth century were divided into three distinct and enduring factions: states' rights planters, Whig-industrialists, and small farmers. This idea originated with Dan M. Robison, who wrote that the states' rights group dominated its party from the end of Andrew Johnson's hegemony in the 1850s to the rise of Bob Taylor, who rallied Johnson's small-farmer constituency and whose leadership ensured that the agrarian revolt was relatively mild in Tennessee. Robison's three-faction hypothesis has permeated the historiography of the last four decades. C. Vann Woodward accepted the distinction between states' rights planters and Whig-industrialists, but, in accordance with his view of the southern Redeemers, he considered the Whig-industrialists dominant in Tennessee politics.[1]

The influential Robison hypothesis is inadequate because it fails to account for several major political realignments between 1870 and 1896, and because it is not supported by evidence on the nature of divisions among the electorate. Whig-industrialists fought both for and against the Redeemer coalition of the 1870s. The new Bourbon Democrats of the 1880s reestablished Democratic control after the

1. Robison, *Bob Taylor,* 14–22, 217; Sharp, "The Entrance of the Farmers' Alliance into Tennessee Politics" (1937), 80; Queener, "East Tennessee Republicans as a Minority Party" (1943), 68–69; Lane L. Boutwell, "The Oratory of Robert Love Taylor," *Tennessee Historical Quarterly,* IX (1950), 42–43; Lewis, "Tennessee Gubernatorial Campaign and Election of 1894" (1954), 235; S. J. Folmsbee, R. E. Corlew, and E. L. Mitchell, *History of Tennessee* (New York, 1960), II, 153–55; Davis, "Arthur S. Colyar" (1962), 320; Folmsbee, Corlew, and Mitchell, *Tennessee: A Short History* (1969), 392–94; Thomas Harrison Baker, *The Memphis Commercial Appeal: The History of a Southern Newspaper* (Baton Rouge, 1971), 146–47; Woodward, *Origins of the New South,* 21.

low-tax revolt split the party. Bob Taylor was not an agrarian leader, but a charming entertainer who worked with New South men and who failed to organize a continuing opposition to Bourbonism. That was done by the Farmers' Alliance, which was a real threat and so was expelled from the party. The Redeemers and Bourbons were not disciplined, cohesive factions, but loose coalitions based more on patronage and symbolic issues than on conflicts among sections or classes with different economic interests. Any attempt to trace continuing factions in the careers of individual politicians ends in a labyrinth of inconsistencies, reversals, and contradictions. For example, Duncan B. Cooper, a sky-blue bolter in 1882, controlled the Bourbon Nashville *American* in 1886 when it battled against tariff protection and the Blair bill; four years later Cooper's Nashville *Herald* backed industrialist Jere Baxter, Colyar's man, for governor.[2] The division between Democrats and Republicans grew increasingly rigid after some attempts to soften it in the 1870s, but differences within the dominant Democratic party did not give rise to continuing, organized, and clearly defined factions.

Though Democratic politicians did not divide consistently, they divided often. Between 1870 and 1896, members or former members of the party appealed directly to the electorate against other Democrats over a dozen times. Can this dissension be explained by economic fluctuations between boom and depression? The growth of low-tax sentiment in the 1870s occurred during the worsening depression of that decade, although the substantial recovery of 1879 did not prevent the climax of the low-tax rebellion in 1880. Farm commodity prices were falling in the 1880s, but there is no relation between cotton production and Populist strength in 1892. The depression beginning in 1893 coincided not with the rise of Populism in Tennessee, but with its decline.[3] It is impossible to prove either a direct relationship between the level of prosperity and the amount of political insurgency, or the absence of any such connection.

2. Jackson *West Tennessee Whig,* January 13, 1886; Nashville *American,* February 20, March 8, 1886; Nashville *Weekly Toiler,* January 9, 1889; Nashville *Herald,* January 1, 1890.
3. Edwin Frickey, *Economic Fluctuations in the United States: A Systematic Analysis of Long-Run Trends and Business Cycles, 1866–1914* (Cambridge, Mass., 1942), graph following p. 338.

Whether or not political behavior depended largely on economic conditions, gross indicators of business cycles could be unrelated to the perceptions of individuals. Late in 1890, for example, which was quite a prosperous year for the national economy, a farmer hauled a load of wood into Jackson, had trouble selling it, and concluded, "Times are a little tighter in this country [*i.e.* area] than I ever saw them before. Money scarcer, don't know where it will end." [4] A precise awareness of current economic conditions was less widespread than the assumption that the Civil War had crippled the southern economy, which had yet to recover.

Tennessee political divisions are as difficult to explain by differences of wealth among the population as by economic changes over time. There is evidence that Populism had more appeal for landless than for propertied farmers (see Table 33 above), and that in 1892, Populism was strong among Middle Tennesseans experiencing the greatest downturn in the rate of growth of the rural landowning class, and in West Tennessee where the greatest amount of new land was being brought under cultivation (see Appendix B, Table 16, Part A). But taken together with other data, this evidence suggests that Populism was linked to frustrated expectations of upward social mobility or to the anomie of unstable growing communities, rather than to simple economic class conflict. The limited analysis possible of the district primary elections of 1890 shows that Buchanan voters were not consistently distinguished by the value of their land (see Table 21 above). Furthermore, statewide correlations of election returns with the value of farmland show that in no elections, with the possible exception of the prohibition referendum of 1887, did relatively affluent and relatively poor areas vote against each other throughout the state (see Appendix B, Tables 2–13). Nor did the rate of mortgage encumbrance affect voting behavior (see Appendix B, Tables 14 and 16). Railroad policies did provoke political opposition in Tennessee, but not from Populists. The absence of any political rhetoric whatsoever, before or during the Populist movement, reflecting a division between rich and poor white farmers is further reason to believe that such political conflict as existed among farmers

4. Cartmell Diary, December 22, 1890.

resulted from different perceptions of their relations to nonfarmers, not from differences in economic interest.

Tennessee politics of the late nineteenth century does not fit well into the progressive framework of interpretation of American history, which has seen the nation's past roughly in terms of a conflict of economic interest between farmers and workers on the one hand and merchants and manufacturers on the other. The major challenge to the progressive school in the last twenty-five years has come from the consensus historians who see political discord not as a clash of basic values and interests, but as competition for social status within the existing order. From the consensus viewpoint, protest groups have often been not rational and forward-looking, but retrogressive and suspicious of real or imagined threats to their status.[5]

One aspect of the irrationality of politics in Tennessee was the paranoid style adopted by some politicians. This is not to say that Tennessee society was fundamentally paranoid, or that men who used that style were clinically ill. The term is borrowed here, as by Richard Hofstadter, to convey "qualities of heated exaggeration, suspiciousness, and conspiratorial fantasy" exhibited by "more or less normal people" who felt that a hostile world was plotting against groups with which they identified. Many southerners had long felt that the North wanted to humiliate them. Governor Isham Harris' war message of April, 1861, though not pervaded by a conspiracy theory, urged secession from "a Government that has developed the coldest and most deliberate purpose to inaugurate a civil and sanguinary war" among its people.[6] A full generation later, a farmer of Madison County wrote in his diary about recent passage by congressional Republicans of a tariff bill and of the Lodge election bill:

> [Their] object being to get control of the Southern states. . . . [A] more corrupt party [than the Republicans] never existed—tyranical [sic], oppressive, and mean, and if not checked will wipe out all State Government . . . They foster trusts, combines, and enrich manufacturers and

5. For the progressive view, see Charles and Mary Beard, *The Rise of American Civilization* (New York, 1927, 1930) and Hicks, *Populist Revolt.* For the consensus view, see Louis Hartz, *The Liberal Tradition in America* (New York, 1955), and Richard Hofstadter, *The Age of Reform: From Bryan to F.D.R.* (New York, 1955).

6. Richard Hofstadter, *The Paranoid Style in American Politics, and Other Essays* (New York, 1965), 3–4; White (ed.), *Messages,* V, 286.

reduce the mass of the people to poverty. Soon the wealth of the nation would be in the hands of a few. . . . There are not words enough in the English language to enumerate all their rascality and evil designs.[7]

There was a strong tendency to locate the source of malevolence in the North, which seemed to be trying to monopolize economic and political power and, in the words of the title of John Savage's autobiography, *to Reduce the Descendents of the Rebels of 1776. . . Down to the Level of the Negro Race.* The Bourbon coalition, and to a large extent the Tennessee Democratic party in general, depended on the feeling that white southerners had to defend their culture, economic interests, and racial status against hostile outsiders.

In a few cases, political leaders spoke as though they personally were victims of evil plotters. Andrew Johnson declared in 1874 that he had been defeated for senator by a "conspiracy." John Savage was not alone in posturing as a martyr for a righteous cause: John R. Beasley claimed that he had been subjected to "vile abuse in the public press," much as Lycurgus, Socrates, the Gracchi, and Christ had been. When McDowell was publicly attacked he retorted that he was the victim of a "conspiracy . . . to ruin me politically because I have the courage to follow my convictions." Governor Buchanan interpreted the coal strike of 1892, in the midst of his campaign for reelection, as a personal attack to make him look bad.[8] But such men were exceptions. Most politicians who spoke of evil forces saw them moving not against themselves as individuals but against the groups of voters they were addressing.

Leaders of particular causes often drew upon the reservoir of popular suspicion of outsiders. Greenbacker R. M. Edwards attacked various "rings" in his 1878 campaign. When A. S. Colyar was running for governor as a low-taxer in the same year, he declared that the state debt was only a surface matter, that the real issue was the money power, which, said Colyar, "has . . . the government by the throat, and with blackened face, addled brain and cramped limbs, it struggles for freedom. . . . It is not the money of this money power

7. Cartmell Diary, December 31, 1890.
8. Memphis *Avalanche,* October 11, 1874; Beasley, *The Conflict Between Liberty and Prohibition;* Memphis *Appeal-Avalanche,* June 26, 1891; Nashville *Banner,* August 16, 1892.

that has made the people jealous and fearful, but it is the purpose now fully developed to humiliate, humble, and degrade labor by first making the laboring people helpless and dependent—without ambition, without hope and without promise." [9]

John P. Buchanan told the 1888 state meeting of the Farmers' Alliance, "We cannot escape the influence of the pools, trusts, corners, and a thousand other rings that have been formed to catch every dollar we raise." J. R. Miles, president of the Tennessee Agricultural Wheel, quoted a London banker as saying that he and his colleagues would control the money supply in order to subjugate workers through their wages. American "money sharks," said Miles, picked up this idea. In 1895 a bellicose member of the nativist American Protective Association proclaimed that "war alone" could save America from conquest by British gold.[10] The diversity of the sources of these statements suggests a continuing assumption by politicians that the public would be receptive to the idea that a hostile, alien conspiracy existed with the deliberate intent of injuring and degrading honest working Tennesseeans.

Such a sense of being oppressed by the deliberate design of evil men is sometimes hard to distinguish from a more general and vague feeling of powerlessness with regard to men or institutions callous enough to push little people around, though not necessarily through conspiracies. This feeling could be grounded firmly in reality. In 1884 one Thomas Edwards, of rural Rutherford County, complained that the local politicos were "robers" because they had taken land from him and his wife Martha and sold it at public auction; Edwards tried to get county officials to take action, but they brushed him off, so he concluded that they would "prosecute just the poor class and not the rich class." Whether he was deprived of his land illegally is unknown, because he and his wife could not afford a lawyer and gave up. Five years later another protest came from Rutherford County, this time in a formal resolution of the county Farmers' Alliance. Armour and other meatpackers had a monopoly, the Alliancemen contended, which permitted the corporations to send

9. Memphis *Avalanche,* March 19, November 1, 1878.
10. Nashville *American,* August 15, 1888; Nashville *Weekly Toiler,* April 10, 1889; Nashville *Sun,* December 28, 1895.

ready-dressed beef into Tennessee cities to take markets from local stock raisers, who then had to ship their beef to Chicago, St. Louis, "or whatever other place those cursed, heartless, cut throats may designate, and then be forced to sell for the cost of raising." The farmers begged for legal remedies from the state government.[11] In both these cases, real grievances did exist: justice was for those who could pay for it, and farmers lacked the unity they needed to bargain with the corporations controlling agricultural markets. Protest against oppression was by no means necessarily unreasonable or misdirected.

Few, if any, Tennessee politicians of the late nineteenth century were customarily anti-Semitic. True, there was a tendency to use the Shylock image to describe greedy bankers or bondholders. John Savage denounced modern "shylocks" in 1879, and Chattanooga politician T. M. McConnell did in 1890. The Dyer County Farmers' Alliance voted to support their congressman against "the shylocks and their allies" who opposed him.[12] The most extended mention of Shylock by an Alliance source is from a newspaper: "And now when the Farmers' Alliance comes to the front with measures of relief for the debtor class who are being daily robbed of their homes, their hopes, and their very lives, Old Shylock prances out on the stage and claims the letter of his bond, 'his pound of flesh,'—poor old foolish Shylock, were he not blinded by his inordinate greed, he could see the modest judge approaching to try his case. . . . Sir, beware of the blood and tears that follow the execution."[13] These uses of Shylock imagery were few and isolated, and did not characterize the rhetoric of any significant politician, group, or newspaper. The most explicit known expression of anti-Semitism occurred in Nashville in 1890. Sam Jones, the popular evangelist, was holding forth when he overheard the sounds of a nearby dance being held on private grounds by a group of Jewish children. He denounced them so

11. Thomas Edwards to W. B. Bate, November 8, 1884, in CGO, TSLA; Nashville *Weekly Toiler,* November 20, 1889.
12. [Savage], *Speech on the State Debt,* 9; Nashville *American,* October 6, 1890; Nashville *Weekly Toiler,* August 6, 1890.
13. Louisville (Tenn.) *Alliance Advocate,* quoted in Washington *National Economist,* July 11, 1891.

fiercely that his hearers rushed outside and disrupted the party, throwing stones and bruising some of the children.[14] These examples are given because they very nearly exhaust the list of evidence for public anti-Semitism in Tennessee during this period. In anti-Semitism, as in Negrophobia, neither Populists nor Bourbons differed significantly from other groups.

Nativist and anti-Catholic feelings were more common than anti-Semitism, but reflected fear of inundation by foreign masses, not of conspiracy. Sky-blue candidate Joe Fussell believed that "Romanism" was subversive of American civilization, and the prohibitionist editor of the Nashville *Issue* also denounced the Catholic Church. When his Nashville *Union* carried front-page headlines about bloodshed in Chicago's Haymarket Square, A. S. Colyar editorialized that immigration had to be cut because foreigners were not being assimilated, but were spreading anarchism and undermining national customs. "American institutions must remain American," Colyar affirmed. Several years later Colyar supported the nativist American Protective Association in Nashville, where it was strong enough in 1895 to force the Democratic party to pull a Catholic off its ticket in a city campaign.[15] The APA was strong only in Nashville and did not exist in rural areas, so that the only possible comparison of the constituencies of the APA and Populism involves the untypically urban county of Davidson. But such a comparison (see Appendix B, Table 20) shows that in the city of Nashville the two movements attracted very nearly the same people. This does not prove that all Populists were nativists, but it does indicate that Populism could appeal to those who soon after followed the APA. Outside Nashville in Davidson County elections, on the other hand, there is no correlation between Populism and APA support. The currents of nativism in Tennessee in the late nineteenth century were mostly connected with prohibitionism or other progressive-reform movements. Populism did not immunize voters against nativism, but it was not the principal source of it either.

14. Nashville *Herald,* May 27, 1890. The *Herald* denounced the incident as a "monstrous outrage."
15. Undated speech by J. H. Fussell, in Fussell Papers; Memphis *Commercial,* January 29, 1893; Nashville *Union,* May 7, 1886; Nashville *Banner,* October 1, 4, 1895.

Some Tennessee politicians used a paranoid style, then, but this assertion must be carefully qualified. Few of them spoke of conspiracies against themselves personally, and even these few were not necessarily clinically paranoid. Much more common was an assumption that the voters would understand and respond to charges that outside forces were moving to threaten them as a group. There was very little tendency to see Jews as enemies. Foreign immigration was feared by reformers who opposed ignorance and anarchism rather than by those who looked out for conspiracies. Greenbackers, low-taxers, Andrew Johnson, and Bourbons, as well as Populists, used the defensive rhetoric which appealed to a sense of grievance against outsiders.

Other Tennesseeans did not find a paranoid style congenial at all, but instead participated in the more general American optimism that national life was basically sound and getting better. The Republican party was one important optimistic group, and New South Democrats were another, although they sometimes had to speak in ways Democratic voters would understand. Prohibitionists and other progressives held to the view that good men could improve society through organized effort. With some exceptions, Bourbons, low-taxers, and Populists found support among voters other than Republicans and prohibitionists (see Appendix B, Table 1).[16] This rough dichotomy expressed a fundamental polarity in Tennessee politics between the former secessionists whose experience of defeat and humiliation prevented them from sharing the general American mood of optimism and those whose opposition to the Confederacy

16. Andrew Sinclair, *Era of Excess: A Social History of the Prohibition Movement* (New York, 1964), Chap. 1, says that prohibitionism and Populism were part of the same antiurban moralism. Although J. H. McDowell belonged to both movements, and some voters from his area favored both, in general Sinclair's analysis does not hold for Tennessee between 1870 and 1896. It might be more valid for the early twentieth century. See Isaac, *Prohibition and Politics.*

The use of the term *progressive* to describe the New South men is not to imply that they felt the concern for social justice which characterized much of the national progressive movement of 1900–1917. The New South men were progressive not in challenging laissez-faire economics or property rights, but (1) in encouraging economic modernization and the accompanying social changes, and (2) in championing the purification of society through businessmen's government, prohibition, and immigration restrictions.

had been vindicated on the battlefield or who could forget the war in the hope of a brighter New South.[17]

Thus Tennessee politics in the late nineteenth century was based largely on status groups, though political movements were not always irrational, retrogressive, or unaware of economic interests. The Democratic and Republican parties were reflections of racial and sectional status groups, and to some degree of antebellum party traditions. There were two types of revolt within the Democratic party, corresponding to the defensive-optimist polarity in attitudes: the low-tax bolt of 1880 and the People's party of the early 1890s represented voters who felt that the country was going amiss, that the distribution of power should be redressed in their favor; the sky-blues of 1882 and the gold Democrats of 1896 were optimistic members of the social elite who could not participate in mass Bourbon Democracy. Economic interests emerged too, especially in the railroad regulation question. The Farmers' Alliance subtreasury plan was not only a litmus test for sincerity of identification with the farmers, but also an extension into politics of the Alliance goal of cooperative marketing, already practiced privately and locally. But even the farmers' co-ops cannot be assigned a purely economic function, because their members needed psychological, as well as economic, independence from the merchants.

There is no implication here that optimistic, progressive politics derived less from status considerations than did defensive, sometimes paranoid politics. The present work does not intend to praise the New South men or to condemn Bourbonism. Long ago, historians friendly to the southern Redeemers tended to describe their motivations in noneconomic terms. For example, J. W. Garner wrote, "The motive back of this policy [of white unity] was the simple instinct of self-preservation." Relatively hostile historians like C. Vann Woodward, on the other hand, have seen the Redeemers as acting for their material interests. This alignment is curiously reversed among historians of Populism. Those most sympathetic toward the party have assumed that they acted for their economic class interest,

17. For the importance of defeat in the southern experience, see C. Vann Woodward, *The Burden of Southern History* (Baton Rouge, 1960), 18–19.

while attacks on Populist motivations have stressed status anxiety. Perhaps it is time to recognize that neither a class nor a status interpretation should discredit or sanctify a political movement. Michael P. Rogin has provided a healthy corrective to the idea that mass movements like Populism are uniquely and wholly status-motivated, hence distinctively irrational and dangerous.[18] Human motivations are never pure, but the contention here is that no major collective political impulses in Gilded-Age Tennessee seem to have been generated primarily by material interests.

A characteristic of Tennessee politics which emerged repeatedly throughout the late nineteenth century was a preference for local associations and loyalties over broader ones. Such a feeling was rooted deeply in the American past.[19] This tendency was no doubt related to the suspicions of Yankees and eastern finance held by Bourbons, Populists, and other "pessimists." But localism is most clearly shown in intrastate politics. It seemed axiomatic that Tennessee was "divided into three sections almost as separate from each other as three several states." [20] The three grand divisions, and sections of them, often behaved quite differently in politics. Votes for the Greenback party in 1878 and for the low-tax Democrats in 1880 were highly concentrated by region, as were delegates' allegiances in the state Democratic conventions, especially those of 1878, 1888, and 1890. The legislature often displayed the same friends-and-neighbors localism, most notably in the United States Senate election of 1875 won by Andrew Johnson, and in the election of temporary House Speaker in 1891. Statewide political structures were loose and weak.

18. J. W. Garner, "Southern Politics Since the War," in *Studies in Southern History and Politics Inscribed to Archibald Dunning* (New York, 1914), 370; M. P. Rogin, *The Intellectuals and McCarthy: The Radical Specter* (Cambridge, Mass., 1967).

19. Cecilia Kenyon wrote, "The fundamental issue over which Federalists and Anti-Federalists split was the question whether republican government could be extended to embrace a nation, or whether it must be limited to the comparatively small political and geographical units which the separate American states then constituted. The Anti-Federalists took the latter view; and in a sense they were the conservatives of 1787, and their opponents the radicals." Kenyon, "Men of Little Faith: The Anti-Federalists on the Nature of Representative Government," in E. James Ferguson (ed.), *National Unity on Trial, 1781–1816* (New York, 1970), 37. Most Tennessee Democrats and Populists in the 1880s and 1890s were conservative in a way the Anti-Federalists would have understood.

20. Isham G. Harris to Grover Cleveland, May 2, 1893, in Cleveland Papers.

The main reason for the survival of the major political parties, despite their organizational weakness, was their iron grip on their voters' loyalties. One indoctrinated Democrat called the opposition "the same old *Federal* party—known at one time as the *Whig* party, then as the American party, and then as the Republican party, when it comes again." [21] Such beliefs were passed down like religion from father to son. Lincoln County voted Democratic by at least a three-to-one landslide in the presidential elections of 1844, 1860, 1872, 1880, 1892, 1908, 1924, 1940, 1960, and very likely all those intervening. Other examples could be cited of the unswerving devotion of white voters to Whigs and Republicans over the same time span.

Daniel Katz has suggested that a factor in the formation and change of public attitudes is "value expression," or finding political views to support and reenforce one's identity and self-image.[22] This valuable concept may do much to explain not only localism, but the high degree of continuity of popular voting habits in Tennessee, behavior which had no consistent relation to economic interests. A very important motive in politics was the desire to put into public office men from a group with which one identified, in order to bestow recognition on that group and enhance its status. The important groups were defined by race, the Civil War, antebellum party traditions, occupation, and local or regional neighborhoods. Sometimes limited economic issues affecting small, alert portions of propertied groups were important political mainsprings; and general economic interests, such as inflationist sentiment among farmers and businessmen, were mingled with powerful irrational feelings. But the major basis of political attitudes and behavior in Tennessee was the need to arrange experience in coherent, meaningful ways—ways that supported the individual's self-esteem and social status.

21. Cartmell Diary, March 27, 1891, emphasis original.
22. Daniel Katz, "The Functional Approach to the Study of Attitudes," *Public Opinion Quarterly,* XXIV (1960), 163–204.

Appendix A
Statistical Methodology

1. Multiple Regression Analysis. A coefficient of simple product-moment correlation between two variables measures the amount of relationship between them; a correlation of zero indicates no relationship, of +1.0, a perfect direct relationship, and of −1.0, a perfect inverse relationship. In layman's terms, a simple correlation shows how well a straight line on a graph can represent the relationship of two variables; the sign of the correlation indicates whether the line is rising or falling from left to right. Multiple regression analysis shows the relationship of a group of independent variables to a dependent variable. This relationship is measured by a coefficient of multiple correlation, which also ranges from +1 to −1. Multiple regression analysis also yields coefficients of partial correlation, which measure the separate relationship of each independent variable to the dependent variable, with the effects of the other independent variables eliminated. In most of the tables in Appendix B, the relationships of one dependent variable to several independent variables are shown by simple, multiple, and partial correlations.[1]

The level of confidence one may place in a statistical relationship is best expressed as the probability that a random ordering of the data would produce as strong a relationship. In the tables in Appendix B, partial correlations with one chance in ten, or less, of resulting from a random

1. Charles M. Dollar and Richard J. Jensen, *Historian's Guide to Statistics: Quantitative Analysis and Historical Research* (New York, 1971), 56–64, 87–90.

ordering of the data (*i.e.* partial correlations with a statistical significance of .10 or less) are identified.

The multiple regression analysis in this study was done with a BIOMED program written at the Health Sciences Computing Facility at the University of California, Los Angeles, and translated at the Computer Center at Princeton University.

2. ϕ (phi). ϕ can be used to measure the degree of relationship between two roll-call votes in a legislative body.[2] If two roll calls are arranged in a matrix like this,

		First Vote	
		yes	no
Second	yes	a	b
Vote	no	c	d,

then $\phi = \dfrac{ad - bc}{\sqrt{(a+c)\ (b+d)\ (a+b)\ (c+d)}}$. ϕ, like the coefficients of simple and multiple correlation, varies from +1 to —1; a zero ϕ indicates that there is no relation between two roll calls, or that the behavior of a legislator on one roll call cannot be predicted at all by his vote on the other. A ϕ of +.60 shows quite a strong degree of relation, as in the following example:

		First Vote		
		yes	no	
Second	yes	40	10	
Vote	no	10	40	$\phi = +.60$

2. *Ibid.,* 71–73.

Appendix B
Statistical Correlations

In the tables of Appendix B, correlations are shown revealing the degree of relationship among political, economic, and social variables for counties or civil districts within counties. In multiple regression analysis, explanation or at least illumination of a dependent variable is sought in its relationships to selected independent variables. In most of the tables of Appendix B after Table 1, eight correlations are given between each independent variable and the dependent variable: a simple and a partial correlation for the whole state and for each of the three grand divisions. (Map 8 shows county locations and grand divisions as used throughout this study, which are not precisely the divisions as defined by law.) Each pair of columns is labeled according to its geographical application, and within each pair, the column of simple correlations is headed by an S, and the partial correlations, by a P. Several counties are usually omitted because of incomplete data, so the number of counties used is indicated in each table. Partial correlations with less than one chance in ten of having occurred in a random ordering of the data (*i.e.* with a statistical significance of less than .10) are marked with an asterisk (*).

Following is a list of the abbreviations used for variables in the tables in Appendix B:

APA-1:   J. H. Acklen's percentage of total vote for Democratic nomination for Davidson County chancellor, 1894 (APA supported Acklen) [1]

1. Nashville *Banner,* July 17, 1894.

APA-2: W. M. McCarthy's percentage of total vote for mayor of Nashville, 1895 (APA supported McCarthy)[2]

black80: percentage of blacks in population, 1880[3]

black90: percentage of blacks in population, 1890[3]

cattle: half-blooded or better cattle per capita, 1890[4]

cotton: cotton production per capita, 1890[5]

Dem80: Democratic percentage (Wright and Wilson) of total vote for governor, 1880[6]

Dem82: Democratic percentage (Bate and Fussell) of total vote for governor, 1882[7]

Dem86: R. L. Taylor's percentage of two-party vote, 1886[8]

Dem90: J. P. Buchanan's percentage of total vote for governor, 1890[9]

Dem92: Peter Turney's percentage of total vote for governor, 1892[10]

Dem94: Peter Turney's percentage of total vote for governor, 1894[11]

density: population per square mile, 1890[12]

diffchg: percentage change, number of farms, 1890–1900, minus same figure for preceding decade[13]

disturban: percentage of population in towns of any size listed by 1890 U.S. Census[14]

$/cap: total assessed property per capita[15]

$change: ratio of average value per acre of farmland in 1890 to same figure for 1880[16]

$farms: average value per acre of farmland, 1892[17]

2. Nashville *American,* October 11, 1895.

3. 1890 Census, *Population,* 428–29.

4. 1890 Census, *Agriculture,* 306–307.

5. *Ibid.,* 396.

6. *Cumberland Almanac,* 1881, p. 24.

7. *Tribune Almanac,* 1883, pp. 72–73.

8. White (ed.), *Messages,* VII, 232–34.

9. *Tribune Almanac,* 1891, p. 312.

10. Shelbyville *Gazette,* November 17, 1892; Columbia *Maury Democrat,* November 17, 1892.

11. Nashville *Banner,* November 8, 1894.

12. 1890 Census, *Population,* 428-29; U.S. Department of Commerce, *City and County Data Book, 1967* (Washington, D.C., 1967), 332, 342.

13. C. E. Allred, S. W. Watkins, and G. H. Hatfield, *Tennessee, Economic and Social: Part II, the Counties* (University of Tennessee *Record,* Extension Series, Vol. II, No. 3, Knoxville, 1929), 53.

14. 1890 Census, *Population,* 317–28.

15. Maury County tax book, 1892, and Bedford County tax book, 1892, film, TSLA; 1890 Census, *Population,* 317–28.

16. Pressly and Scofield (eds.), *Farm Real Estate Values,* 52–53.

17. Maury county tax book, 1892, and Bedford County tax book, 1892, film, TSLA.

$farms80: average value per acre of farmland, 1880 [16]
$farms90: average value per acre of farmland, 1890 [16]
farmchg80s: percentage change, number of farms, 1880–1890 [18]
farmchg90s: percentage change, number of farms, 1890–1900 [18]
foreign: percentage foreign-born in population, 1890 [19]
Fussell: J. H. Fussell's percentage of total Democratic (Bate and Fussell) vote, 1882 [20]
Gback: R. M. Edwards' percentage of total vote for governor, 1878 [21]
gold: J. M. Palmer's percentage of Democratic (Bryan and Palmer) vote, 1896 [22]
growth: ratio of 1890 population to 1880 population [23]
incrTaylor: ratio of Dem86 variable to Dem82 variable *(q.v.)*
Johnson: Andrew Johnson's percentage of total vote for congressman-at-large, 1872 [24]
Johnson/D: Andrew Johnson's percentage of Democratic (Johnson & Cheatham) vote, congressman-at-large election, 1872 [24]
JPB/conv: percentage of delegation for J. P. Buchanan, first ballot for governor, 1890 Democratic state convention [25]
land: ratio of amount of improved farmland, 1900, to same figure for 1890 [26]
low-tax: negative votes as percentage of total, 1879 debt referendum [27]
mortg: average incumbrance on an incumbered acre, 1890 [28]
pers/dw: average persons per dwelling, 1890 [29]
Pop92: J. P. Buchanan's percentage of total vote for governor, 1892 [30]

18. Allred, Watkins, and Hatfield, *Tennessee, Economic and Social: Part II, the Counties,* 53.
19. 1890 Census, *Population,* 554–55.
20. *Tribune Almanac,* 1883, pp. 72–73.
21. *Ibid.,* 1880, pp. 72–73.
22. *Ibid.,* 1897, p. 260.
23. 1890 Census, *Population,* 317–28.
24. Manuscript election returns, Archives Division, TSLA.
25. Nashville *American,* July 16, 1890.
26. 1890 Census, *Agriculture,* 227–28; U.S. Census Office, *Census Reports: Twelfth Census of the United States, Taken in the Year 1900: Volume V: Agriculture, Part I: Farms, Live Stock, and Animal Products* (Washington, D.C. 1902), 297–98.
27. White (ed.), *Messages,* VI, 609–11.
28. U.S. Census Office, *Report on Real Estate Mortgages in the United States at the Eleventh Census: 1890* (Washington, D.C., 1895), map following page 154.
29. 1890 Census, *Population,* 946.
30. For counties: *Tribune Almanac,* 1894, pp. 345–46. For civil districts: Shelbyville *Gazette,* November 17, 1892; Camden *Chronicle,* November 11, 1892; Maryville *Times,* November 16, 1892; Nashville *Banner,* November 10, 1892; Milan *Exchange,* November 19, 1892; Pulaski *Citizen,* November 10, 1892; Chattanooga *Times,* November 11, 1892; Bolivar *Bulle-*

Pop94: A. L. Mims's percentage of total vote for governor, 1894 [31]
Porter78: percentage of delegation for resolution supporting J. D. Porter administration, 1878 state Democratic convention [32]
prohb87: affirmative votes as percentage of total, 1887 prohibition referendum [33]
prohb90: D. C. Kelley's percentage of total vote for governor, 1890 [34]
Rep92: G. W. Winstead's percentage of total vote for governor, 1892 [35]
Rep94: H. C. Evans' percentage of total vote for governor, 1894 [36]
RLT/conv: percentage of delegation for R. L. Taylor, first ballot for governor, 1888 state Democratic convention [37]
Savage: ratio of vote for J. H. Savage for railroad commissioner to vote for W. B. Bate for governor, 1884 [38]
secesh: affirmative votes as percentage of total, June, 1861, secession referendum [39]
slaves: slaves as percentage of total population, 1860 [40]
tariff84: percentage of delegation voting for tariff protection plank, 1884 state Democratic convention [41]
tenancy: percentage of farms operated by tenants, 1890 [42]
tenchg: percentage of farms operated by tenants, 1900, minus same figure for 1890 [43]
tobacco: tobacco production per capita, 1890 [44]

---

tin, November 18, 1892; Savannah *Courier,* November 17, 1892; Knoxville *Journal,* November 16, 1892; Lawrenceburg *Lawrence Democrat,* November 11, 1892; Fayetteville *Observer,* November 17, 1892; Columbia *Maury Democrat,* November 17, 1892; Clarksville *Tobacco Leaf-Chronicle,* November 18, 1892; Memphis *Appeal-Avalanche,* November 11, 1892; McMinnville *Southern Standard,* November 12, 1892; Johnson City *Comet,* November 24, 1892.

31. *Tribune Almanac,* 1895, pp. 312–13; Nashville *Banner,* November 8, 1894.
32. Nashville *American,* August 17, 1878.
33. *Tribune Almanac,* 1888, pp. 78–79.
34. *Ibid.,* 1891, p. 312.
35. Shelbyville *Gazette,* November 17, 1892; Columbia *Maury Democrat,* November 17, 1892.
36. *Tribune Almanac,* 1895, pp. 312–13; Nashville *Banner,* November 8, 1894.
37. Nashville *American,* May 11, 1888.
38. Manuscript election returns, Archives Division, TSLA; Nashville *Banner,* November 28, 1884.
39. *Tribune Almanac,* 1862, p. 59.
40. U.S. Census Office, *Ninth Census: Volume I: The Statistics of the Population of the United States, Embracing the Tables of Race, Nationality, Sex, Selected Ages, and Occupations* (Washington, D.C., 1872), 61–63.
41. Nashville *American,* June 20, 1884.
42. 1890 Census, *Agriculture,* 180–83.
43. *Ibid.;* 1900 Census, *Agriculture, Part I,* 122–25.
44. 1890 Census, *Agriculture,* 450–451.

urban80:   percentage of population in towns over 2,000, 1880 [45]
urban90:   percentage of population in towns over 2,000, 1890 [45]
Whig: John Bell's percentage of total vote for president, 1860 [46]
Wilson: S. F. Wilson's percentage of total vote for governor, 1880 [47]
Wilson/Dems: S. F. Wilson's percentage of Democratic (Wright and Wilson) vote for governor, 1880 [47]

45. 1890 Census, *Population,* 317–28.
46. *Tribune Almanac,* 1861, p. 54. Bell's vote, rather than the result of an earlier election, is used because county boundaries changed before 1860. Simple correlations between the Whig vote for president in 1844 and Bell's vote in 1860 are: Tennessee (75 counties), .92; East Tennessee (28 counties), .92; Middle Tennessee (30 counties), .93; and West Tennessee (17 counties), .90.
47. *Cumberland Almanac,* 1881, p.24.

Table 1
SIMPLE CORRELATIONS AMONG SELECTED ELECTIONS
1860–1894

Part 1. Tennessee
79 counties

Whig
—.45 secesh
—.21 —.02 Johnson
—.04 .45 —.11 Gback
—.29 .47 —.08 .26 low-tax
—.46 .58 .30 .07 .64 Wilson
—.25 .45 —.03 .11 .05 .14 Fussell
—.54 .79 .10 .24 .61 .74 .30 Dem82
—.56 .83 .12 .28 .57 .72 .43 .93 Dem86
 .37 —.53 —.01 —.17 —.47 —.54 —.18 —.46 —.53 prohb87
—.26 .47 .05 .13 .32 .49 .15 .52 .53 —.25 JPB/conv
—.48 .89 .01 .41 .55 .58 .38 .82 .88 —.54 .47 Dem90
—.36 .75 .14 .32 .35 .55 .45 .64 .74 —.54 .55 .73 Pop92
—.26 .69 .15 .37 .24 .46 .44 .54 .65 —.42 .50 .69 .91 Pop94

Part 2. *East Tennessee*
29 counties

Whig
—.44 secesh
—.43 —.13 Johnson
—.14 .07 .12 Gback
—.39 .34 —.14 .38 low-tax
—.57 .62 —.16 .38 .79 Wilson
—.18 .10 .08 .84 .31 .28 Fussell
—.58 .76 —.01 .20 .52 .70 .22 Dem82
—.69 .75 .10 .21 .54 .77 .21 .95 Dem86
 .25 —.09 .01 .07 —.22 —.24 .11 .10 —.03 prohb87
—.09 .30 —.24 —.14 .25 .30 —.04 .39 .40 .05 JPB/conv
—.65 .76 .11 .08 .39 .62 .13 .91 .95 —.09 .45 Dem90
—.66 .47 .20 .05 .11 .43 .00 .28 .40 —.50 .06 .43 Pop92
—.57 .43 .38 .00 —.12 .13 .04 .22 .31 —.35 .06 .39 .82 Pop94

Part 3. Middle Tennessee
32 counties

Whig
—.43 secesh
 .08 .10 Johnson
 .00 .11 —.05 Gback
 .08 —.40 .17 .01 low-tax
—.15 .08 .62 —.29 .49 Wilson
—.09 .35 —.20 .06 —.77 —.40 Fussell
—.50 .52 .22 —.10 .10 .53 —.12 Dem82
—.50 .65 .13 —.11 —.08 .46 .07 .80 Dem86
 .24 —.08 —.06 .07 —.09 —.29 .16 —.22 —.32 prohb87
—.32 .18 .15 —.34 .09 .36 .01 .26 .35 —.17 JPB/conv
—.45 .63 .23 —.08 —.15 .38 .07 .74 .90 —.27 .31 Dem90
—.13 .57 .28 —.17 —.31 .29 .27 .37 .63 —.40 .34 .56 Pop92
—.05 .52 .27 —.09 —.41 .21 .40 .18 .58 —.22 .18 .55 .86 Pop94

Part 4. West Tennessee
18 counties

Whig
—.24 secesh
—.19 .59 Johnson
 .19 .62 .32 Gback
—.04 —.53 .02 —.52 low-tax
—.69 .44 .47 .24 .03 Wilson
—.47 .19 .36 —.30 .00 .32 Fussell
—.12 .19 .54 .14 —.08 .35 .02 Dem82
—.19 .39 .70 .21 —.32 .35 .48 .66 Dem86
 .12 —.14 .15 —.04 .19 .11 .23 .42 .18 prohb87
 .09 .32 .41 .42 —.24 .31 —.09 .42 .32 .35 JPB/conv
—.27 .86 .61 .37 —.37 .27 .21 .17 .40 —.18 .14 Dem90
—.14 .59 .66 .44 —.28 .48 .27 .58 .52 .37 .81 .40 Pop92
—.18 .60 .57 .52 —.26 .58 .06 .51 .40 .26 .80 .49 .89 Pop94

Table 2
MULTIPLE REGRESSION ANALYSIS
ANDREW JOHNSON SUPPORT IN CONGRESSMAN-AT-LARGE
ELECTION, 1872

	Tenn.		E.Tenn.		M.Tenn.		W.Tenn.	
Number of counties	79		29		32		18	
Mean of dep. variable	20.6%		22.7%		23.2%		12.8%	
Multiple correlations	.39		.63		.36		.77	
Dependent: Johnson	S	P	S	P	S	P	S	P
$farms80	.10	.29 *	−.16	.08	.20	.29	.45	.27
slaves	−.18	−.20 *	−.27	−.10	.00	−.30	.00	−.58 *
Whig	−.21	−.25 *	−.43	−.58 *	.08	.13	−.19	.04
secesh	−.03	−.07	−.17	−.42 *	.10	.20	.59	.67 *

Table 3
MULTIPLE REGRESSION ANALYSIS
GREENBACK VOTE FOR GOVERNOR, 1878 ELECTION

	Tenn.		E.Tenn.		M.Tenn.		W.Tenn.	
Number of counties	78		29		31		18	
Mean of dep. variable	8.5%		2.1%		9.4%		17.2%	
Multiple correlations	.58		.35		.53		.72	
Dependent: Gback	S	P	S	P	S	P	S	P
Whig	−.04	.19	−.14	−.07	.02	.17	.19	.46
secesh	.46	.37 *	.08	.02	.08	.18	.62	.55 *
Johnson	−.10	.05	.12	.13	−.01	−.01	.32	−.09
black80	.44	.19	.24	.25	−.05	−.10	.41	−.13
$farms80	.11	−.28 *	.17	−.01	−.06	−.25	.29	−.10
urban80	.23	.18	.10	−.16	.36	.50 *	.21	.02

Table 4
MULTIPLE REGRESSION ANALYSIS
SUPPORT FOR PORTER ADMINISTRATION, 1878
DEMOCRATIC STATE CONVENTION

	Tenn.		E.Tenn.		M.Tenn.		W.Tenn.	
Number of counties	78		29		31		18	
Mean of dep. variable	67.5%		83.5%		48.4%		74.4%	
Multiple correlations	.35		.36		.51		.54	
Dependent: Porter78	S	P	S	P	S	P	S	P
Whig	.25	.05	.15	.05	.20	−.13	−.10	−.02
secesh	−.29	−.20	−.09	−.01	.00	−.25	.00	.40
Johnson	−.04	−.04	−.14	−.15	.16	.21	−.03	−.37
black80	−.05	.01	−.08	−.25	.39	.35 *	−.32	−.49 *
$farms80	.04	.05	−.10	−.01	.33	−.15	.03	.21
urban80	.12	.10	.12	.29	.36	.25	−.18	−.08

* Partial correlations with less than one chance in ten of occurring through a random ordering of the data.

Table 5
MULTIPLE REGRESSION ANALYSIS
LOW-TAX VOTE IN 1879 DEBT REFERENDUM

	Tenn.		E.Tenn.		M.Tenn.		W.Tenn.	
Number of counties	79		29		32		18	
Mean of dep. variable	57.1%		33.1%		72.3%		68.6%	
Multiple correlations	.57		.65		.76		.80	
Dependent: low-tax	S	P	S	P	S	P	S	P
Whig	−.29	.03	−.39	−.36 *	.08	.38 *	−.04	.05
secesh	.49	.40 *	.40	.07	−.40	.02	−.53	−.38
Johnson	−.08	−.09	−.14	−.30	.17	.24	.02	.59 *
Gback	.26	.10	.38	.36 *	.01	.17	−.52	−.32
black80	.09	−.16	.21	.24	−.62	−.42 *	−.51	.14
$farms80	−.04	−.06	.12	−.12	−.47	.00	−.49	−.47
urban80	−.14	−.13	−.02	−.20	−.46	−.34 *	−.37	−.14

Table 6
MULTIPLE REGRESSION ANALYSIS
VOTE FOR S. F. WILSON, 1880

	Tenn.		E.Tenn.		M.Tenn.		W.Tenn.	
Number of counties	79		29		32		18	
Mean of dep. variable	38.3%		20.4%		60.1%		28.2%	
Multiple correlations	.81		.94		.78		.83	
Dependent: Wilson/Dems	S	P	S	P	S	P	S	P
Whig	−.43	−.19	−.56	−.34	−.02	−.08	−.65	−.65 *
secesh	.56	.38 *	.64	.36 *	−.05	.24	.48	.15
Johnson/D	−.27	.35 *	−.62	−.28	.50	.55 *	.33	.41
low-tax	.67	.62 *	.85	.83 *	.53	.37 *	−.06	−.23
black80	.05	−.23 *	.14	.10	−.25	−.26	.11	−.02
$farms80	.13	.25 *	.04	−.35 *	−.03	.29	−.04	−.27
urban80	−.12	−.14	−.07	−.09	−.25	−.32	−.14	−.48

Table 7
MULTIPLE REGRESSION ANALYSIS
VOTE FOR J. H. FUSSELL, 1882

	Tenn.		E.Tenn.		M.Tenn.		W.Tenn.	
Number of counties	79		29		32		18	
Mean of dep. variable	2.6%		0.7%		3.8%		3.6%	
Multiple correlations	.51		.68		.81		.53	
Dependent: Fussell	S	P	S	P	S	P	S	P
Whig	−.20	−.21 *	−.12	−.02	−.02	−.19	−.44	−.45
secesh	.38	.10	.02	−.15	.32	−.17	.15	.09
Johnson/D	−.22	−.05	.00	.37 *	−.09	−.22	.17	.10
low-tax	.04	−.03	.22	−.30	−.78	−.46 *	.06	.03
Wilson/Dems	.08	−.10	.27	.45 *	−.43	.08	.18	−.24
black80	.37	.10	.45	.32	.61	.30	−.07	−.10
$farms80	.35	.21 *	.20	.05	.46	.02	.10	.08
urban80	.24	.05	.38	.04	.43	.15	.04	−.11

* Partial correlations with less than one chance in ten of occurring through a random ordering of the data.

Table 8

MULTIPLE REGRESSION ANALYSIS
DEMOCRATIC SOLIDARITY FOR J. H. SAVAGE FOR
RAILROAD COMMISSIONER, 1884

	Tenn.		E.Tenn.		M.Tenn.		W.Tenn.	
Number of counties	71		26		28		17	
Mean of dep. variable	.88		.96		.79		.91	
Multiple correlations	68		.71		.80		.89	
Dependent: Savage	S	P	S	P	S	P	S	P
Whig	.18	−.25 *	−.25	−.42 *	.04	−.16	.27	.08
secesh	−.47	−.37 *	.13	.00	−.15	−.47 *	−.26	−.56
Johnson/D	.13	−.23 *	−.04	−.06	−.42	−.69 *	−.08	.40
Wilson/Dems	−.41	−.31 *	−.01	−.33	−.12	.25	.00	.32
Fussell	−.42	−.42 *	−.30	−.15	−.12	−.31	−.78	−.76 *
growth	.04	−.07	−.59	−.19	−.22	.48 *	.22	.09
black80	−.20	.24 *	−.25	.10	−.05	.32	−.08	.22
urban80	−.23	−.24 *	−.46	.07	−.23	−.60 *	−.21	−.45
$farms80	−.18	.22 *	.03	−.13	−.02	.66 *	−.05	.18
$change	.05	.11	−.52	−.23	.09	.57 *	−.09	.12

Table 9

MULTIPLE REGRESSION ANALYSIS
SUPPORT FOR PROTECTIVE TARIFF PLANK, 1884
STATE DEMOCRATIC CONVENTION

	Tenn.		E.Tenn.		M.Tenn.		W.Tenn.	
Number of counties	77		29		31		17	
Mean of dep. variable	42%		65%		35%		16%	
Multiple correlations	.62		.65		.71		.83	
Dependent: tariff84	S	P	S	P	S	P	S	P
Whig	−.06	−.13	−.18	−.24	−.16	.37	.13	.11
secesh	−.28	.03	−.01	.19	.22	.29	−.29	−.21
Johnson/D	.35	.29 *	.27	.33	−.15	.10	.15	−.08
Porter78	.02	−.05	−.02	−.01	−.08	−.04	−.12	−.14
Wilson/Dems	−.24	−.26 *	−.15	−.18	−.14	−.23	−.35	.16
Fussell	−.15	−.04	−.09	−.19	.03	.25	−.02	.09
Dem80	−.15	.07	.01	.09	.38	.20	−.21	−.19
growth	.41	.22 *	.28	.45 *	.40	.10	.45	.38
black80	−.34	−.22 *	−.06	.04	−.27	−.49 *	.01	−.09
$farms80	−.12	−.06	−.01	−.15	−.16	.06	.28	.21
$change	.28	−.18	.01	−.28	.28	−.01	.23	−.16
urban80	.17	.23 *	.09	.02	.21	.14	.53	.43

* Partial correlations with less than one chance in ten of occurring through a random ordering of the data.

Table 10
MULTIPLE REGRESSION ANALYSIS
SUPPORT FOR BOB TAYLOR, 1886 ELECTION

	Tenn.		E.Tenn.		M.Tenn.		W.Tenn.	
Number of counties	79		29		32		18	
Mean of dep. variable	52.6%		37.0%		65.8%		54.4%	
Multiple correlations	.95		.97		.91		.92	
Dependent: Dem86	S	P	S	P	S	P	S	P
Whig	−.56	−.20 *	−.69	−.59 *	−.50	−.16	−.19	−.39
secesh	.84	.20 *	.80	.13	.65	.40 *	.39	−.32
Dem82	.93	.71 *	.95	.85 *	.80	.64 *	.66	.62 *
black90	.22	.15	.24	.29	−.14	.10	−.08	.00
growth	−.31	−.12	−.11	−.10	−.09	−.34	.39	−.36
cotton	.00	−.25 *	.40	.25	−.19	−.44 *	−.39	−.19
urban90	.03	.00	.23	−.19	−.25	−.12	.40	.33
tenancy	.15	.15	.33	.02	−.21	.37 *	−.07	.18
$farms90	.06	−.03	.17	.12	−.28	−.08	.72	.56 *
farmchg80s	−.22	−.09	.16	.17	.05	−.07	−.15	−.46

Table 11
MULTIPLE REGRESSION ANALYSIS
CHANGE IN DEMOCRATIC VOTE, 1882–86

	Tenn.		E.Tenn.		M.Tenn.		W.Tenn.	
Number of counties	79		29		32		18	
Mean of dep. variable	0.9930		1.0094		0.9666		1.0133	
Multiple correlations	.58		.78		.78		.88	
Dependent: incrTaylor	S	P	S	P	S	P	S	P
Whig	.03	−.10	.04	−.36	−.07	−.15	−.15	−.14
secesh	−.10	.26 *	−.33	.29	.30	.48 *	.31	−.28
Wilson/Dems	−.15	.12	−.20	.12	−.07	.27	.09	.22
Dem82	−.35	−.46 *	−.54	−.59 *	−.19	−.48 *	−.26	−.42
black90	.10	.14	−.17	.09	.30	.18	.35	−.06
growth	.13	.23 *	.23	.46 *	−.44	−.28	−.07	−.35
cotton	.03	−.23 *	−.06	−.06	.07	−.47 *	−.02	−.33
urban90	.02	.00	−.14	.06	−.10	−.08	.51	.32
tenancy	.04	.03	−.07	−.27	.21	.46 *	.10	.23
$farms90	.08	−.23 *	−.26	−.31	.02	−.19	.40	.53
farmchg80s	.00	−.05	.06	.00	−.07	−.14	−.37	−.27

* Partial correlations with less than one chance in ten of occurring through a random ordering of the data.

Table 12
MULTIPLE REGRESSION ANALYSIS
PROHIBITIONISM IN 1887 REFERENDUM

	Tenn.		E.Tenn.		M.Tenn.		W.Tenn.	
Number of counties	79		29		32		18	
Mean of dep. variable	45%		56%		35%		45%	
Multiple correlations	.70		.59		.66		.90	
Dependent: Prohb87	S	P	S	P	S	P	S	P
Whig	.37	.00	.25	.33	.24	−.04	.12	.73 *
secesh	−.54	−.09	−.09	−.12	−.08	.08	−.14	.13
Wilson/Dems	−.51	−.31 *	−.22	−.10	−.28	−.40 *	.02	.56
Dem86	−.53	−.05	−.03	.33	−.32	−.19	.18	−.31
black90	−.22	−.20	.02	−.17	.24	−.18	−.47	−.11
growth	.24	−.10	−.04	−.18	−.14	−.07	.11	−.35
cotton	−.10	.24 *	−.30	−.17	.15	−.09	−.43	−.19
urban90	.03	−.15	.11	.26	.07	−.45 *	−.35	−.59 *
tenancy	−.22	−.18	−.35	−.26	.14	−.11	−.47	−.32
$farms90	.16	.38 *	.18	−.04	.36	.54 *	.14	.57
farmchg80s	.24	.19	.00	.07	−.06	.14	.12	.64 *

Table 13
MULTIPLE REGRESSION ANALYSIS
FIRST-BALLOT VOTES FOR BOB TAYLOR, 1888
DEMOCRATIC STATE CONVENTION

	Tenn.		E.Tenn.		M.Tenn.		W.Tenn.	
Number of counties	79		29		32		18	
Mean of dep. variable	43%		48%		32%		55%	
Multiple correlations	.56		.74		.65		.88	
Dependent: RLT/conv	S	P	S	P	S	P	S	P
Whig	.12	.04	.09	−.03	−.02	.10	.19	.04
secesh	−.04	.08	.13	.05	.13	.16	−.05	.05
Wilson/Dems	−.08	.01	−.08	−.13	.26	.32	−.08	.24
prohb87	.25	.14	.48	.37	−.15	−.12	.05	.39
black90	.07	−.29 *	−.02	−.22	.06	−.24	.09	−.52
growth	−.08	−.28 *	−.27	−.45 *	.10	.15	−.03	−.34
cotton	.24	.46 *	−.06	.27	.35	.54 *	.32	.77 *
urban90	.11	.22 *	.01	−.06	.14	.09	.19	.74 *
tenancy	−.01	−.27 *	−.35	−.15	−.01	−.01	.05	−.07
$farms90	.10	.16	.22	.43 *	.17	.08	−.14	−.13
farmchg80s	.10	.18	−.01	.18	−.02	−.18	.26	.54

* Partial correlations with less than one chance in ten of occurring through a random ordering of the data.

Table 14, Part A
MULTIPLE REGRESSION ANALYSIS
FIRST-BALLOT VOTES FOR J. P. BUCHANAN, 1890
DEMOCRATIC STATE CONVENTION

	Tenn.		E.Tenn.		M.Tenn.		W.Tenn.	
Number of counties	79		29		32		18	
Mean of dep. variable	48%		28%		68%		47%	
Multiple correlations	.63		.78		.54		.86	
Dependent: JPB/conv	S	P	S	P	S	P	S	P
Whig	−.26	.06	−.09	−.14	−.32	−.25	.09	.67 *
secesh	.48	.29 *	.35	.09	.18	.00	.32	.52
Wilson/Dems	.47	.23 *	.29	.22	.31	.27	.33	.56
black90	.11	.02	.23	.03	−.13	.17	.02	.00
urban90	−.20	−.26 *	−.03	.02	−.29	−.20	−.26	−.52
mortg	−.11	.09	−.08	−.15	−.12	−.02	−.03	.44
tenchg	.11	.17	.68	.58 *	−.12	−.18	−.29	.51
tenancy	−.02	−.03	−.26	−.08	−.24	−.06	.13	.19
farmchg80s	−.23	−.13	−.04	−.07	−.08	.04	−.18	−.25
diffchg	.08	−.13	.00	−.10	.05	.11	.01	−.41
land	−.10	.18	−.33	.21	.06	−.08	.27	.39

Table 14, Part B
MULTIPLE REGRESSION ANALYSIS
VOTE FOR J. P. BUCHANAN FOR GOVERNOR, 1890

	Tenn.		E.Tenn.		M.Tenn.		W.Tenn.	
Number of counties	79		29		32		18	
Mean of dep. variable	56%		37%		66%		67%	
Multiple correlations	.92		.88		.80		.98	
Dependent: Dem90	S	P	S	P	S	P	S	P
Whig	−.48	−.15	−.65	−.45 *	−.45	.00	−.27	−.78 *
secesh	.89	.73 *	.80	.64 *	.63	.70 *	.86	.85 *
Wilson/Dems	.53	.16	.61	.00	.18	.32	.29	−.70 *
black90	.48	−.11	.27	−.02	−.11	−.38	.61	−.52
mortg	−.04	.05	.07	.16	−.02	.08	.60	−.26
tenchg	−.11	.13	.09	.14	−.12	−.05	−.45	−.81 *
tenancy	.42	.36 *	.34	.03	−.10	.29	.56	−.06
farmchg80s	−.19	−.03	.15	−.21	.10	.21	.00	.68 *
diffchg	.11	−.05	−.20	−.29	−.01	.24	.36	.79 *
land	−.16	.15	−.22	−.03	.14	−.10	.10	.00
urban90	.11	−.01	.26	.04	−.08	.03	.57	.29

* Partial correlations with less than one chance in ten of occurring through a random ordering of the data.

Table 15, Part A
MULTIPLE REGRESSION ANALYSIS
VOTE FOR D. C. KELLEY FOR GOVERNOR, 1890

	Tenn.		E.Tenn.		M.Tenn.		W.Tenn.	
Number of counties	91		35		37		19	
Mean of dep. variable	4.4%		2.6%		6.4%		3.9%	
Multiple correlations	.42		.57		.69		.40	
Dependent: prohb90	S	P	S	P	S	P	S	P
black90	.24	.02	.26	.21	.50	−.18	−.27	−.14
growth	−.01	−.19 *	.22	−.39 *	.16	−.09	.32	.31
urban90	.37	.35 *	.43	.52 *	.67	.53 *	−.07	−.12

Table 15, Part B
SIMPLE CORRELATIONS BETWEEN VOTE FOR
D. C. KELLEY AND OTHER POLITICAL VARIABLES

	Tenn.	E.Tenn.	M.Tenn.	W.Tenn.
Number of counties	91	35	37	19
Dependent: prohb90	S	S	S	S
Fussell	.29	.14	.04	.25
prohb87	.00	.47	.30	.42

Table 16, Part A
MULTIPLE REGRESSION ANALYSIS
VOTE FOR J. P. BUCHANAN, 1892

	Tenn.		E.Tenn.		M.Tenn.		W.Tenn.	
Number of counties	79		29		32		18	
Mean of dep. variable	12%		5%		16%		14%	
Multiple correlations	.80		.83		.77		.94	
Dependent: Pop92	S	P	S	P	S	P	S	P
Whig	−.36	.07	−.66	−.42 *	−.13	−.11	−.14	.42
secesh	.76	.54 *	.48	.34	.57	.44 *	.59	.83 *
Wilson/Dems	.50	.20	.38	−.07	.21	.44 *	.44	.47
black90	.36	.06	−.12	.07	.36	.35	−.05	−.56
urban90	−.32	−.12	−.10	−.14	.09	−.01	−.10	−.22
mortg	−.13	−.06	−.22	−.23	.02	−.21	.03	−.05
tenchg	−.07	.07	−.24	.13	.21	.07	−.28	.34
tenancy	.24	.04	.53	.47 *	−.14	.07	.02	.28
farmchg80s	−.22	−.16	−.03	−.24	.12	.45 *	−.20	−.10
diffchg	.08	−.20 *	−.10	−.20	−.01	.42 *	.04	−.23
land	−.08	.29 *	.14	.34	.00	−.20	.26	.64 *

* Partial correlations with less than one chance in ten of occurring through a random ordering of the data.

Table 16, Part B
MULTIPLE REGRESSION ANALYSIS: VOTE FOR
J. P. BUCHANAN IN CIVIL DISTRICTS, 1892. LARGER SAMPLE
(279 DISTRICTS) INCLUDES ALL DISTRICTS IN BEDFORD,
BENTON, BLOUNT, DAVIDSON, GIBSON, GILES, HAMILTON,
HARDEMAN, HARDIN, KNOX, LAWRENCE, LINCOLN, MAURY,
MONTGOMERY, SHELBY, WARREN, AND WASHINGTON COUNTIES,
EXCEPT THE CITIES OF NASHVILLE, MEMPHIS, KNOXVILLE,
AND CHATTANOOGA, AND THOSE DISTRICTS CHANGING THEIR
BOUNDARIES BETWEEN 1880 AND 1890. SMALLER SAMPLE
(101 DISTRICTS) INCLUDES ALL THOSE OF THE 279 IN
WHICH BUCHANAN RECEIVED AT LEAST 25% OF THE
COMBINED POPULIST-DEMOCRATIC VOTE IN 1892
(see Map 8 for counties)

	Larger Sample		Smaller Sample	
Number of districts	279		101	
Mean of dep. variable	15.5%		31.4%	
Multiple correlations	.20		.17	
Dependent: Pop92	S	P	S	P
disturban	−.17	−.14 *	−.12	−.11
growth	−.14	−.09	−.14	−.13

Table 17, Part A
MULTIPLE REGRESSION ANALYSIS
VOTE FOR J. P. BUCHANAN IN MAURY AND BEDFORD COUNTY
CIVIL DISTRICTS, 1892

	Maury & Bedford		Maury		Bedford	
Number of districts	44		25		19	
Mean of dep. variable	12.9%		16.4%		8.2%	
Multiple correlations	.29		.40		.55	
Dependent: Pop92	S	P	S	P	S	P
disturban	−.22	−.06	−.19	.04	−.31	−.52 *
$farms	−.27	−.02	−.39	−.16	−.08	.38
$/cap	−.26	−.11	−.36	−.04	.07	−.02
growth	−.05	−.02	.00	.01	−.01	.25

* Partial correlations with less than one chance in ten of occurring through a random ordering of the data.

Table 17, Part B
MULTIPLE REGRESSION ANALYSIS
VOTE FOR PETER TURNEY IN MAURY AND BEDFORD COUNTY
CIVIL DISTRICTS, 1892

	Maury & Bedford		Maury		Bedford	
Number of districts	44		25		19	
Mean of dep. variable	56.0%		57.6%		53.9%	
Multiple correlations	.24		.44		.21	
Dependent: Dem92	S	P	S	P	S	P
disturban	.16	.16	.20	.36 *	.13	−.01
$farms	.15	−.10	.18	−.25	.10	.06
$/cap	.16	.13	.25	.26	.05	−.04
growth	−.05	−.11	−.14	−.29	.17	.16

Table 17, Part C
MULTIPLE REGRESSION ANALYSIS
VOTE FOR G. W. WINSTEAD IN MAURY AND BEDFORD COUNTY
CIVIL DISTRICTS, 1892

	Maury & Bedford		Maury		Bedford	
Number of districts	44		25		19	
Mean of dep. variable	31.1%		26.0%		37.9%	
Multiple correlations	.17		.62		.38	
Dependent: Rep92	S	P	S	P	S	P
disturban	.01	−.13	−.08	−.58 *	.07	.34
$farms	.07	.13	.17	.54 *	−.05	−.29
$/cap	.04	−.06	.03	−.38 *	−.09	.05
growth	.10	.14	.21	.45 *	−.16	−.31

* Partial correlations with less than one chance in ten of occurring through a random ordering of the data.

Table 18
MULTIPLE REGRESSION ANALYSIS
VOTE FOR A. L. MIMS, 1894

	Tenn.		E.Tenn.		M.Tenn.		W.Tenn.	
Number of counties	79		29		32		18	
Mean of dep. variable	9.8%		3.2%		13.9%		13.2%	
Multiple correlations	.76		.84		.76		.93	
Dependent: Pop94	S	P	S	P	S	P	S	P
Whig	−.26	−.02	−.57	−.40	−.05	−.16	−.18	.50
secesh	.70	.40 *	.40	.58 *	.52	.37	.60	.58
Wilson/Dems	.42	.10	.11	−.37	.14	.38 *	.58	.44
cotton	.24	.09	−.13	−.13	.13	−.13	.13	−.26
tobacco	.31	.25 *	.08	.15	.32	.09	−.02	−.03
black90	.44	.00	−.07	.21	.45	.30	.11	−.07
tenchg	−.01	.00	−.21	.11	.31	.16	−.25	.36
tenancy	.26	.06	.38	.27	−.04	.21	.15	.37
farmchg90s	−.04	−.14	−.13	−.25	−.03	.19	.17	.04
diffchg	.13	.12	.08	.25	−.07	−.12	.26	.15
urban90	.02	−.18	.00	.15	.19	.16	−.12	−.67 *
land	−.13	.09	.33	.44 *	−.15	−.31	.15	−.17
$farms90	.14	.18	−.11	−.40	.24	−.20	.36	.53

Table 19
MULTIPLE REGRESSION ANALYSIS
GOLD DEMOCRATS IN 1896

	Tenn.		E.Tenn.		M.Tenn.		W.Tenn.	
Number of counties	91		35		38		18	
Mean of dep. variable	0.8%		1.0%		0.8%		0.7%	
Multiple correlations	.47		.46		.59		.70	
Dependent: gold	S	P	S	P	S	P	S	P
growth	.35	.34 *	.43	.43 *	.20	.17	.36	.45 *
density	.32	.00	.15	−.02	.46	.15	.56	.08
tenancy	.02	−.17	.04	−.02	−.11	−.14	.25	−.32
$farms90	.28	.00	.12	−.06	.43	−.07	.36	−.13
black90	.22	.28 *	.06	−.03	.44	.35 *	.41	.46 *

* Partial correlations with less than one chance in ten of occurring through a random ordering of the data.

Table 20, Part A
MULTIPLE REGRESSION ANALYSIS
POPULISM AND NATIVISM IN NASHVILLE,
1894–95

	Nashville	
Number of wards	20	
Mean of dep. variable	51.5%	
Multiple correlation	.72	
Dependent: APA-2	S	P
black90	.08	−.18
foreign	−.70	−.60 *
pers/dw	−.48	−.07

	Nashville	
Number of wards	20	
Mean of dep. variable	12.2%	
Multiple correlation	.74	
Dependent: Pop94	S	P
black90	−.21	−.47 *
foreign	−.57	−.47 *
pers/dw	−.60	−.36

Table 20, Part B
SIMPLE CORRELATIONS
POPULISM AND NATIVISM IN NASHVILLE,
1894–95. 20 WARDS

APA-2			
.40	Rep94		
.84	.41	Pop94	
−.67	−.91	−.75	Dem94

* Partial correlations with less than one chance in ten of occurring through a random ordering of the data.

Table 20, Part C
Simple Correlations
Populism and Nativism in Davidson County, 1894

	Nashville	Rural Davidson	All Davidson
Number of wards and/or districts	20	22	42
Dependent: APA-1	S	S	S
Dem94	−.85	−.11	−.48
Rep94	.71	.16	.41
Pop94	.75	.00	.20

* Partial correlations with less than one chance in ten of occurring through a random ordering of the data.

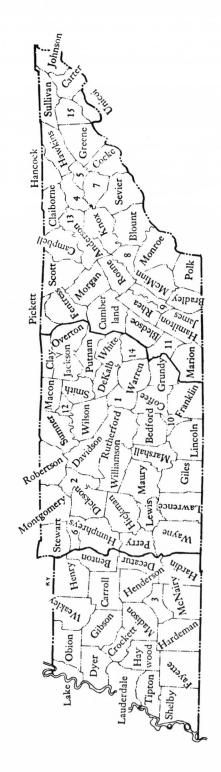

Map 8
COUNTIES AND GRAND DIVISIONS OF TENNESSEE

Counties identified by number:

1 Cannon	6 Houston	11 Sequatchie
2 Cheatham	7 Jefferson	12 Trousdale
3 Chester	8 Loudon	13 Union
4 Grainger	9 Meigs	14 Van Buren
5 Hamblen	10 Moore	15 Washington·

259

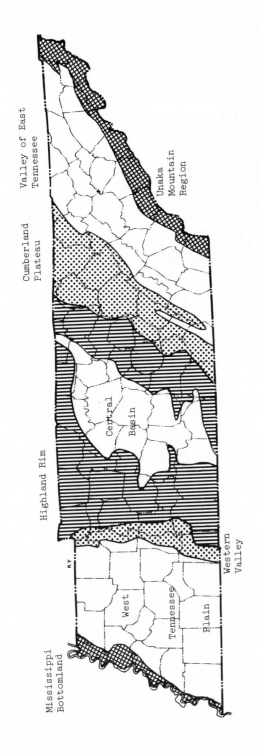

Map 9
PHYSICAL REGIONS OF TENNESSEE

Mississippi Bottomland

Highland Rim

Cumberland Plateau

Valley of East Tennessee

Unaka Mountain Region

Central Basin

Western Valley

West Tennessee Plain

KY

Source: U.S. Census Office, *Report on Cotton Production in the United States; Also Agricultural and Physico-Geographical Descriptions of the Several Cotton States and of California. Part I: Mississippi Valley and Southwestern States* (Washington, 1884), 383.

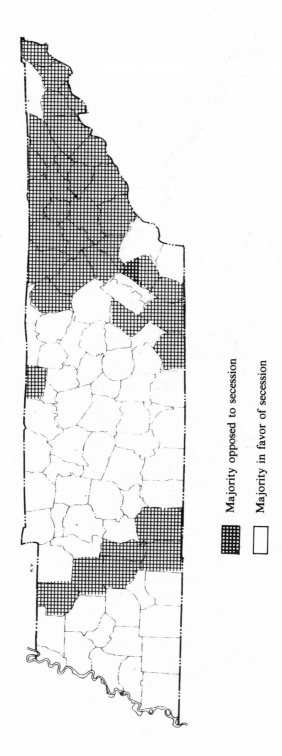

Map 10
VOTE ON SECESSION, JUNE 8, 1861

Majority opposed to secession

Majority in favor of secession

Source: White (ed.), *Messages*, V, 304–306.

Appendix C
Populist Platforms

We, the representatives of the great laboring and wealth-producing classes of the country, assembled as the first convention of the People's party of the State of Tennessee, brought together by the centripetal force of the undying principles for which our patriotic ancestors fought, and which they formulated into a government in order to secure the blessings of liberty to themselves and their posterity, hereby declare our everlasting adhesion thereto, and emphasize our opposition to all violations and departures therefrom, under whatever name or on whatever pretense they may be perpetrated.

We charge both the old parties with the abandonment of the spirit of those principles, while loudly professing loyalty to them. The suffering people are denied the relief which it is the province of their government to provide, and the old parties regard their positions as if they were the idle vaporings of outcasts, thus forcing us to form a party of the people in order that this may be a government of the people, by the people, and for the benefit of the people.

We charge that the corrupt use of aggregated capital threatens the destruction of the liberties of the people, guaranteed to every man by the constitution of our fathers, and unless there is a change in governmental affairs the great common people will soon be reduced to a condition of

1. Nashville *Banner*, June 29, 1892.

degraded servitude to which the manhood of no American citizen can submit. [W]e charge that the Democratic party of our Nation, with its 148 majority in the lower house of Congress, has violated the most sacred pledges made to the people in refusing to give them free and unlimited coinage of silver, and the failure to pass in the lower house a general bill reducing the tariff tax within the bounds of strictest economy.

We charge that both the Democratic and Republican parties are controlled in legislation by the influence of corporate wealth, and that the only hope for the perpetuity of this government is in the organization of all patriotic, liberty-loving, industrial reform forces into a People's party, untrammeled [*sic*] with political leaders, pledged to or owned by aggregated wealth.

We therefore submit the following as the platform of the People's party and urge all true and honest men to join us and help us maintain its principles.

We demand a national currency[,] safe, sound, and flexible, issued by the general government only, a full legal tender for all debts, public and private, without the use of banking corporations; a just, safe, equitable, and efficient means of distribution to the people on a safe and sound security at actual cost.

We demand that silver be restored to an equal footing with the bondholders' gold by the free and unlimited coinage thereof at the ratio established by our forefathers and in force until 1873.

We demand that the amount of circulating medium be speedily increased to not less than $50 per capita.

We demand a graduated income tax.

We believe that the money of the country should be kept as much as possible in the hands of the people, and hence we demand all national and state revenue shall be limited to the necessary expenses of the government economically and honestly administered.

We demand the rigid and just state and national governmental control and supervision of the means of public communication and transportation.

We demand that Congress shall pass such laws as will effectually prevent the dealing in futures of all agricultural and mechanical productions, providing a stringent system of procedure in trials that will secure the prompt conviction and impose such penalties as shall secure the most perfect compliance with the law.

We oppose Federal interference with elections in the states and favor the right of every citizen to cast his vote untrammeled by unnecessary legislation and that every man's vote shall be honestly counted as cast.

We demand that the Congress of the United States submit an amendment to the constitution providing for the election of United States Senators by direct vote of the people of each state.

We demand an abolition of the lease system and condemn the working of convicts with free labor.

We demand the prohibition of the employment of children under 14 years of age in factories and workshops.

We are in favor of equal rights for all and special privileges for none.

We are opposed to the present excessive salaries of state and county officials, and favor a reduction in accord with the strictest economy in governmental affairs.

[The following was offered from the floor of the convention and accepted by the platform committee before the ratification of the platform:]

We favor the abolition of the internal revenue law.

STATE POPULIST PLATFORM OF 1894 [2]

We, the People's party of Tennessee in convention assembled, arraign before the public bar of the country the party in power for criminal neglect of duty in its persistent refusal to correct the evils with which this country is afflicted: The great financial depression which has spread ruin and consternation in every industrial avocation throughout our land, is but a culmination of a past pernicious policy, dictated by home and foreign gold standard capitalists, which is being pursued with increased vigor and tyranny by the Democratic Administration.

This party refuses, by inaction, to protect the best interests of the masses or in any way to give hope to a distressed people, crying and praying for relief. This party, after professing for years to favor reform and promising repeatedly, if placed in power and given a chance, would [sic] repeal bad laws and enact others as [sic] would bring relief, have utterly failed to carry out a single promise made, but, to the contrary, in times of profound peace increased the interest-bearing bonded indebtedness of an already overtaxed people, refusing to coin the millions of silver bullion in the United States Treasury.

We regard the action of Grover Cleveland in the use of the veto power to degrade silver and contract the silver currency, as one of the greatest crimes of the age, and deserving the severest condemnation of the outraged people regardless of party. Divested of his Democratic robes, his back

2. Nashville *American,* April 12, 1894.

turned upon Democracy, his face fixed upon Wall Street, while he controls and manipulates his party in the interest of home and foreign capitalists, he presents to the American people a spectacle which should bring a blush of shame to every lover of our free institutions of Government, handed down to us by our Revolutionary fathers.

We arraign the Democratic party of Tennessee for the recent issue of $600,000 of interest bearing bonds while the people of Tennessee are unable to pay the interest on the present bonded indebtedness of the State. We arraign the Democratic party of Tennessee for the iniquitous election laws of the State passed for partisan purposes and which deprive more than 50,000 citizens of the right of suffrage.

Realizing the controlling influence of the representatives of Eastern capitalists, who dominate both the Democratic and Republican parties in the halls of Congress, we hail with delight the disposition of the people of the great Northwest and South to unite against the plutocratic East in a determined effort to hurl from power the heartless destroyers of our nation's prosperity, believing that this union is the only hope to perpetuate the liberties and prosperity of the American people.

We, the People's party of Tennessee, make the following demands, and cordially invite all good citizens who love their country, their homes, their families and humanity, who prefer principle to party name, to unite with us in an honest effort to hurl from power the enemies of the people.

1. We demand a national currency, safe, sound, and flexible, issued by the general government only, a full legal tender for all debts, public and private, and that without the use of banking corporations, a just, equitable, and efficient means of distribution, direct to the people [, be established].

(a) We demand free and unlimited coinage of silver at the present legal ratio of 16 to 1.

(b) We demand that the amount of circulating medium be speedily increased to not less than $50 per capita.

(c) We demand a graduated income tax.

(d) We believe that the money of the country should be kept as much as possible in the hands of the people, and hence we demand that all State and national revenue shall be limited to the necessary expenses of the Government economically and honestly administered.

We demand the abolition of the internal revenue laws.

We demand that the Congress of the United States shall submit an amendment to the Constitution providing for the election of United States senators by direct vote of the people in each State.

We demand an abolition of the lease system and condemn the working of convicts in competition with free labor.

We are in favor of equal rights for all and special privileges for none.

We are opposed to the present excessive salaries of State and county officials, and favor a reduction in accord with the strictest economy of governmental affairs.

We believe that the will of a majority of the people should control on all local questions pertaining to the public welfare.

We demand the repeal of that part of the poll tax law which makes the presentation of a poll tax receipt a prerequisite to the right of every free citizen to cast untrammeled his vote in the ballot box.

We demand the repeal of the uniform ballot law, which requires that tickets be exact in width and length, as unnecessary and liable to abuse.

We demand the repeal or modification of the Dortch law, which deprives thousands of taxpayers of limited education of the right to suffrage.

We demand that the revenue laws of the State be so changed that all double taxation shall be eliminated.

J. H. McDowell, Chairman, Frank P. Dickey, S. S. Aughey, Wm. M. Preston, J. F. Black, W. M. Watkins, J. W. B. Hamilton, W. D. Gold, Secretary, A. E. Smith.

Appendix D
Black Disfranchisement in
Tennessee: The Election Laws
of 1889-90

Modern southern liberals, trying to make a political alliance between blacks and poor whites, have invoked the example of the People's party of the 1890s to prove that it could be done. They have been encouraged by a historical interpretation of southern Populism as willing to overlook race for the sake of economic issues. One widely read historian, for example, declared that "A number of important Populist leaders . . . sought something that no American political party has achieved before or since: a political coalition of the poor whites and the poor blacks of the South." [1] A corollary of this proposition is that disfranchisement of southern blacks was not a part of the farmers' protest movement, but came after Democratic-Populist bidding for black votes revealed that a split among whites would endanger their supremacy by giving the balance of power to voting blacks. One of the Populists' most influential friends wrote recently that the "standard devices for accomplishing disfranchisement on a racial basis and evading the restrictions of the Constitution were invented by Mississippi, a pioneer in the movement and the only state that resorted to it before the Populist revolt took the form of political rebellion." [2] This view, however, does not take account of Tennessee, where Farmers' Alliance legislators helped enact racial disfranchisement laws before the Mississippi constitutional convention of 1890.

1. Eric F. Goldman, *Rendezvous with Destiny: A History of Modern American Reform* (Rev. ed.; New York, 1956), 39.
2. C. Vann Woodward, *The Strange Career of Jim Crow* (Rev. ed.; New York, 1966), 83.

Race and the ballot were associated in Tennessee long before 1890. The constitutional convention of 1834 barred free Negroes from the polls, though they had voted under the state's first constitution. The former Confederates who controlled Tennessee's third constitutional convention in 1870 erased the word *white* from the franchise clause, but added a requirement that voters present poll-tax receipts. The convention incurred the opposition of white diehards by the first change and of some blacks by the second. The statute enacting the poll-tax requirement remained a dead letter until its repeal in 1873, the year the Tennessee legislature received its first black member.[3]

After lying dormant for a few years, the franchise question was revived again in 1885 with the introduction of a voter-registration bill in the legislature. About twenty Republicans jumped from their seats, vaulted the railing at the back of the House chamber, and escaped before the sergeant at arms could lock the door, thus preventing a quorum and blocking the bill's passage. During the next four years calls for election reform were raised again by newspapers of both parties. The Democratic Nashville *Herald,* referring to South Carolina, suggested that an eight-box law, combined with registration, might do a lot to eliminate ignorant voters. In any case, continued the *Herald,* it was "incumbent on the [General A]ssembly to consider some plan especially for the immediate relief of those parts of Tennessee which are most burdened with dense ignorance and the evils which flow from a besotted voting class." Five days later the Republican Knoxville *Journal* warned that "somebody's meal tub ha[d] a large rat in it."[4] The Republican party was in trouble, because for the first time in six years and the second time in a decade, the Democrats numbered more than two thirds of each legislative house. The majority party was in a position in 1889 to use this power to cut off debate or constitute a quorum by itself, because Democratic legislators were more united than they had been in over twenty years.

The Democrats owed some marginal seats and much of their unity to the Farmers' Alliance, which had turned out in such numbers as to control many local party nominating conventions in 1888. The Alliancemen were almost half the legislature, but exerted no control over the Democratic

3. Folmsbee, Corlew, and Mitchell, *Tennessee: A Short History,* 175; Memphis *Avalanche,* March 30, 1870; Williams, "The Poll Tax as a Suffrage Requirement in the South, 1870–1901" (Ph.D. dissertation, Vanderbilt University, 1950), 49; Stephen B. Weeks, "The History of Negro Suffrage in the South," *Political Science Quarterly,* IX (1894), 693.

4. Nashville *American,* July 13, 1885, October 2, 1887, April 13, 1888; Knoxville *Journal,* January 8 (quote), March 22, 1889; Nashville *Herald,* January 3, 1889.

caucus or the course of legislation.[5] The farmers' organization was not yet the bitterly divisive issue it would soon become; during the Forty-Sixth General Assembly's sessions, Alliancemen and nonfarmer Democrats cooperated to establish the secret ballot, voter registration, and the poll-tax requirement for voting.

The bill sponsored by United States Representative Henry Cabot Lodge of Massachusetts for federal supervision of elections has been suggested as a motivation for the Tennessee legislation for a secret ballot and voter registration.[6] However, Congress did not witness a flurry of Republican election bills until after December, 1889, and the Lodge bill itself was not introduced until June, 1890. The origins of the Tennessee laws must be traced primarily to the state's longstanding awareness that black voting threatened white supremacy, to the renewed Democratic strength in the legislature, and to the influence of a national trend toward election regulation which saw ten states enact secret-ballot laws during 1888 and 1889.

The secret-ballot law, sponsored by Senator Joseph H. Dortch of Fayette County, required each voter to mark and deposit his ballot in secret, with no assistance, and without showing it to anyone. At one point the bill contained a stipulation that illiterates who could vote before May 1, 1857, could receive assistance from the officials. This loophole was closed after the Knoxville *Journal* correctly branded it as racially discriminatory. Perhaps this exemption for whites was expected to operate extralegally, however, by discretion of local officials. The law had a largely urban application, including only Chattanooga, Knoxville, and the counties containing Memphis and Nashville. Before final passage, a clause extending the bill to most county-seat towns was deleted. Clearly the framer's intent was not to protect the voter's anonymity and independence, because he was not concerned with rural districts where those with economic power and social status could influence their neighbors the most. The effect of the Dortch law, to keep illiterates from voting in and near the cities, was to hurt blacks since they were less literate than whites.[7]

Senator J. C. Myers of Pikeville, located in a county north of Chattanooga where few blacks lived, introduced the successful voter-registration bill. The Myers law, as amended in 1890, applied to Shelby and Davidson counties (Memphis and Nashville) and to all towns and districts with over 2,500 population; in other words, it covered the area of the Dortch bill plus

5. Nashville *Weekly Toiler,* January 23, 1889.
6. Frank B. Williams, Jr., "The Poll Tax as a Suffrage Requirement in the South, 1870–1901," *Journal of Southern History,* XVIII (1952), 483.
7. Knoxville *Journal,* March 1, 16, 31, 1889; *Tennessee Acts,* 1889, pp. 364–71.

some county seats. If satisfied of an applicant's eligibility, the registrar would enter his name in a book and issue him a certificate of registration. No person could vote in the wards and districts covered by the bill without presenting a valid certificate, despite the availability of the official registrar's book listing all voters.[8]

Discussion of these bills in the Democratic caucus and in the press centered on the question of partisan advantage. Knowing that they would lose votes if blacks were disfranchised, Republicans fought the bills bitterly: one of them declared that the literacy-test effect of the Dortch law was "injustice and cruelty," especially because it had been illegal to teach slaves to read. Democrats, on the other hand, tended to think of Negroes as less than full citizens. A Memphis paper referred to them as "the class which is unfitted to exercise the right of suffrage." [9] The highly partisan nature of the debates and divisions over these election laws indicates that the issue was not the mere innocuous reform described by some scholars.

The House of Representatives also considered a bill sponsored by Farmers' Alliance member J. D. Pearson of Madison County to enforce the poll-tax clause of the state constitution, a bill the Democrats failed to endorse in the regular session. When it came to a vote on the floor, Farmers' Alliance representatives supported the Pearson bill, twenty to six, while other Democrats opposed it, fifteen to eleven. Therefore the Republicans, calling the poll-tax bill "the meanest type of demagoguery," were able to defeat it by a vote of thirty-two to thirty-nine.[10]

The Democratic caucus, which usually confined itself to nominations for offices, formally endorsed the Dortch and Myers bills, along with a gerrymander designed to defeat a Republican congressman from Chattanooga. The Democracy then rammed these three bills through the House in rapid order, beating down Republican obstructions. A minority protest for the *House Journal* objected strongly that the Democrats had passed the Dortch bill illegally while a GOP amendment was still on the floor, and that the Myers bill had not been read a third time as the constitution required. The Democrats refused to allow this protest to be printed in the official record. All the roll-call votes on that turbulent spring afternoon were strictly partisan, with one important exception: on final passage of the Dortch secret-ballot bill, nine Democrats went over into opposition. Seven of them were from the highland area of Middle Tennessee, where Negroes were

8. *Tennessee Acts,* 1889, pp. 414, 416–17; *Tennessee Acts,* 1890 extra session, pp. 59–60.
9. Nashville *American,* March 12, 27, 1889; Knoxville *Journal,* February 1, April 9 (quote), 1889; Memphis *Avalanche,* March 19, 1889 (quote).
10. *House Journal,* 1889, pp. 472–73.

fewer and farmland less valuable than in the state as a whole. Only two Alliancemen voted against the Dortch bill in the ninety-nine-member lower house.[11]

The legislature met in extra session early in 1890, before the Lodge bill was written, because of minor inconsistencies among the Dortch and Myers laws and another law providing for separate boxes for state and federal ballots.[12] "The Dimacrats are in a sweet [*i.e.* sweat]," wrote a Republican leader. "Election Laws ar the watch ward with they will ad the poll Tax Law [and?] change all the others."[13] In the spirited House debate, John H. Savage reversed his earlier position against the poll tax, citing political corruption at his reason. An unsuccessful Democratic amendment to exempt holders of registration certificates from the poll-tax requirement revealed an attitude that the poll tax was not primarily a revenue measure, but a bar to voting. A Democrat of Franklin County suggested that there was a "negro in the woodpile," and after the laughter at this pun on a colloquial expression subsided, he charged more directly that what the Republicans feared was a barrier to the importation of out-of-state Negroes to vote in Memphis and Chattanooga. A Republican leader retorted that the bill's purpose was to "crush out" his party's vote.[14] The poll tax was a highly partisan issue because it was quite obvious that its effect on the franchise would be a severe blow to the Republican party, which relied heavily on black voters in many areas.

The Republicans boycotted the legislature, leaving one sentry in each house, when the poll-tax bill came up for its final reading in 1890. Democrats opposed to the measure were content to vote against it and thereby ensure its passage by helping to form a quorum. One scholar, trying to dissociate the poll tax from the racial issue, has suggested that possibly "the Democrats in the [Tennessee] black counties controlled the Negro votes and did not want to use the poll tax as a suffrage qualification."[15] This conclusion is not supported by the roll call on passage of the poll-tax requirement: of the 132 members of both houses, 56 lived in counties at least 25 percent black, but of these only 4 were among the 11 Democrats voting against the bill. Significantly, only 1 of these 11 was from West Tennessee. A mere 10

11. Nashville *American,* March 9, April 3, 4, 1889; Knoxville *Journal,* April 6, 1889; 1890 Census, *Population,* 428–29; Pressly and Schofield (eds.), *Farm Real Estate Values,* 52–53; *House Journal,* 1889, pp. 742–43.
12. Nashville *American,* February 14, 1890.
13. J. C. Hale to L. C. Houk, March 5, 1890, in Houk Papers.
14. Nashville *Banner,* February 26, 1890; *House Journal,* 1890 extra session, p. 100.
15. Williams, "The Poll Tax as a Suffrage Requirement" (1952), 482.

percent of the Farmers' Alliance legislators voted against this bill, an indication that the organization was not worried about disfranchisement of white farmers.[16]

A few argued that the new election laws were not racially discriminatory. Adolph Ochs's Chattanooga *Times,* which held that "the ignorant colored citizen now ha[d] more rights than he [knew] what to do with," considered the laws fair. The Memphis *Appeal* was content that the Dortch law denied no one the right to vote, but "merely raise[d] that right above the reach of the vicious, ignorant, and purchasable voter." The poll-tax law was welcomed as a constitutional necessity by the Nashville *Herald,* which considered "indiscriminate enfranchisement" of Negroes to have been a mistake in the first place.[17] Because of the combined influence of racism and partisanship, these judgments of fairness and justice mean little.

Recent historians, however, have continued to uphold the view that the Tennessee election laws were not racist in intent. One student found it "difficult to connect the [Tennessee] poll tax with Negro suffrage," claiming inexplicably that "the question of Negro suffrage was not mentioned as an issue" when the poll tax was before the legislature. Another historian remarked that although some had tried to include Tennessee among the southern states legislating against Negro suffrage, "such a view cannot be historically demonstrated. Neither the Dortch law nor the poll tax law, both [*sic*] enacted in 1890, were [*sic*] designed primarily for the elimination of the colored voter[.]" It is impossible to sustain these assessments in the face of the evidence to the contrary.[18]

Frequent contemporary references were made to the effect of the new laws in cutting the black vote. One newspaper mentioned "the accepted belief that the registration law knocks the negro vote sky high," and a Nashville daily remarked that the new laws had "very effectively disposed of the negro vote." A Republican politician privately despaired that they were "almost insurmountable." Two years later an editor explained that the poll tax had been "adopted as a means of making sure the rule of the white majority in this state," and of removing locally the "pressure of an ignorant negro majority threatening utter destruction to the community."

16. 1890 Census, *Population,* 428–29; *House Journal,* 1890 extra session, pp. 99–100; *Senate Journal,* 1890 extra session, p. 66.

17. Chattanooga *Times,* January 18 (quote), June 10, 1890; Memphis *Appeal,* November 5, 1890; Nashville *Herald,* March 16, July 13 (quote), 1890.

18. Williams, "The Poll Tax as a Suffrage Requirement" (1950), 76; *ibid.* (1952), 481; Corlew, "Negro in Tennessee," 139. One scholar who differs with Williams and Corlew is J. A. Sharp, in "The Entrance of the Farmers' Alliance into Tennessee Politics," 85.

Such examples of the contemporary presumption of discrimination could be multiplied manyfold, all from white sources.[19]

After the 1890 election one Democratic editor conceded that the Dortch law had helped cut the vote in the four urban counties and that the poll tax had reduced the vote in Republican East Tennessee; but he claimed that the election returns showed that the laws were not racially discriminatory. Comparison with the previous nonpresidential election of 1886, however, shows the reverse. The decrease in the Republican vote from 110,000 to 76,000 [20] occurred mostly among black people.

Table 1

EFFECT OF TENNESSEE ELECTION LAWS OF 1889–90 [21]

	Number of Counties Used	Simple Product-moment Correlations Between Decrease in Republican Vote, 1886–90, and Black Population, 1890
Tennessee	95	+.79
E. Tenn.	37	+.40
M. Tenn.	38	+.88
W. Tenn.	20	+.89

The racial effect of the new laws was not only very distinct; in West Tennessee, it was persistent. Twenty-three of the state's ninety-six counties registered a drop of over 40 percent in the Republican vote from 1886 to 1890. Ten of these were in East and Middle Tennessee, and generally recovered their Republican losses after 1890. The other thirteen, all in cotton-planting West Tennessee, did not need to worry about the Republican threat again for generations.

Contemporaries were well aware of the relevance of Tennessee's experience for the rest of the South. After the local elections of August, 1890, a Memphis paper noted that the Mississippi constitutional convention was considering ways to keep political power from Negroes without overt racial discrimination, and the paper suggested that the delegates consider how well the secret ballot and poll tax had worked in Shelby County, Tennessee,

19. Memphis *Avalanche,* July 15, 1890; H. B. Lindsay to L. C. Houk, August 8, 1890, in Houk Papers; Memphis *Commercial,* June 3, 1894; Memphis *Commercial Appeal,* December 18, 1894; Nashville *Herald,* September 4, October 12, 1890; Nashville *Banner,* August 9, October 11, November 6, 11, 1890, May 5, 1892, December 7, 1893, October 29, 1895.

20. Nashville *American,* November 26, 1890; White (ed.), *Messages,* VII, 234, 364.

21. White (ed.), *Messages,* VII, 232–34; *Tribune Almanac,* 1891, p. 312; 1890 Census, *Population,* 428–29. For explanation of simple correlations, see Appendix A.

Table 2
LONG-RANGE EFFECT OF ELECTION LAWS ON CERTAIN
WEST TENNESSEE COUNTIES [22]

Year	Republican vote	
	State	W. Tenn. Counties (13) Showing Over 40% Drop in GOP Vote, 1886–90
1882	90,660	19,100
1886	109,837	21,785
1890	76,081	7,068
1894	105,104	8,380
1918	59,519	5,123
1930	85,558	8,448

where the "party of ignorance" had met its "Waterloo" without being cheated illegally. In Alabama the Birmingham *Age-Herald* regretted that the entire South had not adopted such excellent laws right after Reconstruction, and it expected the Mississippi convention, in search of a bulwark against "hordes of black illiterates," to take due notice of Tennessee's laws. In November a Tennesseean proposed that Arkansas copy the Dortch law to prevent the "ignorant hordes of the black counties" from threatening white supremacy.[23]

Disfranchisement of blacks was not as thorough in Tennessee as in the lower South, because white voters were in secure majorities in most of the state's counties, and because some local white politicians like E. H. Crump of Memphis organized blacks to vote Democratic. But the southern trend of disfranchisement of blacks after 1890 by ostensibly legal methods, rather than by extralegal or fraudulent ones, began in Tennessee in 1889–1890. The Farmers' Alliance was not wholly responsible for Tennessee's partial disfranchisement of blacks, but Alliance legislators were generally very cooperative. Some of these same Alliancemen soon found themselves in the People's party and opposing, for purely practical reasons, the same election laws they had helped to pass for the good of the Democratic party.

22. White (ed.), *Messages,* VII, 19–21, 232–34, 555–57; *Tribune Almanac,* 1891, p. 312; Shirley Hassler, *Fifty Years of Tennessee Elections, 1916–1966* ([Nashville], n.d.), 92, 120. The thirteen counties are Crockett, Dyer, Fayette, Gibson, Haywood, Henry, Lake, Lauderdale, Madison, Obion, Shelby, Tipton, and Weakley.

23. Memphis *Appeal,* August 21, November 15, 1890; Birmingham (Ala.) *Age-Herald,* quoted in Nashville *Banner,* August 11, 1890.

Bibliographical
Essay

The following abbreviations are used in the Bibliographical Essay: *THQ, Tennessee Historical Quarterly; ETHSP, East Tennessee Historical Society's Publications; JSH, Journal of Southern History.*

MANUSCRIPT MATERIALS

A useful and neglected collection is the Correspondence of the Governor's Office of Tennessee (abbreviated CGO in footnotes), Tennessee State Library and Archives, Nashville (abbreviated TSLA). The correspondence of Governors John C. Brown (1871–75), James D. Porter (1875–79), Albert S. Marks (1879–81), William B. Bate (1883–87), Robert L. Taylor (1887–91), John P. Buchanan (1891–93), and Peter Turney (1893–97) all yields insight into patronage. Of this correspondence, the Taylor, Porter, and Buchanan sections are the least limited to routine official business. The well-indexed Andrew Johnson and Grover Cleveland papers, in the Library of Congress, include correspondence from many Tennessee Democrats, much of it very useful. The Harding-Jackson Papers, in the Southern Historical Collection of the University of North Carolina Library, Chapel Hill, are the largest and most helpful collection of private papers of Tennesseans in the period of this study; Judge Howell E. Jackson and General W. H. Jackson were both politically active. A smaller collection, and one more confined to personal and family matters, is the Howell Edmunds Jackson Papers, TSLA. Two small but useful collections of Tennessee politicians in the TSLA are those of S. A. Champion, Bourbon state senator and president of a Paris bank, and Joseph H. Fussell, sky-blue nominee for governor in 1882 and prohibitionist leader. The R. H. Cartmell Diaries, TSLA, extend over several years and include information about farming in Madison County and occasional comments on politics; they are indexed. There is a very large but mostly unorganized collection of the papers of Republican congressmen L. C. Houk and John C. Houk in the Lawson-McGhee Library, Knoxville. Collections in the TSLA, the usefulness of which was somewhat limited by chronology or content, were those of the Cooper, Jones, and Trousdale families, and of Jacob McGavock Dickinson, Walter W. Faw, Joseph B. Killebrew, and W. W. Fergusson. The James C. Napier Papers, in the Negro collection of Fisk University, contain mostly clippings and souvenirs, with few political items. County records, especially tax books showing landholdings and assessments, have been partially microfilmed by the Archives Division, TSLA.

NEWSPAPERS

The State Library Division, TSLA, publishes mimeographed progress reports listing its excellent microfilmed collection of Tennessee newspapers. The Nashville *American* (which replaced the *Union and American* in 1875) is the best source of political news through the period, although its frequent shifts in point of view are confusing, and it lost its preeminence in the 1890s. The Nashville *Banner* became an increasingly informative paper through the 1880s, surpassing the *American* in the nineties, though the *Banner*'s outlook on some matters is colored by its connection with the L & N Railroad. The dailies outside Nashville providing the most political news, though as strongly partisan as the *American,* are the Memphis *Appeal* (*Appeal-Avalanche* from 1890 to 1894) and the Memphis *Commercial* (*Commercial Appeal* after 1894).

Several newspapers are most significant for their editorial attitudes. In the 1870s the Memphis *Avalanche* and *Public Ledger* voiced discontent with the Redeemers. Adolph S. Ochs's Chattanooga *Times* was a mugwump, New South paper, usually opposing the Bourbon Knoxville *Tribune.* A series of ephemeral Nashville papers demonstrated the reliance of rival politicians on editorial mouthpieces: the Bourbon *World* (1882–84), A. S. Colyar's *Union* (1886–87), the prohibitionist weekly *Issue* (1887–88), the *Democrat* (1888), the *Herald* (1889–91), and the free-silver *Sun* (1895–96). The Knoxville *Journal* replaced the Knoxville *Chronicle* in the mid-1880s as the leading Republican daily in the state. Several county papers reflect small-town opinion and institutions, most notably the Bolivar *Bulletin,* the Clarksville *Tobacco Leaf-Chronicle,* the Fayetteville *Observer,* the Jackson *West Tennessee Whig,* and the Pulaski *Citizen.*

The absence of black newspapers in the TSLA collection is a severe handicap. The Farmers' Alliance and Populist press are somewhat better represented. The *Weekly Toiler* of Nashville, official organ of the state Alliance, is indispensible; it is supplemented by two issues of the *State Wheel* of Jackson and one issue of the *Tennessee Populist* of Trenton. The Carthage *Record* was a Democratic weekly that switched to Populism. The *National Economist* of Washington, D.C., occasionally quoted Tennessee Populist papers.

Election returns for units smaller than counties must be found in newspapers. Of Tennessee's ninety-six counties in this period, precinct election returns are available for about fifteen, which may be identified in the TSLA list of microfilmed newspapers.

GOVERNMENT PUBLICATIONS

The published reports of the United States censuses of 1860, 1870, 1880, 1890, and 1900 (Washington: Government Printing Office) provide statistics on population, agriculture, wealth, and other useful data for counties, wards, and civil districts. The U.S. Department of Commerce produced the *City and County Data Book, 1967* (Washington: Government Printing Office, 1967). Another convenient compilation is Thomas J. Pressley and William H. Scofield (eds.), *Farm Real Estate Values in the United States by Counties, 1850–1959* (Seattle: University of Washington Press, 1965). Prices of farm products by states are given by the *Annual Report of the Commissioner of Agriculture* (Washington: Government Printing Office, 1863–94).

The official records of the Tennessee legislature are the *Journal* of the House of Representatives and the *Journal* of the Senate, published for each biennial regular session and each extraordinary session. Their principal value is in showing roll-call votes, the significance of which is usually not evident from the journals alone. The legal results of each legislative session were published in the *Acts of the State of Tennessee.* Robert H. White has collected the *Messages of the Governors of Tennessee* for 1869–1899 in Vols. VI and VII (Nashville: Tennessee Historical Commission, 1963 and 1967). Some information on railroads, and much more on the troubles of the first railroad commission, is in the *First and Second Annual Reports of the Railroad Commissioners for the State of Tennessee* (Nashville: Albert B.

Tavel, 1884). The record of the contested gubernatorial election of 1894, including testimony and some precinct returns, is *Contest for Governor in Tennessee: Complete Proceedings of the Joint Convention and Investigating Committee, the Evidence in Full and Arguments of Counsel* (Nashville: Franc M. Paul, 1895). Also useful is the *Journal of the Proceedings of the Convention of Delegates Elected by the People of Tennessee, to Amend, Revise, or Form and Make a New Constitution for the State* (Nashville: Jones, Purvis, & Co., 1870).

A semiofficial promotional work from the Redeemer decade is the solid *Introduction to the Resources of Tennessee,* by Joseph Buckner Killebrew, assisted by J. M. Safford, C. W. Charlton, and H. L. Bentley (Nashville: Tavel, Eastman, and Howell, 1874, 2 vols.). During the first three decades of this century the periodical *Field Operations of the* [U.S.] *Bureau of Soils* included surveys of several Tennessee counties; at least nine more have been covered since 1946 by the irregular periodical *Soil Survey* of the U.S. Department of Agriculture.

Facts about Tennesseans who served in Congress are in the *Biographical Directory of the American Congress, 1774–1927* (Washington: Government Printing Office, 1928). Daniel Robison began compiling a similar reference work for the Tennessee legislature.

CONTEMPORARY PUBLISHED SOURCES

More biographical information is available in W. S. Speer, *Sketches of Prominent Tennesseans: Containing Biographies and Records of Many of the Families Who Have Attained Prominence in Tennessee* (Nashville: A. B. Tavel, 1888). More extensive and less detailed is *Who's Who in Tennessee: A Biographical Reference Book of Notable Tennesseans* (Memphis: Paul & Douglas Co., 1911). John Allison (ed.), *Notable Men of Tennessee* (Atlanta: Southern Historical Association, 1905) also offers biographical data.

Some Tennesseans revealed something of themselves in published works. A. S. Colyar's *Life and Times of Andrew Jackson: Soldier, States-man, Patriot* (Nashville: Marshall and Bruce, 1904, 2 vols.) praises Jackson as a successful man of business. The title of a speech by Peter Turney speaks for itself: "They Wore the Grey—The Southern Cause Vindicated: An Address by Hon. Peter Turney, Chief Justice of the Supreme Court of Tennessee, before the Tennessee Association of Confederate Veterans, at Nashville, August 8th, 1888," in *Southern Historical Society Papers,* XVI (1888), 319–39. *Gov. Bob Taylor's Tales* (Nashville: DeLong Rice & Co., 1896) is a collection of his lectures as performed on stage. Taylor is colorfully, if imaginatively, described in William Allen Dromgoole (pseud.), "Fiddling His Way to Fame," *Arena,* II (November, 1890), 719–31. John H. Savage's several pamphlets include *Extracts from the Speeches of John H. Savage, Delivered in the Canvass of 1882* (Nashville: no publ., 1882); *Railroads in Tennessee: Their War upon the People!* (n.p.: no publ., [1884]); *Speech of Hon. John H. Savage, as Delivered in the Senate and Before the People, on the So-Called State Debt Question* (McMinnville: no publ., 1879); *An Open Letter from the Old Man of the Mountains: The Incorruptible Statesman Scorns a Masked Battery, And Gives Some Reasons Why the Proposed Prohibitory Amendment Should Not Pass* (n.p.: no publ., [1887]); and *Col. Savage's Defense: He Is Not an Enemy of Senator Harris: Harris' Friends Make War on Him* (n.p.: no publ., [1888]). The man is character- ized in the title of his memoir: *The Life of John H. Savage: Citizen, Soldier, Lawyer, Congressman: Before the War Begun and Prosecuted by the Aboli- tionists of Northern States to Reduce the Descendents of the Rebels of 1776, who Defeated the Armies of the King of England and gained Independence for the United States, Down to the Level of the Negro Race* (Nashville: John H. Savage, 1903). John H. McDowell revealed his own values to a lesser degree in his *History of the McDowells, Erwins, Irwins, and Connections* (Memphis: C. B. Johnston & Co., 1918). Low-taxer and Greenbacker J. R. Beasley wrote *The Conflict between Liberty and Prohibition; an Inquiry into the Most Practicable Method of Reforming the World: With Other Essays on Political Subjects* (Chattanooga: no publ., 1886).

The *Official and Political Manual of Tennessee,* by Charles A. Miller (Nashville: Marshall and Bruce, 1890), is a valuable compilation of state officials, current political platforms, recent election returns, and similar data; unfortunately it was not periodical. *Poor's Manual of the Railroads of the United States* (New York: Henry V. Poor, 1868–1924, annual) shows routes and officials. *Dow's City Directory of Memphis, for 1891* (Memphis: Harlow Dow, 1890) lists the city's institutions, including newspapers, and the addresses and occupations of residents; though not extensively used for this study, this and other directories for Memphis and Nashville are valua- ble sources for urban social history. Election returns by counties are accessi- ble, if sometimes slightly unreliable, in *The Tribune Almanac and Political Register* (New York: 1838–1913, annual, title varies), and in the *Cumber- land Almanac* (Nashville: 1826–94, annual).

W. Scott Morgan, *History of the Wheel and Alliance, and the Impending Revolution* (Hardy, Ark.: W. Scott Morgan, 1889), is written from a Wheel point of view. Charles H. Otken, *The Ills of the South; or Related Causes Hostile to the General Prosperity of the Southern People* (New York: G. P.

Putnam's Sons, 1894), stresses the oppression of farmers by town merchants. The TSLA has a copy of the *Ritual for Subordinate Lodges Working under the Jurisdiction of the Farmers' and Laborers' Union of America* (Nashville: The Weekly Toiler, n.d.). Party and Farmers' Alliance platforms are collected in Thomas Hudson McKee (ed.), *The National Conventions and Platforms of All Political Parties, 1789–1901: Convention, Popular, and Electoral Vote: Also the Political Complexion of both Houses of Congress at each Biennial Period* (Baltimore: Friedenwald, 1901); and George B. Tindall (ed.), *A Populist Reader: Selections from the Works of American Populist Leaders* (New York: Harper & Row, 1966).

SECONDARY SOURCES—TENNESSEE

Historical books and articles specifically about Tennessee are listed topically in *A Guide to the Study and Reading of Tennessee History,* compiled by William T. Alderson and Robert H. White (Nashville: Tennessee Historical Commission, 1959). A more recent and more extensive, though nontopical and uncritical, list of published works is included in S. J. Folmsbee, R. E. Corlew, and E. L. Mitchell, *Tennessee: A Short History* (Knoxville: University of Tennessee Press, 1969). The TSLA mimeographed a thirty-three-page list of *Writings on Tennessee Counties* in 1967.

The multivolume *History of Tennessee, from the Earliest Time to the Present* (Nashville: Goodspeed, 1886–87) is still quite useful for local history; less so is W. R. Garrett and A. V. Goodpasture, *History of Tennessee: Its People and its Institutions, from the Earliest Times to the Year 1903* (Nashville: Brandon, 1905). Two more recent works combining general history with biography are Philip M. Hamer (ed.), *Tennessee: A History, 1673–1932* (New York: American Historical Society, 1933, 4 vols.); and Stanley J. Folmsbee, Robert E. Corlew, and Enoch L. Mitchell, *History of Tennessee* (New York: Lewis Historical Publications, 1960, 4 vols.). The latter is condensed in *Tennessee: A Short History* (Knoxville: University of Tennessee Press, 1969), by the same three authors.

The important studies of the period 1865–70 in Tennessee are E. Merton Coulter, *William G. Brownlow: Fighting Parson of the Southern Highlands* (Knoxville: University of Tennessee Press, 1971, reprint); and Thomas B. Alexander, *Political Reconstruction in Tennessee* (Nashville: Vanderbilt University Press, 1950). Both are unfavorable to the Republicans. There is no general history of the state in the 1870s. David M. Abshire, *The South Rejects a Prophet: The Life of Senator D. M. Key, 1824–1900* (New York: Praeger, 1967), is stronger on Key himself than on Tennessee politics.

Thomas B. Alexander offers a light sketch in *Thomas A. R. Nelson of East Tennessee* (Nashville: Tennessee Historical Commission, 1956). Another leading figure is portrayed by Clyde L. Ball in "The Public Career of Colonel A. S. Colyar, 1870–1877," *THQ,* XII (1953), 23–47, 106–28, and 213–38. Colyar is more extensively treated by Thomas Woodrow Davis in "Arthur S. Colyar and the New South, 1860–1905" (Ph.D. dissertation, University of Missouri, 1962). Other aspects of industrial development are touched in Samuel Boyd Smith, "Joseph Buckner Killebrew and the New South Movement in Tennessee," *ETHSP,* XXXVII (1965), 5–22; Constantine G. Belissary, "The Rise of Industry and the Industrial Spirit in Tennessee, 1865–1885," *JSH,* XIX (1953), 193–215; and Jesse C. Burt, "Four Decades of the Nashville, Chattanooga, and St. Louis Railway, 1873–1916," *THQ,* IX (1950), 99–130. The state-debt issue of the 1870s is described by Alice Lynn in "Tennessee's Public Debt as an Issue in Politics, 1870–1883" (M.A. thesis, University of Tennessee, 1934); and William A. Stanton, "The State Debt in Tennessee Politics" (M.A. thesis, Vanderbilt University, 1939). Another topical study, with an appropriately modest title, is "The Background for Regulation of the Railroads in Tennessee" (M.A. thesis, University of Tennessee, 1939), by Edward Cameron Duggins.

The fullest source of information about black Tennesseeans in the postwar period is Alrutheus A. Taylor, *The Negro in Tennessee, 1865–1880* (Washington: Associated Publishers, 1941). Robert E. Corlew, in "The Negro in Tennessee, 1870–1900" (Ph.D. dissertation, University of Alabama, 1954), argues that the racial situation slowly improved in this period, despite the efforts of "well-meaning outsiders." The Tennessee railroad-segregation law of 1891 is put in its legal context by Stanley J. Folmsbee in "The Origin of the First 'Jim Crow' Law," *JSH,* XV (1949), 235–47. Joseph H. Cartwright has demonstrated that blacks were not mere passive pawns in politics in "Black Legislators in Tennessee in the 18[8]0's: A Case Study in Black Political Leadership," *THQ,* XXXII (1973), 265–84.

Tennessee urban history in the late nineteenth century is almost unexplored territory. The best work is on Memphis, but Gerald M. Capers' *Biography of a River Town: Memphis, Its Heroic Age* (Chapel Hill: University of North Carolina Press, 1939) closes with the effects of the yellow fever epidemics of 1878–79, and William D. Miller, *Memphis During the Progressive Era* (Memphis: Memphis State University Press, 1957), deals with the early twentieth century. The crucial intervening decades invite scholarly attention. Unfortunately, William Henry McRaven, *Nashville, Athens of the South* (Chapel Hill: Scheer and Jervis, 1949), and Shields McIlwaine, *Mem-*

phis, Down in Dixie (New York: Dutton, 1948), are little more than collections of anecdotes. William Waller, in *Nashville in the 1890's* (Nashville: Vanderbilt University Press, 1970), "makes no pretense to scholarly merit" (p. xv). A fine work touching on urban history is Thomas Harrison Baker, *The Memphis Commercial Appeal: The History of a Southern Newspaper* (Baton Rouge: Louisiana State University Press, 1971).

Bob Taylor has attracted relatively much attention, beginning with the sentimental, eulogistic *Life and Career of Senator Robert L. Taylor* (Nashville: Bob Taylor Publ. Co., 1913), by his brothers James P., Alf A., and Hugh L. Taylor. The first serious, scholarly book on post-Reconstruction Tennessee was Daniel Merritt Robison, *Bob Taylor and the Agrarian Revolt in Tennessee* (Chapel Hill: University of North Carolina Press, 1935). Rupert P. Vance, "Tennessee's War of the Roses," *Virginia Quarterly Review,* XIV (1940), 413–24, adds very little, but Lane L. Boutwell, "The Oratory of Robert Love Taylor," *THQ,* IX (1950), 10–45, is more useful. Robert L. Taylor, Jr., "Apprenticeship in the First District: Bob and Alf Taylor's Early Congressional Races," *THQ,* XXVIII (1969), 24–41, does not challenge Robison's interpretation.

The Tennessee Farmers' Alliance was sketched by Corinne Westphal in "The Farmers' Alliance in Tennessee" (M.A. thesis, Vanderbilt University, 1929). J. A. Sharp, "The Entrance of the Farmers' Alliance into Tennessee Politics," *ETHSP,* IX (1937), 77–92, and "The Farmers' Alliance and the People's Party in Tennessee," *ETHSP,* X (1938), 91–113, provide an accurate narrative.

Three articles by Verton M. Queener illuminate the Republican party: "A Decade of East Tennessee Republicanism, 1867–1876," *ETHSP,* XIV (1942), 59–85; "The East Tennessee Republicans as a Minority Party, 1870–1896," *ETHSP,* XV (1943), 49–73; and "The East Tennessee Republicans in State and Nation, 1870–1900," *THQ,* II (1943), 99–128.

Legislation on prohibition is summarized in Grace Leab, "Tennessee Temperance Activities, 1870–1899," *ETHSP,* XXI (1949), 52–68. Paul E. Isaac, *Prohibition and Politics: Turbulent Decades in Tennessee, 1885–1920* (Knoxville: University of Tennessee Press, 1965), with emphasis on the early twentieth century, is a good survey of prohibitionism, Tennessee's major statewide progressive movement.

Miscellaneous monographs on Tennessee of the late nineteenth century include A. C. Hutson, Jr., "The Coal Miners' Insurrections of 1891 in Anderson County, Tennessee," *ETHSP,* VII (1935), 103–21; Hutson, "The Overthrow of the Convict Lease System in Tennessee," *ETHSP,* VIII (1936), 82–103; Jesse Crawford Crowe, "Agitation for Penal Reform in

Tennessee, 1870–1900" (Ph.D. dissertation, Vanderbilt University, 1954), which draws on Hutson; J. Eugene Lewis, "The Tennessee Gubernatorial Campaign and Election of 1894," *THQ,* XIII (1954), 99–126, 224–43, and 301–28; and Thomas D. Clark, "The Country Store in Post–Civil War Tennessee," *ETHSP,* XVII (1945), 3–21.

SECONDARY SOURCES—GENERAL

The most important historical work on the post-Reconstruction South is still C. Vann Woodward's *Origins of the New South, 1877–1913* (Baton Rouge: Louisiana State University Press, 1951). Sheldon Hackney analyzes its extraordinary influence and its relation to subsequent New South historiography in *"Origins of the New South* in Retrospect," *JSH,* XXXVIII (1972), 191–216.

Woodward's monograph, *Reunion and Reaction: The Compromise of 1877 and the End of Reconstruction* (Boston: Little, Brown, 1951), shows great insight into the tangled relationship of public policy and private interests. Irwin Unger, *The Greenback Era: A Social and Political History of American Finance, 1865–1879* (Princeton: Princeton University Press, 1964), provides background for the important currency question. A short, clear summary of the development of the free-silver crusade is in Richard Hofstadter, "Free Silver and the Mind of 'Coin' Harvey," in Hofstadter, *The Paranoid Style in American Politics, and Other Essays* (New York: Knopf, 1965), 238–315.

The extensive literature on the Farmers' Alliance and People's party in the South is surveyed by Allen J. Going in "The Agrarian Revolt," Chapter 15 of Arthur S. Link and Rembert W. Patrick (eds.), *Writing Southern History: Essays in Historiography in Honor of Fletcher M. Green* (Baton Rouge: Louisiana State University Press, 1965), 362–82. An excellent capsule summary of the historiography and problems of Populism in South and West is Sheldon Hackney's introduction to his collection of readings, *Populism: The Critical Issues* (Boston: Little, Brown, 1971), which also contains a full bibliography of the Populist revolt.

Frank M. Drew, a contemporary of the Alliance, wrote sympathetically and informatively about agrarianism in "The Present Farmers' Movement," *Political Science Quarterly,* VI (1891), 282–310. A brief early work on the subject is Hallie Farmer, "Economic Background of Southern Populism," *South Atlantic Quarterly,* XXIX (1930), 77–91. *The Populist Revolt:*

A History of the Farmers' Alliance and the People's Party (Minneapolis: University of Minnesota Press, 1931), by John D. Hicks, was the first full treatment of American Populism, but slighted the South; that defect has been remedied by Woodward's *Origins of the New South* and by Theodore Saloutos, *Farmer Movements in the South, 1865–1933* (Berkeley: University of California Press, 1960, reprint), a sound and cautious account. Hicks's view of the movement was persuasively challenged by Richard Hofstadter in *The Age of Reform: From Bryan to F.D.R.* (New York: Knopf, 1955), which helped stimulate a debate on the nature of Populism (see Hackney's bibliography, cited in the preceding paragraph). Among the several state studies of Populism, two of the most helpful are Roscoe C. Martin, *The People's Party in Texas: A Study in Third Party Politics* (Austin: University of Texas Press, 1970, reprint), which provides a much-ignored example of how to compare election returns and rural neighborhoods; and Sheldon Hackney, *Populism to Progressivism in Alabama* (Princeton: Princeton University Press, 1969), which sees Populism as a backward-looking movement based on social alienation, and discontinuous with urban-based progressivism. Herbert Shapiro clears away some misconceptions in "The Populists and the Negro: A Reconsideration," in August Meier and Eliott Rudwick (eds.), *The Making of Black America: Essays in Negro Life and History* (New York: Atheneum, 1969), II, 27–36. A recent work, misleading with respect to Tennessee, is Gerald H. Gaither, "The Negro in the Ideology of Southern Populism, 1889–1896" (M.A. thesis, University of Tennessee, 1967).

C. Vann Woodward, in *The Strange Career of Jim Crow* (2nd rev. ed.; New York: Oxford University Press, 1966), outlines the rise of the system of segregation. Joseph B. Bishop, "The Secret Ballot in Thirty-Three States," *Forum,* XII (1892), 589–98, approves the reform as a way for the South to get rid of Negro voters legally; L. E. Fredman, *The Australian Ballot: The Story of an American Reform* (East Lansing: Michigan State University Press, 1968) is a more recent assessment. Frank B. Williams, Jr., "The Poll Tax as a Suffrage Requirement in the South, 1870–1901" (Ph.D. dissertation, Vanderbilt University, 1950), takes a benign view of that reform, as the same author does in an article of the same title in *JSH,* XVIII (1952), 469–96. Jack Temple Kirby, *Darkness at the Dawning: Race and Reform in the Progressive South* (Philadelphia: Lippincott, 1972), shows that racism and reform were quite compatible in the South. Historians of both blacks and Populists will benefit by the demonstration of oral traditions as a useful source in Lawrence C. Goodwyn, "Populist Dreams and

Negro Rights: East Texas as a Case Study," *American Historical Review,*
LXXVI (1971), 1435–56.

METHODOLOGY

Lee F. Anderson, Meredith W. Watts, Jr., and Allen R. Wilcox, *Legislative
Roll-call Analysis* (Evanston: Northwestern University Press, 1966), is a
manual of techniques. Two useful handbooks of quantitative methods are
Hubert M. Blalock, *Social Statistics* (2nd ed.; New York: McGraw-Hill,
1972), and Charles M. Dollar and Richard J. Jensen, *Historian's Guide to
Statistics: Quantitative Analysis and Historical Research* (New York: Holt,
Rinehart, & Winston, 1971).

Index